ACKNOWLEDGEMENTS

The Editors would like to thank all the people who contributed their ideas and energy to this project, in particular Lisa Power, Sir Ian McKellen and Anya Palmer at Stonewall and Ruthie Petrie and Becky Swift, our excellent editor at Virago.

José Arroyo would like to thank Chris West, Richard Dyer, Ross Jennings and especially Tom Waugh for their comments while writing this piece.

Olivette Cole Wilson would like to thank all the lesbians who contributed to her piece, in particular Gail Lewis for her advice and support.

Emma Healey would like to thank Jane Held and Jeni Bremner for their many hours of support and encouragement.

Andy Medhurst would like to thank Stephen Maddison, Tony Pilgrim and Andy Simmons for sharing television reminiscences and his parents for not staying in that evening in 1975.

Sally Munt would like to thank Caroline Freeman, Geoff Hemstedt, Lisa Henderson and Andy Medhurst for sharing their ideas with her for her piece which will be appearing in a more extended form in her forthcoming book.

CONTENTS

STONEWALL
25

The Making of the
Lesbian and Gay Community
in Britain

Edited by Emma Healey and Angela Mason

Published by VIRAGO PRESS Limited June, 1994
42–43 Gloucester Crescent, Camden Town, London NW1 7PD

*A CIP catalogue record for this book is available from the British
Library*

Typeset by Florencetype Ltd, Kewstoke, Avon
Printed in Great Britain by Cox & Wyman Ltd, Reading, Berks.

3. LESBIAN AND GAY CULTURE AND LIFESTYLE

Foreword

MARTIN SHERMAN

MARTIN SHERMAN was born in Philadelphia and now lives in Britain. His play *Passing By* was performed by Gay Sweatshop in 1975. *Bent* was first performed in 1979 and starred Ian McKellen; it was revived in 1989 at the Royal National Theatre. Other plays include *Messiah* starring Maureen Lipman, *A Madhouse in Goa* and *When She Danced*, both starring Vanessa Redgrave. In 1993, *Clothes in the Wardrobe* starring Jeanne Moreau and Joan Plowright was produced by the BBC.

A hot night in June. New York, 1969. I was walking up Seventh Avenue with a friend discussing the imminent end of the decade. I was a hippie or, at least, hippie-like. I didn't think the sixties *would* end. We crossed Christopher Street and saw a crowd in front of the Stonewall, a popular Village gay bar. Policemen were tossing drag queens into a van! The queens were feisty and angry and funny. Well, it was hot and Judy Garland had just died and there was a lot of emotion in the air and those days every day had some kind of street theatre. I wasn't fond of the Stonewall. It seemed to belong to decades past, and Janis Joplin had replaced Judy

1

Garland for me. Gay men were not especially hippied and often seemed unresponsive to my generation. I had no idea that the scene playing in front of me would change those attitudes for ever. A friend of mine, an actress called Jonelle Allen, walked by. Jonelle watched the commotion for a while and then decided to go home. She tried to hail a cab. Empty taxis passed her by; Jonelle was black, and they did not want to chance a fare to Harlem. I hid Jonelle behind a car, hailed a taxi, and when it stopped, rushed her inside. Walking home I pondered how little had been achieved in the civil rights movement if someone like Jonelle still could not get a taxi. Jonelle and the taxi are my prevailing image of that evening. It was later – much later – that I realised that I had witnessed the birth of another movement, one that would colour my life and that of every lesbian and gay man from that moment on. There had been a raid, and queens had fought back. Fought back! I was there, but I wasn't. Actually only the drag queens were really *there* that evening. I had seen it, but I hadn't. I had stumbled across history. And I didn't know it.

Introduction

It would be difficult not to sense a feeling of optimism and hope about lesbian and gay politics. At the 'fag' end of the twentieth century, as other progressive movements fail and falter, lesbians and gay men are the one social group for whom life seems to be getting better.

Not only that. There is an emerging political movement centred on demands for civil rights for lesbians and gay men. In America, the election of Clinton as US President gave a new visibility to the lesbian and gay lobby, even if the new administration did not deliver on its key demands. The 1993 march on Washington of over half a million lesbians and gay men was the largest civil rights gathering in history. In international law lesbian and gay rights are being accepted as part of the language of human rights. Constitutional challenges have succeeded in Canada, Australia and New Zealand. This year Stonewall was involved in producing a major report for the European Commissioner of Social Affairs which traces the emerging legal status of lesbians and gay men in the European Community. In South Africa the ANC has incorporated lesbian and gay rights in its charter.

Nor does this new civil rights movement lack glamour.

The support of 'stars' from the world of sport and entertainment and new gay lifestyles create a climate for the
movement which is self-confident, expansive and fun.
Despite the many problems still to be dealt with, the new
movement is one of the few places where men and women,
black and white, old and young, are working together
around common demands.

Even in the Stygian gloom of British politics as we move
towards the millennium this starry new force is making a
breakthrough. In 1993 we saw *Camp Christmas*, TV's first
lesbian and gay Christmas show, a welcome breakthrough
to the TV 'family' Christmas, but when the Queen spoke to the
nation did she have a message for her lesbian and gay subjects? How far are we from gaining what Jeffrey Weeks, the
historian of gay life in Britain, has called sexual citizenship?

The short answer is – a long way. Perhaps the distance
will not be so great this summer, which sees the 25th anniversary of the Stonewall riots, but Britain remains alone amongst
western democracies in failing to accord lesbians and gay men
legal status or public recognition. Not only that, Section 28
of the Local Government Act 1988 which proscribed the promotion of homosexuality by local government and the teaching of homosexuality as a 'pretended family relationship',
was an unprecedented attack on the public status of homosexuality. We still have an unequal age of consent for gay men
despite the recent shift from 21 to 18, and lesbians and gay
men are banned from serving in the armed forces.

Yet lesbian and gay life has flourished in Britain in the
last twenty-five years. Many essays in this volume explore
the development of a lesbian and gay style, even a new
aesthetic and a new humour. We have a flourishing gay press
which may soon be able to rely on mainstream advertising.
The new gay scene has provoked a torrent of articles on the
importance of the pink pound. Lesbian and gay sex is
acknowledged, described, written about and filmed. AIDS has

ushered in homophobia but also a new sexual honesty and awareness. We seem to be strong on lifestyle and poor on politics and legal rights.

Civil rights movements in Britain have always clung to stony soil. The great franchise movements of the nineteenth century, including the women's suffrage movement, have no analogue in the twentieth century. Britain does not have a written constitution and the new social movements based on identity politics have not been able to achieve their aims through litigation.

So on the face of it a group like Stonewall, which was set up in 1989 as a professional lobby group, trying to construct a civil rights agenda, faced an uphill struggle, but there are strong grounds for optimism. The history of the lesbian and gay movement post-Stonewall has made it possible for the first time to build a confident and coherent movement for civil rights, which is not just about acceptance but also suggests a new social and sexual order based on tolerance, freedom and individual responsibility.

When the Stonewall Group was set up much was made of its differences from more 'radical' groups like Outrage. Clearly differences in tactics are important, but discussions about reform and revolution often obscure the deeper historical process. It may seem self-evident in a democracy that every citizen will demand equality, and organise to get it, but history makes it plain that this is not so.

Lesbian and gay political activists have never been able simply to mobilise a constituency. First we have had to create it. The need to create a shared sense of identity, a shared understanding of injustice, is common to all emancipation movements. In English history it is as characteristic of the Chartists as of the modern women's liberation movement where it was actually called consciousness-raising. But for us this process of claiming an identity is particularly complex and difficult. Whatever the status of the gay gene we are not

5

biologically visible. Historically we have had no natural communities, no ghettos or areas where we all lived. We do not grow up in gay families who can tell us our story. Until the post-Stonewall movement we had no access to our own history. We have been invisible to each other and to the world.

The Stonewall riot changed all that. The New York Mattachine Society, one of the earliest American homophile movements, called the Stonewall riot 'The hairpin drop heard all around the world'. The Mattachine Society was set up in 1950 by ex-communists to liberate, as they saw it, a 'social minority trapped in a dominant culture'. It was the Stonewall riot and the liberation movement that followed it that made that minority visible: it did so by challenging the dominant culture. In welcoming the queens on to the historical stage, the Mattachine headline alludes to the challenge the Stonewall rebellion made to the dominant male culture. Unpacking the stigma of homosexuality, being able to come out as lesbians and gay men has meant above all challenging old sexual roles which homosexuality was used to police.

These questions have a particular relevance in British culture. After all, in 1885 we gave the world the Labouchère amendment, which created the offence of gross indecency. This was the offence under which Oscar Wilde was arrested, tried and imprisoned, and which has been and still is responsible for countless blackmails, suicides, broken careers and lives. There has always been a slippage in English law between homosexuality as a condition or preference and homosexuality as a sexual act. This was apparent in relation to Clause 28 and is true of the gay sex crime of gross indecency. The only specificity of the crime is the sex of the parties not the nature of the sexual act; and the only offence derives from offending prevailing sexual norms that emphasise the purity of the family and household.

The stigmatisation of homosexuality in English society arises now not so much from religious sanctions as from the role which homosexuality has played as, in a sense, the arbiter of 'decency', of 'maleness' and 'femininity'.

In opposition to the despised category of the homosexual a new concept of masculinity flourished. The dominant upper-class English male was inscribed with a set of characteristics of control, possession, strength and racial purity which were defined by the exclusion of the low, the dirty, the effeminate and the contaminating. In this model homosexuality was seen as a pollutant; as undermining true masculinity and its complex structure of power. No wonder male homosexuality was despised and stigmatised. The same process constructed lesbians as asexual, dependent and inferior. It wasn't so much lack of knowledge of lesbianism, which was well explored in earlier pornographic literature, but rather the impossibility of speaking of female sexual desire which made it impossible to include lesbianism in definitions of gross indecency. Queen Victoria's supposed ignorance was a symbol of society's silence. As homosexuals were depicted as effeminate, lesbians were constructed as assertive, male, unfeminine; literally hairy and uncontrollably aggressive.

These constructions were enforced in a series of show trials from Wilde to Radclyffe Hall's *The Well of Loneliness*. The closet was effectively policed, and still is, by arrest and press exposure. In fact, the press has always played a crucial role. Coverage of sexual scandals by popular journalism has helped articulate a code of sexual behaviour which is part of a unifying national identity. Homosexuals have been the ritual sacrifices needed to construct a self-congratulatory British identity which has been jingoistic, xenophobic and complacent. The very real association in the public mind between homosexuality and treason has been reinforced by a succession of homosexual spy scandals which surely have no parallel outside English society.

This complex sense of British identity which was created

7

during the second part of the nineteenth century was never seriously challenged by the Labour movement, and survived into the second half of the twentieth century with remarkable force. The election of a reforming Labour government after the Second World War challenged many elements of the old class order but, as feminists have outlined, the postwar settlement was sexually conservative with a renewed emphasis on traditional sexual roles.

In this climate, which flourished with almost no challenge right up to 1969, it is not surprising that the first moves for homosexual law reform were timid and apologetic. In his influential autobiography, *Against the Law* (1955), Peter Wildeblood who was involved in a famous scandal in the early 1950s with himself and Lord Montagu of Beaulieu and imprisoned for gross indecency, pleaded his case in the language of the time.

> When I ask for tolerance it is not for the corrupters of youth, nor even the effeminate creatures who love to make an exhibition of themselves, although by so doing they probably do no harm; I am only concerned with the men who despite the tragic disability which is theirs, try to lead their lives according to principles.

Why was Stonewall able to substitute pride for shame and apology? Part of the power and magic of the event was that the citadel seemed to fall as soon as we marched round Jericho and blew our trumpets. The credibility of the white Anglo-Saxon male bestriding an empire abroad and wife and children at home had expired, and when the whistle was blown the ideological edifice began to collapse very quickly. But it took the new understanding of sexual politics which had been generated by the women's movement, which had reached out on to the streets, to demonstrate that the Emperor had no clothes. When women started to be angry then faggots could be proud. And who knows how unassailable the white male ruling class would have seemed without the movements for national liberation in Vietnam and Algeria? If peasants on bicycles could challenge the mightiest military industrial empire in the world what else would be possible? If black could be beautiful why not us?

When we shouted, 'Out of the closets, on to the streets!' it wasn't rhetoric. It was a psychological truth. Coming out and being visible had been made possible by collective political confrontation. The conundrum of the identity politics that Stonewall and gay liberation created was that you can't live your whole life on the streets in riot mode. Nor can a political movement organise itself through a weekly general meeting. And the very radicalism which shattered the old stigmas was itself exclusive, the property of a particular group, unable to unite a people who by their very nature came from all sections of society with an enormous variety of political views and interests.

The unfolding of these dilemmas has occupied the twenty five years since Stonewall. We have had a seemingly contradictory development: as the essays in this volume attest the lesbian and gay world, not only 'the scene' but a wider culture, has flourished, but political groups and movements have often faltered and lacked coherence. This in part derives from a more general feature of British society in which an intensely urban, tolerant and non conformist tradition coexists with a formal political culture which is often didactic, closed and repressive, but equally we have had to wrestle with problems of difference, of strategy and tactics as well as the renewed attacks provoked initially by the AIDS crisis.

The essays which deal with the development of the community try to unpick some of that history. It is a history that will require more writing and discussion but tentatively three themes emerge. Firstly the building of unity. What is significant about the modern movement is that it is a lesbian and gay movement. This would not have been possible without feminism and the women's movement, but it is not something which can just happen in the past and be forgotten. An understanding of the oppression of others which made Stonewall '69 possible needs constantly to be reinscribed and renegotiated in our movement today. The essay on the black experience underlines this point. It is a failure of this book that in the short time it was put together there is no contribution from the disabled movement.

This is not an issue of political correctness. It is one of the great strengths of the lesbian and gay movement that far from being isolated from society we are indeed everywhere. This gives our cause a richness and depth and above all a humanity which is a source of great power and vision. Nowhere has this been more apparent than in the response of the community women and men, young and old to the AIDS panepidemic. At moments of great attack we have been able to unify, but again that initial resistance needs to be recodified in our more general struggle for civil rights.

Secondly we have slowly learnt to build a political movement that is autonomous but not separatist, that seeks allies throughout society but remains in control of its own agenda. This is particularly significant in the British context. Progressive social movements in Britain have naturally tended to look to the Labour Party and the trade union movement as vehicles for social change. Indeed the dominance of the party system in British political life makes it difficult to gain any access to political power outside party politics. During the 1980s a coalition of forces which brought together identity politics and 'left' groupings within the Labour Party seemed to hold out the promise of undreamt of political influence. In the event neither the left forces nor the new sexual politics had a constituency which could sustain them against the hostile response they invoked. This attack culminated in the passing of Section 28 of the Local Government Act 1988.

It seems clearer now that Section 28 was part of a wider attack on Labour strongholds in local government and that 'homosexuality' was used, fairly cynically, for that end. But whilst the government won the argument about politics on the rates they lost the argument on homosexuality. The movement that came into being against the Clause recaptured its own autonomy and was finally able to mobilise a constituency which has been emerging from the ghetto, growing in size, influence and importance in the last twenty five years. It was these larger developments which created the context for the formation of the Stonewall Group. Set up to provide an all party political lobby, backed by high profile public figures it seemed a new departure in lesbian and gay politics, but with hindsight it seems clear that the will to enter the public political domain, on our terms, was part and parcel of that very process that began in New York in 1969.

Thirdly there is an emerging unity around the struggle for civil rights for lesbians and gay men. For us this is never a simple matter of incorporation. The process that was begun at Stonewall has created a new political constituency which is no longer willing to be denied equality and recognition. Demands for equality do challenge sexual politics. This book has been prepared during the age of consent campaign but before we knew the outcome of the vote. That campaign was, perhaps, the most visible sign of the strength of the new constituency that we have seen. It involved an unprecedented discussion of lesbian and gay issues in the media, a full scale Parliamentary debate and intensive national lobbying. Although at the time of writing the Bill still has to go to the House of Lords the narrow majority against equality in the House of Commons naturally led to intense disappointment and anger. But behind this anger, and the renewed discussion on tactics that will naturally follow, it is possible to see a new political constituency taking shape. Predictions are always difficult, but in the immediate defeat on the age of consent it is possible to see all the ingredients of victory. It is not so much what we have achieved at any one instant but whether the tide of events is turning against us or running in our favour.

In Britain movements of sexual emancipation have often come to the fore in epochs of wider social and political change. The suffragette movement was part of a gale of social protest that shattered Liberal England at the end of the nineteenth century. The sexual reforms of the 1960s on abortion, divorce and homosexuality were part of a political shift in the 1960s which ushered in a new Labour government, although their commitment to a new moral settlement was only partial and the conventional morality of Harold Wilson himself was never challenged.

Today again there is considerable disenchantment with our political system which is paralleled by a profound moral angst. The lesbian and gay movement has necessarily had to forge itself outside that system and those values, to generate itself economically, socially and now at last politically. We invoke the most resonant traditional values of society – equality and freedom – and suggest and initiate a debate on the most potent and silenced human issue – sexuality. This book can only provide a very partial snapshot of those demands and that debate, but hopefully the many different lives, communities and styles represented here suggests ways in which the voice of sexual freedom can speak to a political hope that reaches beyond its own interest, so we, like those twenty five years ago, may be the harbingers of a new order.

Lesbian and Gay Lives

Questioning
Everything

Michelle Jones

YONI EJO – SOCIAL
WORKER

YONI EJO worked in the Hotel and Catering industry for some years. Her first social work job was as a residential social worker. She also ran playschemes, creches and volunteered for Lesbian Line. Since qualifying as a social worker she has worked in Child Protection in a Northern inner city. She is now Placement Worker with the Albert Kennedy Trust.

My father was a black American and my mother was white. I was her third child and the only one who was black. I was also the only one she had adopted, which I still find rather difficult to accept. I was adopted by a white couple who already had two foster children. We lived in the south of England, a very white part of Britain. It seems incredible now, but I didn't actually have a conversation with a black woman until I was 18 years old.

I knew I was gay when I was at school. But I did not really know what lesbianism was; I just felt interested in and attracted to women. Lots of lesbians and gays I know talk about 'feeling different' at school and they put this difference down to their sexuality. People at school saw I was different,

15

but most put it down to my colour. I think a few of my close friends knew I was gay, but I never talked about it. I was never able to talk about being black either.

When I came out to my parents at the age of 15, they threw their hands up in horror. My mother was particularly upset. She said I couldn't be gay because I was much too young and seemed to think it was something I had thought up just to disgust her. I couldn't really handle my parents' reaction and so decided to keep quiet about being gay. I even 'experimented' with going out with boys. This was just a cover, and not a very successful one at that – the local boys really weren't interested in going out with a black woman.

Somehow I found out that the Campaign for Homosexual Equality (CHE) had meetings locally and so I started to attend. I told my parents I was going to the youth group, and managed to fool them for quite a long time. At the meetings I met a married couple I knew, and they were very supportive. But it was inevitable that my parents would eventually find out about the meetings, and when they did they were very shocked and very angry. I had stopped talking to them about my sexuality so they probably thought that the problem had gone away. Still, despite their anger, I think they began to realise that I was serious about my sexuality. Coming out to my parents for a second time, I fought much harder to get more freedom. I can be very stubborn, so I really fought to be allowed to go out and to meet other lesbians and gays and at last my parents did let me go out.

We had moved to an area which had quite an active gay scene. I started to lead a bit of a double life: I was out on the scene at night and a 'good' girl during the day. I would sleep with a woman and then have to get up at three or four in the morning to get home before my parents woke up. It was an anxious and stressful time – I was always over-sleeping and having to creep home. It was almost as if I was staying out just to rebel rather than for support, enjoyment or sexual fulfilment. It was only when I left home that I had the confidence to start having relationships.

I was 19 when I left home and headed for London. I couldn't stand the small-town atmosphere of where I was living and I needed independence. When I moved to Hackney, I had no idea that it was London's lesbian Mecca. My parents helped me move but I don't think they would have let me go if they had known where I was heading for. I shared a flat with a black gay man and had a great time. I didn't have a job but I wanted to do a social work course. I wanted to do something real and useful, and had this feeling that I wanted to 'help' people. I became close friends with a social worker and I suppose I wanted to emulate her. Although I didn't become a social worker just because of her, I think she showed me that social work was something I could do. My own experiences made a difference as well: I had been through the adoption system and felt and still feel that I should use my experiences in a positive way. My beliefs about good practice and about meeting young people's needs are things I can back up with personal experience. My parents did their best for me, but I did suffer for being placed trans-racially. I sometimes wonder how I got the strength to survive prejudice and insensitivity.

I got a place on a social work course, then started to do my CQSW. This was when I really settled down in London. I didn't mix much with my fellow students, which I regret slightly now, but I did make the most of the London lesbian scene. It was a time of great discovery and a time when I became strong enough to have deeper relationships with women. I did well on the course and gained a lot of confidence from work experience. I think I got one place-ment because I was a lesbian, which showed me that my lesbianism did not always have to be hidden at all costs.

I also began to meet other black lesbians and gay men. It took me a long time to be comfortable with black people because I felt they could tell that I had been brought up by a white family. I didn't know how to speak the language and was afraid that I would be judged for not being black enough. I have really only come to terms with my colour relatively recently. For a lesbian it is very hard to find a way into the wider black community when you know that there is so much homophobia there. And although I started to go to various lesbian groups, these were also often intimidating. It was the time when the movement seemed to be dominated by loud, confident white women who felt they could tell you how you should live your life. I was much more at home in the free and easy atmosphere of the clubs and bars.

After I left college I spent some time in residential work, but though I had started the job with lots of ideas, I soon found all that energy disappearing. So I decided to make a move and look for a full-time social work job: I found one doing family support and child protection work in Manchester. I didn't know Manchester well, but I had been there once for the massive rally against Section 28. It had been a marvellous day, so I took that as a good omen.

Being a lesbian and a social worker is something of a stereotype. I don't know why there are so many lesbians in social work, but I did imagine that as an out dyke I would be much more respected and, indeed, much safer as a social worker than I would be in other professions. Social work training stresses the importance of equal opportunities, so you believe that this will be reflected in your place of work. I have been lucky – quite a few of the people I worked with in Manchester were out lesbians so it was a very supportive environment. I worked there for two years. Child protection is immensely stressful and although we all tried to support each other as much as possible, the stress began to get too much. I stopped sleeping properly at nights. When my friends began to notice how the job was affecting me, I realised that it was time to move on.

I now work for the Albert Kennedy Trust, a small voluntary organisation that provides safe accommodation and support for homeless young lesbians and gay men. I have always been out but working for the trust takes this one step further. It is an incredibly supportive environment to work in: I never have to pretend to be something I am not. But sometimes I can feel very exposed. Recently, when I visited a young gay person in a residential home I could feel the homophobia and the antagonism of the staff. It is my job to deflect all that negativity and concentrate on the young person's needs. When you work for local government or a straight organisation, you can hide behind that organisation; it gives some anonymity. Working for a lesbian and gay organisation you lose that safety net. When I walk into a meeting as the worker from the Albert Kennedy Trust, everyone knows I am gay.

Young people who come to the Trust are at the end of their tether: they don't know what they are going to do or where they are going to be. We offer security, some time and space, and at the end of that we can help them to live independently. That is the biggest buzz: we help young lesbians and gays for as long as they need us. When you are a social worker for a local authority there comes a time when you can no longer be involved in a young person's life. At the Trust we watch young lesbians and gay men grow in strength and confidence; it is they who decide when they no longer need us.

I enjoy being a dyke and I enjoy what I do. I like the freedom and I like the choices that being an out dyke gives me. Lesbians and gays look at society in a very different way: our experiences make us question what society wants and what society thinks. We end up re-evaluating and rethinking everything from our own special perspective. We don't immediately assume that there is only one way of doing things: we learn to question everything.

Strong Enough to Survive

JUSTIN FASHANU – FOOTBALLER

JUSTIN FASHANU was born in 1961. He made his professional football debut at Norwich City in 1979 and became Britain's first one million pound black footballer when he transferred to Nottingham Forest in 1981. Since then he has played for a number of major clubs and most recently played for Heart of Midlothian in Scotland.

I had just been given a £1 million transfer to Nottingham Forest and there was a big party. I had a few drinks and ended up in bed with my best friend. It wasn't planned. From then on, I started to experiment more and more.

Coming to terms with my sexuality has been a painful process; all I ever really wanted was to choose who I go to bed with. It has taken me a long time to reach the point when I can say that I am not interested in what anybody else thinks any more.

We all want to be happy, contented and fulfilled in our sexuality, but society puts up so many barriers that it becomes hard for us to be what we want. We are all expected to fit a certain label. We should all be heterosexual, and if we have to be lesbian or gay then we are expected to keep quiet about it. The trouble starts if we turn round and make a fuss. I think everyone has a little gayness in them but it is so subdued that the slightest display of difference is deeply threatening. There is so much fear and ignorance about what makes up a lesbian, gay man or bisexual.

But the gay world wants us to have an identity that is just as fixed. Lesbians and gays feel very threatened by bisexuality. They seem to say that you can only be gay or straight. Some of my biggest critics are the people who you would have thought would understand what prejudice and intolerance is all about – blacks and gays. I am not underestimating the prejudice of the heterosexual world but lesbians and gays have not always understood my situation, nor have they really wanted to listen.

When I came out I thought I would meet my true family. Sometimes I would listen to transsexuals and they would talk about how they were trapped in a body that wasn't theirs. I knew exactly what they meant: I felt I was living my life as a lie. I thought that when I came out all my problems would be over; all I would have to do was stand firm and I would be welcomed into the gay community. But it didn't happen like that. I felt isolated and alone and none of the people who could have helped me did. I felt used and abused by the gay machine, which seemed to say that I was just another celebrity to be exploited for the cause.

Everyone wants you to be their spokesman and as long as you are the one standing in the firing line then everything is fine. I got to the point when I decided it was someone else's turn to put themselves on the line. Suddenly, I felt that everyone thought I was a traitor to the cause. I don't do Outrage or go on marches because that is not my style, it just doesn't make me comfortable. But I will do my bit by living my life, coming out and saying that it is just as normal for me to love a man as it is to love a woman. Sadly, many gay people thought that was not enough.

I don't think the lesbian and gay community is supportive enough. It is like the story in the Bible: one of the old heroes was given the mantle of power by God and every time he held his staff up the battle went his way but as soon as his arm got tired and the stick went down the opposition started to win. So the people gathered round him and held up his arm. You can't always be the person standing up, you have got to have the people standing round you in support. The heterosexual world makes lesbians and gay men so insecure and frightened that as soon as they see someone in trouble they move away, not because they mean to but because they can't deal with any more aggravation. We may have enough to put up with in our own lives, but we must do more.

Young people in particular need our support. They come into the gay scene very naive, longing to find a home, and they finish up after a couple of years feeling let down, used and abused. If we can nurture them and help them to be balanced and strong, we create a great picture.

I came out publicly because I met a young 17-year-old who had told his parents he was gay. They gave him a choice – either to get out or to change his lifestyle. He walked out and became a rent boy on the streets. He felt that his life was so empty that eventually he committed suicide. This had a profound effect on me. I felt angry at the waste of his life, and guilty because I had not been able to help him. I wanted to do something positive to stop such deaths happening again, so I decided to set an example and come out in the papers.

I have been greatly criticised for coming out in the tabloid press. Many people thought I just did it for the money, I suppose they have never stopped to consider that my world is based around *Sun* and *Daily Star* readers; the football world has that kind of mentality, it doesn't read the *Sunday Times*. I genuinely thought that if I came out in the worst newspapers and remained strong and positive about being gay, there would be nothing more that they could say. Of course, I was wrong and lost three years of my career. It cost me much more to come out than I ever received. I don't regret that but I do object to people thinking that I took the easy way out. It certainly wasn't, and my colour made it even more difficult. The tabloids don't like black people being successful, so they take any opportunity to bring us down. Saying I was gay was the perfect excuse for them to attack me.

It was a dreadful time because I couldn't even rely on my family. My brother, John, was saying some terrible things. He was the classic example of someone whose prejudice is fuelled by ignorance. I think he was influenced by his so-called friends, who saw having a gay brother as a threat to business and a threat to them. He was going around with a crowd of black guys at the time and for them homosexuality was worse than murder. I thought John would have shown enough strength to overcome that. John is brilliant now, he has said in public that he doesn't feel he was as supportive then as he should have been. My sister Dawn was a rock, she has always been totally supportive; and my parents were fine. In fact I had more problems with them than they had with me. I kept thinking I was letting them down and that they would be very disappointed; I am still working that one through. I regret that I didn't feel I could tell my parents earlier, but I would still do the same again. We all need to understand that we will make mistakes and we all need to forgive. I don't think you ever forget those mistakes or the mistakes that other people make that wound you, but it is important to forgive.

So, coming out for me was incredibly, almost suicidally, lonely. I am a very private person, but I couldn't even walk out of my house without someone hassling me. I am also a very proud person. I pride myself on the fact that I can match any person in anything, but once I came out people stopped giving me a chance. Today people still call me names and insult me. Three or four years ago I was their role model but now, because of my sexuality, they think they have the right to judge me. They never bother to listen to my side of the story. It can be horribly cruel.

There have been some very positive things about coming out. I have had to rely on my own resources, I have had to start growing from within. I spent so much of my time just holding myself together that I stopped looking forward, I just got on with living my life day by day and hour by hour. This made me look deep inside myself and helped me to reassess all my values. It made me look at why I was doing certain things, whether I was motivated simply by my ego. It was a very good experience for me. I am a born-again Christian and coming out has made me look at my faith very hard. I got no support from the Church and so really had to think about the place of God in my life. I could very easily have rejected my faith, but although I don't go to church any more I do feel that I have a much deeper understanding of my faith. I believe there are still many things that God wants me to achieve and that if you change one thing in your life, then that brings about many other changes, some good, some bad. For all the negative changes, there are always so many more positives; the secret is to find them. So for all the times that coming out has been lonely or difficult, I have never once regretted doing it.

I don't think there would have been any point in coming out if I could not give people the benefit of everything I have experienced. I hope that in the future I will be able to work in the media so that I can pass on all these experiences. People have killed themselves, they have led miserable and unfulfilled lives because society tells them it is wrong to be

24

gay. The more people who can stand up and show how they have overcome this sort of prejudice, the better it will be for every lesbian and gay man. All the things that have happened to me have shown me that I am strong enough to survive without bitterness and without anger.

I would love the time to come when gay people can express themselves in a dignified, proud, confident way because they have been nurtured both by themselves and by society. I compare it to how my family taught me to be proud of being black. When prejudice made me feel like the odd one out, my family showed me how to hold my head up high. They taught me not to try to be something I am not but to change the world by being dignified and proud of who I am. The gay community must learn to do the same.

Gayness is automatically an indication of expressive brilliance in many different ways. Lesbians and gays are so creative, so dynamic, so loving and caring and spiritual that together we can create a joyous, rich environment. Lesbians and gay men have so much potential; with a little bit more courage, dignity and pride we will be absolutely great.

My Sexuality is Me

Sorin Masca

REVEREND PAUL FLOWERS — METHODIST MINISTER

PAUL FLOWERS was born in Portsmouth in 1950. A Methodist Minister since the 1970s he is currently Superintendent Minister of the Bridlington Circuit in Humberside. A past member of the Advertising Standards Authority, he was also Vice Chair of the National Association of Citizens' Advice Bureaux and a Labour Councillor. He is Chair of the Lifeline Project in Manchester.

I had always been involved with the church. When I was 16 I became a lay preacher – I was far too precocious. Here I was, this spotty, callow youth with zits all over the place daring to get into a pulpit and preach to all these lovely elderly people who knew much more of the world than I. But it was these people who, over the years, encouraged me to enter the ministry.

I started my training as a Methodist minister in 1972, when I was packed off to Bristol and did a degree in theology at the same time as my training. And then I got a scholarship from the World Council of Churches and spent a year studying in Geneva. This was a sort of ecumenical hothouse. There were sixty of us from twenty-five countries and because we were all living so closely it became quite easy, and indeed quite natural, to talk about oneself. I think this was the culmination of a coming-out process which had been gathering steam while I was at college.

When I returned to England I was appointed as a university chaplain in an ecumenical chaplaincy in west London. This was my probationary period as a minister and before I was fully ordained I insisted on seeing my district chairman (the Methodist version of a bishop). I wanted it to be on my record that I was gay. Now, he was very much a minister of the old school. I don't think he liked it very much but it was not regarded as a bar to my ordination. That was fifteen years ago, so I think the Methodist church was way ahead of lots of other churches.

That doesn't mean it has always been easy to be out. Sometimes you are treated by some people in the Church as less than fully human. There have been times when I went into a particular pulpit that I could almost cut the air because of the *frisson* of tension in the place. It was unreal because it was based upon prejudice and no real or adequate knowledge of me as a human being at all. But it is up to people like me to break down all that. It is particularly important to do this in the churches that have fears and problems, because I don't think we can ever change the basic culture of the country unless there are people who are prepared to persevere and to relate to and work with those who have problems with gay men and lesbians.

It is easy to be gay in certain professions, it is tolerably easy to be gay in some metropolitan centres, but the biggest battle is within the small towns and communities where it is unacceptable to be gay and where it is impossible for us to lead lives of dignity and integrity. The church has a real role to play in these areas once we break down the barriers of people's fear. So it makes me very angry indeed when I think about clergy who choose to remain closet and how openly gay clergy are treated within the Church. My college was twinned with the Anglican college, Salisbury Wells. Richard Kirker, who later became General Secretary of the Lesbian and Gay Christian Movement, was a student there and was beginning his gay campaigning. But he ran into great difficulties about his openness and the Church refused to ordain him. That still makes me angry.

There are still pressures in the Methodist Church. The 1993 Methodist Conference passed a motion upholding chastity outside marriage and fidelity within it but at the same time went on to pass a motion to 'celebrate, affirm and welcome the contribution of lesbians and gays within the life and ministry of the Church'. This has left a tension in the Church. I think that is all right. There is a large number of people who are very welcoming, warm and accepting, who have no problems at all with lesbian and gay people. Equally, a large number of people do have great problems with lesbians and gay men. They are there, but because we have opened up the debate we can deal with them.

I don't think things will ever change in the Church of England until people who are gay and lesbian are prepared to come out of those wretched little closets. They don't have to do so dramatically or with enormous style but they do have to do so with dignity. They simply have to say that they will not put up with this rubbish any longer. The whole tenor of the debate in the Church of England and the Roman Catholic Church will change if that happens. If gay men were denied ministry in the Anglican or the Roman Catholic Church then the whole damn shebang would simply collapse. It would be like taking all the gay men out of Harrods – it just couldn't carry on.

It is upsetting and aggravating when gay clergy refuse to come to terms with themselves, pretending to do so privately while publicly denying themselves and their very being. I think this probably makes them flawed in the work they do.

The church institutions are also to blame for being so timid and fearful about dealing with their fellow human beings in an honest and straightforward manner. I would put the debate on a par with issues of racism. As we have tried to come to terms with the inherent racism in all of us, so there is an implicit duty upon church institutions to do exactly the same with homophobia.

There are times when it is important to put myself on the line. I don't particularly want to put myself on the line, nor do I want to be seen as a representative or token person. And I don't want to be seen as Paul Flowers, gay minister, because it is almost irrelevant. I don't mean to say that it is not important; it is very important, but it is not relevant to my work. What is relevant is whether I can do the job and how well I do it, or how badly. My sexuality should be almost immaterial to that. But there will always be times when it is important to make a public statement and to make people aware that you are there. That you are certainly not about to resign or run away, just because you are gay.

I learnt this during the Rochdale child abuse case when I was vice-chair of the Social Services Committee. As spokesperson for the Labour group I made many appearances on television and radio. It was then that a number of newspapers felt it right to remember that I was gay and to write some fairly vicious stories about me. I was front-page news for quite some time. They questioned whether a gay man should be involved in child abuse cases and, inevitably, they tried to make the equation of gay man therefore child abuser, which I found especially painful.

And, of course, they used the fact that I was a minister. The papers featured a whole range of pictures which were always the most awful shots, managing to make me look not remotely decent or human. They take pictures when you are looking away, yawning, picking your nose; and always I was wearing my dog collar. I was harassed by photographers who would come to my home. At one stage I had police cars outside keeping the baying hounds away, and that was awful. It leads in my experience to crank letters, always anonymous and always from people who sign themselves 'loving Christian person' but who mercilessly abuse and attack you. It also leads to anonymous and very obscene phone calls which are extremely upsetting. But despite all the attention and vilification, the support from my colleagues, both in politics and in the Church, was quite extraordinary.

And I don't believe that my sexuality ever became a barrier between myself and my congregation. Often it is quite the reverse: if people see that you have been vulnerable, they can then express their own vulnerability and talk openly about things which are of concern to them at the deepest of levels. These are often the most harrowing and difficult of issues which cause people great anxiety but which they cannot talk about because they are trapped by their environment or their relationships. My sexuality and the public awareness of it is actually a great help in this process.

My faith is simple, simplistic even. My basic faith is in the teaching of a very fine man, who I think was the best teacher about human relationships there has been: about how people should live together and grow into a maturity where possessions are irrelevant and where their relationships with other people are pre-eminently important. My faith and the way I try to carry it out in the Church and the community as a whole is about encouraging people to see the best in themselves. It is most helpful when the teaching of Christ is translated into people's actual experiences, and that's my job. My faith is firmly rooted in a non-materialistic approach to life; it is about putting value on people and not things.

My sexuality is me, and I cannot conceive of Jesus Christ

denying the basic humanity which is within me or any other person whatever their sexuality. I find my sexuality entirely consonant with his teaching and therefore with my faith. So when I hear about people being very negative about my sexuality I react on lots of different levels. I laugh at the stupid comments that some come out with. But, at another level, I think I see people who need to love themselves a bit more. Having learnt to love themselves, they can then learn to love others. I don't see people I want to hate; I see people who need to open their eyes more, who need to see people for who they are and not what they are.

Going My Own Way

DEB FORSTER — DRIVING INSTRUCTOR

DEB FORSTER was born in Jersey in 1955. She settled in North London in the mid-70s, eventually setting up her own business as a driving instructor. Out of car interests include music (she was a drummer in a couple of women's bands) and walking the dog. More recently her interests have broadened to world travel; an extended trip to South East Asia and Australia with her partner is planned for the Summer.

I was born and brought up on Jersey. Life is all mapped out for nice, quiescent Jersey girls, a string of pearls on your eighteenth birthday followed by a large 'deb' party, and a nice little secretarial job while you wait for Mr Right to sweep you off your feet. All that was never for me. Unsure of what I wanted, I certainly knew what I didn't want. I had always known that I was different but I knew it was important to keep my mouth shut about it. I even had a 'boyfriend' for two years, just to be like everybody else. He was a really nice guy and we were close friends.

In my last year of school, few teachers could tolerate me. I wasn't GCE material and I was disruptive. My only passion, my drum kit purchased with my life savings, impressed no one. At the end of every term my parents made the trip to The Jersey College for Girls to beg them not to expel me and, as this was a fee-paying school, they succeeded, much to my dismay. The school managed to get rid of me three days a week to learn shorthand and typing at the local College of Further Education. My parents, spurred on by my success at shorthand and typing despatched me off to London for a year, to a very expensive Park Lane secretarial college where they awarded diplomas!

My move to London was financed by my parents and included residence in a hostel full of women. It was there that I met my first girlfriend. I had had closet crushes on different women every term until I met Jody. Neither of us had had a lesbian relationship before and, in early 70s London, we knew that the quality of our relationship depended on not publishing our feelings. I made the first drunken move, but it was pretty mutual, though more of a surprise for Jody. Any lingering doubts about my sexuality were immediately dispelled.

Before I met Jody, I thought I was the only lesbian in existence – then suddenly there were two of us. We didn't go to gay bars because we didn't know they existed.

Jody had been sent to the College by her employers in Bermuda and, on completion of the course, had to return to fulfil her contract. Before flying back to Bermuda, we paid a brief visit to Jersey and my parents naively made up two beds in the same room! Jody loved the island, but we maintained a low profile. I temped for six months to save the money and joined Jody in Bermuda. We lived together but it was a case of out of the frying pan and into the fire. Bermuda was no different to Jersey in its small island mentality. We remained closet (although in fact Jody's mum knew and was very supportive . . .). However, I loved the island, eighteen years old, living in paradise, halfway across the world, out of the clutches of my parents and blissfully in love. Jody disliked Bermuda in much the same way as I hated Jersey, and, when her bank contract ended eighteen months later, we left for Jersey to visit my parents before our 'intended' world travels. They never happened. We were broke and had to find work and accommodation back in Jersey.

A year later Jody returned to Bermuda to visit her parents. I was working in a factory and met another dyke there, Maureen, the first 'real' lesbian I had ever met. Our close friendship was instant, always platonic as it remains to this day. We were, however, out and outrageous together and entertained the whole factory floor with our camp activities and total disregard for the niceties of island proto-col. I met Marlene, the secretary to the Managing Director, at her Hen Party, but within a couple of months Marl and I set up home together, having painfully dealt with Jody's return from Bermuda and dismembering Marl's recently acquired marital status. Our employers were outraged and Marl was threatened with the sack and finally sent off on an all expenses paid trip to the Canary Islands to get over her 'problem'. I was also threatened with the sack, but my Union stepped in and, as a compromise, I was demoted from the office upstairs to the factory floor where a custom built metal office was constructed for me, presumably to protect the rest of the workforce. It was great. I had no-one to oversee me, I had music blaring across the factory floor and Maureen and her mates for company. Marl returned to the factory and was given an ultimatum: either get over it or get out, she resigned. It was a traumatic time, particularly for Marl, but she got an even better job almost immediately.

Six months later, in 1975, Marl and I moved to London. I couldn't get a job, largely because of my dress and appear-ance. It was the days of 'butch and femme' and I was definitely butch, and, though not consciously setting out to make a statement about my sexuality, I realise now that's

34

exactly what I did. Eventually, I got a job with a credit card company which I hated but couldn't afford to leave. Then one day a colleague spotted an advert for a driving instructor and I thought 'Yes. I want that'. I rang them and went for an interview. The owner asked me to drive his car round the block and told me that he had one more person to see. I thought 'Oh yeah. I've heard that before.' But they phoned next day and offered me the job. At last I had found something that I really wanted to do . . .

Marl and I were out and living in Finchley but didn't really know how to find the women's scene. We would drink in the William IV pub, Hampstead and the Black Cap, Camden, but these were haunts for gay men. Friday nights in the upstairs room at the Sols Arms by Capital Radio was our first lesbian venue, followed by a Saturday night basement 'dive' in a King's Cross pub. This place was actually the cellar, used for storing booze during the week, it was pretty foul with mould everywhere, damp running down the walls and generally dark, dank and depressing. We went to the legendary Gateways when Maureen came to visit from Jersey to show her a 'real' women's club which was open all week. I found Gateways cliquey and posey and much preferred the Sols Arms with its good music, good laughs and more relaxed, informal atmosphere. Marl and I split up in 1980 at about the time when the lesbian scene began to develop a higher profile. Rackets was my favourite lesbian haunt where I met some of my closest dyke friends. The music was brilliant and there was always a good crowd which helped me develop an awareness of the size of the lesbian community. I moved from Finchley to Haringey just because it was on a bus route home from Rackets. They closed soon after. It was the end of an era – nothing really ever replaced Rackets. I bought my second drum kit when I moved to Haringey, joined various women's bands and 'gigged' around London's gay venues.

At this time I worked for a small Driving School in King's Cross. Lesbian Line, Women's Aid, Homeless Action were all just around the corner. The first recognisable lesbian to book lessons with me reportedly informed one and all that 'there's a dyke working at the local School of Motoring' and thereafter I received a regular stream of enquiries which produced a workload which was the envy of my four male colleagues.

In 1983 I became self-employed and there was plenty of work around. It was the good old days of the GLC and ILEA. Women and young people who would otherwise have had little opportunity or financial resources to pursue driving instruction could join Youth Clubs or register on GLC/ILEA and local authority funded courses which included driving tuition. There weren't enough hours in my day and I didn't need to advertise. But my work with the Youth Services and local authority funded courses disappeared almost overnight due to the abolition of ILEA, the GLC and subsequent public sector cuts and restructuring. Many women who were working in lower and middle management were targeted for redundancy and therefore unable to pursue plans to learn to drive. Many of us are still waiting for John Major's 'upturn in the economy' . . .

Some pupils treat the car like a confessional, knowing full well that their secrets and intrigues go no further than 'those four doors'. I hear who is seeing who, for how long, who knows, who doesn't, how often, how good, bad . . . but this is my livelihood and I know when to be discreet. One scenario really sticks in my mind. (The following names are fictitious.) Before I dropped Jane at her home at the end of her lesson, I picked up my next pupil, Claire. Jane became distraught as we pulled up outside Claire's home and explained that she had recently discovered that her lover had been having an affair with her. Although they were aware of each other's existence, they had never met. Jane declined my offer to take her home first. All things considered, they found that they quite liked each other. Later they met up again and have been living together now for a number of years. I, too, met my current partner in my car some years ago. She passed her test!

To this day I have not come out to my parents. Of course they know, I never tried to hide my sexuality, but any discussion would be futile. They are the product of Jersey's small island mentality: male homosexuality was only decriminalised in Jersey in 1992 and then only as a direct result of pressure from, and threats of expulsion from the EEC.

I have seen lesbians progress from hidden away bars and lonely isolation to thriving nightclubs and marches on Pride. Although I have never been in a heterosexual relationship, I can see much more equality and quality in lesbian relationships.

Jody returned and settled in Bermuda, got married and now has two teenagers. We still keep in touch. Marl and her partner of twelve years have a two-year-old son. They were fortunate enough to avail themselves of NHS donor facilities before the recent media hype about lesbians and donor insemination. Me, I'm out of here, off to Indonesia with Bridget. Wonder if they need any driving instructors?

Out and Proud in the Athens of the North

ELLEN GALFORD — WRITER

ELLEN GALFORD is an adopted Scot who emigrated from the USA in 1971.

She has worked as a book editor, copywriter, TV researcher, restaurant critic, and freelance writer on subjects ranging from the home life of the Egyptian Pharaohs to the rise of the Sicilian Mafia. She is the author of four novels: *Moll Cutpurse: Her True History* (1984 reissued by Virago 1992), *The Fires of Bride* (1986), *Queendom Come* (Virago 1990) and *The Dyke and the Dybbuk* (Virago 1993). She lives in Edinburgh.

On the night of New York's great Stonewall riot, in 1969, I was living about twenty minutes' walk away, in another part of downtown Manhattan, probably sitting down to write thank-you letters for the wedding presents received a few weeks before.

I remember feeling, when the news broke, a nagging sense that I should have been there. But it was only in the mid-seventies, in the cool, blue light of Scotland, that I finally came out as a dyke. Scotland did for me what Greenwich Village didn't. I made up my mind about it in the wilds of

Argyll, had my first relationship with another woman in Glasgow, and headed eastwards to Edinburgh to be out, proud and loud.

Fresh off the train from Glasgow, where the lesbian scene felt much smaller and more precarious despite the city's greater size, I felt I'd arrived somewhere throbbing with Amazonian energy. But I blanched when, at a newly formed 'lesbian feminist discussion group', one woman announced that we might as well face the facts and accept that we were all destined to become each other's lovers. I don't think the group lasted for too many meetings after that.

The women I knew had closer ties to the women's liberation movement than to the mixed-sex Scottish Minorities Group (ancestor of Scotland's campaigning group, Outright). We had even fewer links to the apparently apolitical women in the gay bars: I remember, and blush for it now, that we sometimes referred to the latter as 'straight dykes', in snooty contrast to our politically sussed, counter-cultural, radical-activist, far-too-right-on-to-engage-in-old-fashioned-role-playing selves.

But Scotland is a land that likes its schisms (ask any historian of the nineteenth-century Kirk), and even inside the small world of Edinburgh lesbian feminists there were debates and divisions: working class vs. middle class; radical feminist vs. socialist feminist; separatist vs. anybody who ever gave the time of day to a man. In retrospect, I can laugh about some of it, but there were emotional firestorms and very real traumas: changing the world was easier than changing our lives.

It was in Edinburgh too, finally, after years of frustrated silence, that I found the voice as a writer I thought I'd lost way back in New York. A friend invited me to join a new feminist writers' group: half a dozen of us, lesbian and otherwise, met every few weeks in an old house on the beach at Lower Largo, in Fife, to read, discuss and, in scrupulously

39

sisterly fashion, criticise each other's work. The intellectual stimulation and support we gave each other (in the short pauses between walks on the beach and five-star vegetarian meals) have, over the years, borne fruit: every member of the group has become a published writer, of fiction, poetry or journalism.

Nevertheless, in 1979 my Glaswegian partner and I took the well-worn Scottish path to London: the streets down there, at the moment just before Tory tyranny descended upon us all, seemed paved not only with gold and better jobs, but with mortgages for single-sex couples (when we'd tried for the same in Scotland, the building society managers just showed us the door). But London, even with its massive lesbian population, felt like exile: I now considered myself more Scottish than anything else. This was hard for Londoners to understand: the accent was still transatlantic, but the sentiments were militantly Scottish.

So, in 1987, we were glad to come home. And it seemed that while we'd been away, Edinburgh's visible lesbian and gay population (and Glasgow's, too) had grown by what felt like a hundredfold. Why the sea change? Was it something in the drinking water, piped in from the reservoirs in the Pentland Hills? Was it the distinctly lavender colour of the northern winter light?

I am reluctant to offer any simplistic explanations, but lesbian Edinburgh by itself now has a larger population than some fairly substantial Scottish towns. Add to this our friends from Glasgow, Dundee, Aberdeen, down in the Borders and up the glens, and we'd probably qualify for regional status on our own.

This may come as a surprise to many members of the heterosexual Edinbourgeoisie: the academic and medical mandarins, the legal elite, the old boy networks who run the country and ruin the economy from their golf courses, all of them labouring under the illusion that their douce

Georgian dining rooms are the only nerve centres of the capital's life. Such folk as these do not let their hair down at the gay clubs or women-only discos, nor browse in our landmark lesbian and gay bookshop, West and Wilde, nor drop into the Blue Moon, neighbourhood café for all local and visiting sexual outlaws, nor stomp off into the hills with the inter-city dykey walking group, the Lilydots.

Before this slips any further into Scottish Tourist Board prose (now there's the germ of an idea ...) let me offer a bit of amateur social theorising as to why things have changed.

Tired old homophobic fulminations by the more Jurassic breed of politicos and certain contributors to the *Scotsman* letters page may bore us stiff, but they also stiffen our backbone. In Scotland, as in the rest of Ukania, their inscribed Sieg Heil, in the form of the contemptible Section 28, has strengthened our insistence that we will never let ourselves be invisible again. But I think there is also a specifically Scottish factor: the death, in the dyke world and elsewhere, of the Caledonian Cringe. People, urban and rural alike, have long since stopped looking southwards, to London, to pick up their cultural and political cues. And although there is a venerable, and international, tradition of lesbian and gay migration (I suppose I'm part of it), such movements are no longer essential for survival. Scots who want to be part of a visible, and richly varied, lesbian and gay culture don't have to go into exile to do it. The cutting edge, now, is right here.

Before, Now and In Between

Jane Bown

SIR IAN McKELLEN — ACTOR

SIR IAN McKELLEN was born in Lancashire in 1939. When he was eight he saw the romantic leading man, Ivor Novello on stage in Manchester and fell chronically in love with the theatre.

He has worked consistently since 1961. He came out when he joined the Arts Lobby against Section 28. Thereafter he co-founded Stonewall. He is a patron of Gay Sweatshop and London Lighthouse and is an associate director of the National Theatre.

There is a fantasy as old as the modern gay rights movement, that if all our skins turned lavender overnight the majority, confounded by our numbers and our diversity and recognising a few of our faces, would at once let go of prejudice for evermore.

In the United Kingdom today, the reality is that closet doors are opening, gingerly or defiantly, all over the place but not yet at such an enthusiastic rate that the imminent fulfilment of gay rights is inevitable. The powers that be are not yet convinced that we are a force to be reckoned with.

Meanwhile, some of us lobby and some try to frighten

the horses and together we make steady but minimal progress towards equality under the law. The recent whole-sale repeal of leftover English anti-gay statutes by the Irish Parliament is an inspiration. This seems to have been achieved without the benefit of a popular national campaign. That's not surprising, when anyone openly objecting to the old laws on his own behalf would have been declaring himself a criminal.

On the other hand we can also be inspired by the tactics of activists in the USA, who are funded by very large numbers of supporters. Together they have forced Congress, the Presidency and the media to debate and re-stress the basis of their constitution: *all* men are created equal. There is an abundance of gay rights organisations, recruiting in every state. When these groups work together, as they did for the 1993 march on Washington, they produce a miracle akin to skins turning lavender.

The media coverage was ubiquitous. The Washington story, for those marching as well as for those watching on cable television, was of a mighty coalition from every area of gay life, united in their demand for justice. Leading the parade was a collection of good and famous people none of them more dominant than any of the million who walked behind. This popular movement didn't need a lone leader. Heaven preserve us from a Führer, a pope or even a martyred King.

Rainbow-striped balloons, streamers, flags, ribbons and sashes decorated the route. Men and women were half-naked. It was too hot for too many costumes. Judging from the hugely supportive bystanders, only a handful of crack-pots objected that we had completely taken over the nation's capital, so that wherever you went, the straights were bent for a day. From the rally stage, with the Capitol's dome for a backcloth, the rhetoric flowed through the loudspeakers along the Mall to the George Washington monument. Old campaigners like Larry Kramer and new ones like Martina Navratilova. There were professional politicians – Jesse Jackson, the two out-gay congressmen – and a recorded message from Senator Kennedy, weekending with his new bride up north. But in the nation of big showbusiness, where were the big performers?

It's a sad fact that there isn't yet one leading American actor of either sex who is out. Movie agents and Hollywood executives are falling out or being pushed out of their closets. They ostentatiously fund pro-gay enterprises. But the stars themselves just won't twinkle.

Over the years there has been a long list of emigré gay Brits who have acted in Los Angeles. To a man and to a woman they too have nestled down in the cosy closet of the Californian sunshine, unshamed by their proximity to Christopher Isherwood and David Hockney. Only posthumously has Cary Grant (from Bristol) been identified and, with less confidence, Laurence Olivier in the latest biography. (Joan Plowright says that her husband was latterly boastful about his sexual adventures and would surely have included the spice of Danny Kaye, had there actually been an affair. Anyway she says, 'we must get love wherever we can'.)

There is a middle-aged British actress who used to introduce herself at London benefits by name, adding, 'and I'm a dyke'. Now that she is in the movies, she isn't out any longer and, with no joy, has wittingly entered the Hollywood closet, policed by the commercial need that we should all be the same, so that we shall all buy the same.

She's like another British colleague who during rehearsal for a Broadway show confided that he wasn't gay in New York. That was twelve years ago. When Sean Mathias and I went to the end-of-season Tony awards *à deux*, we were clandestinely congratulated for our daring in being out together. Well, if you share a home and a bed, you might as well share a couple of complimentary tickets. Today, America is awash with openly gay playwrights. Their example and the bravery of people with HIV/AIDS are beginning to transform the very close society of New York theatre and a few eminent young stage actors have also come out. That is possible because Broadway and off-Broadway are a community. By contrast, Hollywood and its suburbs are a commercial conglomerate.

I am proud to belong to a growing group of openly gay theatre people in the UK. Some of the most productive theatre enterprises are run by them: Greenwich, the Lyric Hammersmith, the Royal Court, Stratford East, Cheek-by-Jowl, DV8, Gay Sweatshop and the managements of Michael Codron and Cameron Mackintosh. There are actors, too, across the generations from Simon Russell-Beale and Anthony Sher to Alec McCowen and Nigel Hawthorne. Yet, even at a time of lesbian chic, there isn't a leading lesbian theatre actress of any age who is out in the UK. Should we expect otherwise? 'It's hard enough surviving as a woman in British theatre. Don't ask me to be a dyke as well!' This from a renowned actress who is out to her family, friends and working colleagues. So she tries to protect her job prospects with a lie.

Famous actors have long promoted non-theatre causes. Edward Alleyn spent a fortune 500 years ago on education. Fanny Kemble campaigned against slavery. The Redgraves publicised the PLO. Anthony Hopkins has acknowledged his debt to Alcoholics Anonymous. Brian Rix abandoned farce to run MENCAP and has now joined Attenborough in the House of Lords. In the Commons, Gyles Brandreth and Glenda Jackson have followed Andrew Faulds into the fray. Tenniel Evans is an actor-priest. With the same combination of private impulses and public service, some actors now work for gay rights. But we are outnumbered by others who, not hesitating to do an AIDS benefit or be photographed signing a poll tax petition, yet continue to disguise their sexuality even in their autobiographies. What a joy not to be part of that any longer.

At the outset of their careers, there are two obvious types of theatre actor: the super-confident seeking an extra outlet for their exhibitionism and the under-confident like me. I was attracted to the security of daily rehearsals, so that for three hours each evening on stage the confusion of every-day life was kept at bay. Looking back, my own confusion lay in society's disapproval of me. When I became an actor in 1961, it was illegal for me to make love. Ever since I had fallen for Ivor Novello when I was nine, I had wanted to work in the theatre, where I expected to meet other queers. I did.

Working in regional theatre in the 1960s, I missed swinging London and never discovered gay bars. When the law was somewhat relaxed in 1967, I noted that my role models, freed from the threat of blackmail, still didn't declare themselves. I half-believed that Gertrude Lawrence really was Noel Coward's greatest love. Later, I didn't realise that Gay Liberation was fighting for my freedom. My closet was comfortable, protected by the family structure of theatre companies, in which each person's individuality was cele-brated. If Betty Bourne or Martin Sherman ever suggested that I come out like them when I worked with them, I was too engrossed in my career to hear them.

I believed the nonsensical convention that audiences wouldn't accept a young actor in a straight romantic part if they knew he was gay. Does that mean that a law-abiding actor can't play a convincing murderer? Michael Winner considered me for a film in 1966 and asked if I was gay. I prevaricated long enough for him to say that 'queers often make the best screen lovers'. Twelve years on, Sam Spiegel offered me the lead in a Pinter screenplay but hastily withdrew it when I mentioned my boyfriend.

Meanwhile, in the theatre, I had played three wonderful gay roles: Marlowe's *Edward II*, Shaffer's farcical queen in *Black Comedy* and Max in Sherman's *Bent*. The dimmest theatregoer could have drawn the correct conclusion. At the time, I agreed with John Schlesinger, who used to think there was no need for him to come out, as his work made it obvious that he was gay. Conversely, when Simon Callow discussed his homosexuality in press interviews, the journalists declined to report it. He eventually managed to get himself out, by writing his own book!

The straight media has long wavered between thinking of homosexuality as a libel or a chastisement. That didn't, every so often, prevent their dropping hints about me. The *Daily Express* used to misplace the apostrophe by calling me 'The Queens' favourite actor'. The *Sunday Telegraph* posted me on a list of 'unavailable bachelors' alongside Prince Charles and Rudolf Nureyev. The *Guardian* mentioned that I shared my home with another man. I was spared the indignity of a tabloid exposé because I wasn't newsworthy. No journalist ever asked me whether I was gay, not even Nicholas de Jongh. If he had, I might have asked him the same.

I finally came out of my own accord in 1988. I had spent the previous year working all over the USA. My last stop was California. In San Francisco, three men helped me decide to come out. Steve Beery had been Harvey Milk's lover at the time of his assassination. Like Steve, Terry Anderson was a determined gay activist and helped to organise the annual Pride parade out of the Castro district. His partner, Armistead Maupin, was still writing his *Tales of the City* sextet. All three lives concentrated on gay politics and their example to me was clear: until you're out you don't know what you are missing. So it proved for me and, as far as I can see, for everyone else who ever came out. My three godfathers in San Francisco also stressed the absence of any out American actors but we realised that at 49, I was well enough established to resist any backlash of disapproval from employers, critics or fans. So it proved.

What I hadn't anticipated was the support system in waiting, as for converts backstage at a revivalist mission. I've made new friends galore who work among the 500 specifically lesbian and gay groups in the UK. Of late, gay-oriented commerce is thriving against the tide of recession. In Soho, there are the sproutings of the first exclusively gay area in central London. There does, after all, seem to be a powerfully pink pound. I help to spend it on gay literature, on as much gay theatre as possible and in my gay local pub.

That is now. I didn't do these things before. 'Before and Now': and, in between, saying 'As a gay man' was much less daunting than having to tell Gladys, my Quaker stepmother for forty years. That involved a trip to her home in the Lake District. We drove out into the friendly hills, the most beautiful in the world. I began with a warning that I had something important to tell her. She ended it by saying, 'I thought it was going to be something dreadful. I've always known you were gay.' 'Poor Gladys,' said an ancient friend of hers, 'now she'll have to leave the village.' Of course she didn't. Anyway the Society of Friends has an impeccable record on gay issues. My relationship with Gladys has never been so loving.

Friendships and working for equality through Stonewall have filled an emotional vacuum of which I hadn't been aware. If I'm also a better actor because of that, I shouldn't be surprised.

Making the Argument by Example

PAM ST CLEMENT — ACTRESS

PAM ST CLEMENT is best known as Pat Butcher in *EastEnders*. Her career has included a considerable amount of work in film, theatre and television. She is a Trustee of the Iris Trust and an original member of the Stonewall Group. She is a campaigner for animal charities and is actively involved with AIDS organisations.

In 1969 I was a student at drama school in Kent. It was a time of exploration and discovery for me, but I never thought about my sexuality, I was too busy bonking boys. I had never even heard of the Stonewall riot.

I was thinking about my career. When I left school I wasn't sure if I wanted to be a vet, a journalist or an actress. My father sent me to a public school to teach me to be a young lady and being an actress was something that nice young ladies didn't do. I acted at school and became president of the school drama society; I always felt that I had a feeling for expressing other people's emotions.

Before drama school I had an unusual childhood which I am still trying to piece together. My father was an East

49

Ender, a dashing, romantic man who married several times. He was Errol Flynn with a rather vicious subtext, the sort of man who should never have entered a long term relationship with a woman. My mother was Irish and died when I was young. During the war I was evacuated to Devon where I grew up in a not very well off hill farm with two elderly ladies who became my adoptive aunts.

My first job was as a teacher in an East End school. I loved the children but couldn't get on with the politics of the staff room. From there I moved into youth theatre and then began to get acting work. Even when I was going out with boys I was conscious that I had meaningful relationships with women. I got married in 1971. When I met my husband he was in the Navy, we had a fling and there seemed to be no reason why we shouldn't get married. It was when I was a young actress that I realised that I was physically attracted to women. I had my first affair and decided that I wasn't prepared to say that it was just a phase. I knew it was not fair on either myself or my husband to pretend. Although acting is about being someone else, I have always tried to be true to myself. I think actresses need to be quite private people; if you allow your own personality to dominate a role then you lose the magic. But you have to have a bottom line when you will stand by yourself and stand up for what you are. I don't mean that I was a complete adventurer, a sexual Freya Stark, but I did want to climb over the hill and look on the other side. I came out in 1976 and felt wonderfully free to club and enjoy myself. I was 'in lust' if not 'in love'. I used to go to the Gateways and knew Gina and Smithy who ran it for years. I could see then that there was a big cross section in the lesbian scene. There were the political lesbians and the old fashioned dykes. People often assumed that I was a butch because I didn't wear very femme clothes and the old back couldn't cope with six inch stilettos, but coming out actually made me feel more like a woman. It gave me permission to be comfortable with myself and to enjoy my 'femaleness'. I think women are lovely. If being femme is being lovely for yourself and everybody else that's fine with me.

I wasn't at all involved with gay politics, but the women's movement hit me. I went on International Women's Day Marches. It was gloriously exciting and I was involved with the National Abortion Campaign, I helped organise their first theatrical fundraising event. I was never involved in women's theatre, I always worked in the mainstream. I wasn't really worried that being a lesbian would affect my career. I always played character parts and there is never a graph of success for jobbing actresses.

I first appeared in *EastEnders* in 1986. At that point, Pat, my character, was so nasty and vitriolic that I thought that they would never want to keep her in the series. But the producers assured me that I had only seen one dimension of her character, the aggressive defensiveness. They would peel away all those layers and a different person would emerge. When I was offered the part I not only had to think about being out as a public figure but also about how I would cope with the recognition, being someone that everybody knew in their own homes. I talked a lot with my partner, I felt I could take it all if she could. I'd dropped a pebble in a pond and I wanted to follow it through. I decided that I wasn't going to hide my lesbianism, but I wasn't going to make a song and dance about it either. Certain people at work knew, it was never a secret. Although I got 'outed' by the tabloid press, in fact I had never been 'in'.

I first got involved in gay politics in the campaign against Section 28. Ian McKellen and Michael Cashman approached me about taking part in a big benefit, *Before the Act* that the Arts Lobby was putting on. I knew Michael from *EastEnders*. I think there had been a few gay characters on TV shows before but 'Colin', Michael's character was the first major one and certainly the first to kiss.

Both Ian and Michael were very conscious about the difficulties that I might face, particularly as a woman, in publicly supporting the campaign, but I felt that it was something that had to be done. I did a sketch with other cast members of *EastEnders* for the show and it was the most wonderful night of comradeship, entertainment and raucousness. It was wonderful to appear with so many great stars like Peggy Ashcroft and Alan Bates all supporting us. When I left the theatre I was walking by myself to the car and a journalist literally crept up on me and started asking questions about why I had taken part in the show. I said something about supporting personal freedoms, but very shortly afterwards, my personal life was splashed across the front page of the *News of the World*. After feeling all the strength of the show and solidarity, I was suddenly alone and vulnerable. It wasn't dramatic, I didn't think that the bottom had dropped out of my world. It was like being abused by rather nasty rats.

Despite all their doorstepping, questioning neighbours and shouting through the letterbox, the journalists got it all a bit confused. They could never decide which of us was Gertrude and which was Alice. They depicted us both as 'bull dykes', wrongly describing my partner as a mannish six footer and myself as a beer-swilling pubcrawler.

I think there is something especially vicious in the male response to women choosing women. It was that viciousness that came out in the tabloids. It's true men do eroticise lesbians, but that's when we are under their control. If women are independent, if they choose to be with other women, men hate it. Sometimes I feel that hatred underneath the surface, sometimes it's blatantly above the surface. It makes me very angry.

The BBC and the cast were very supportive. My friends and colleagues found it hard to believe that we were being treated like this just because we were gay. They weren't all right on radicals; they just understood that we were normal people entitled to the same rights as everyone else.

To me, Stonewall is about what I call 'normalisation'. In demanding equal rights under the law we are a counter-weight to those elements of the tabloid press who want people to hate us and to be vocally and physically aggressive. By being dignified and 'out' and at ease with ourselves we win the argument by example. I don't want to be the exception and the headline. I want people to see lesbians and gay men as individuals who are all different, good and bad.

I have felt incredibly sustained by the gay movement. Just after I was 'outed', I was helping in the Stonewall tent at Pride and everyone was enormously kind and supportive. It felt like being part of the family.

I suppose now I am something of an icon, both in my TV character and because I am still one of the very few out lesbians in this country. It's silly to talk about this as a burden, but I do feel a bit alone, I don't believe in outing, but I wish other lesbians would join me.

I prefer to call *EastEnders* a bi-weekly drama, rather than a soap opera. It is a very special programme, it was one of the first popular TV shows which took up some of the social issues of the time and made them ordinary people's problems. It didn't try to be comfortable and nostalgic. That's why it was always gay friendly. Now after the Conservatives have been in power for fourteen years some of that hope and optimism has been rubbed away; the programme is blander now.

I now have a big following of gay men. I think they like 'Pat' because there's that sense of grittiness and endurance shining through the tragedy and the harsh knocks. It's the Dorothy Squires, Judy Garland syndrome. I suppose in that sense I am a camp character. Perhaps they also like the strong maternal image.

I think I have shown that you can be out and survive, but I don't overestimate the progress we have made, it is still incredibly difficult for young actresses. But one of the great strengths of the movement now is that men and women are working together. I think that one of the reasons that CHE (Campaign for Homosexual Equality) split up was that the men and the women couldn't work alongside each other. The women were into politics and the men wanted to cruise. Stonewall for me is about men and women working equally together. It's part of the vision of what life could be like.

I am still changing and exploring different aspects of myself, although I am not sure that I live so close to the edge any more. Perhaps in some ways I have put the lid on my spiritual development; it's a room in the house that I haven't dusted for a while. But I still feel that moment of sheer anger when the press try and crucify some Council just because they recognise the existence of gay people. Gay people pay their taxes and they have a right to expect a society which is integrated and tolerant, not one that shuts people out. In the face of that I will not be silent.

Glad to be Square

HEATHER SAVAGE — CHEF

HEATHER SAVAGE was born in Belfast in 1961. She graduated from the University of Stirling in English Literature and History. She has worked as a sandwich board woman, Santa's elf, Media Sales Manager, Chef and Bagel Shop Proprietrix. She lives in Scotland with her cat Maurice.

My family's, particularly my mother's, expectation of me was so high that upon entry into the real world via my first primary school I was sorely disappointed when teachers and fellows neglected to kneel before me bearing gold, frankincense and myrrh.

My schooling was patchy and often interrupted, owing to the nomadic lifestyle of my family, whose chief pastime seemed to be emigrating to various countries *en masse*, when the mood came upon them, and my own ill-health in early childhood (my grandmother had decreed that I was 'delicate'). So I never fitted in at school. Not at any of my eleven schools. Being the only girl in the fourth form who wore a liberty bodice had a profound effect upon me, and a lasting one. The mass hysterical laughter in that games changing room must echo yet.

I discovered that my orientation was different from other girls' when I was eight or nine, if not earlier. So I cannot blame the liberty bodice. But wherever I went, whoever I mixed with, and whatever I did, I always felt like the outsider, the one who didn't fit. I knew why I was different, but I could not accept being so very different. The only gay people I had ever seen were a journalist on the *Bangor Spectator*, who dyed his eyelashes blue and wore perfume, and a maths teacher who wore tweed skirts and men's shoes and reputedly smoked a pipe. These people, I was told, were not normal, nor could they ever be happy, and in any case it was illegal to be like that. My grandmother refused to discuss my Great-uncle Freddie, who was a nurse in London, and knitted the most wonderful Fair Isle pullovers. He was, I remember, also fond of cravats.

I promised myself that I would wait until I was a great success, at something or other, before I lived in that very different way. I was prepared to shelve my real self, knowing even at the age of 20 and naive as the average 14-year-old, that my life would be hellish if I didn't.

Ironically, it was within the dreary university confines that I finally decided to let go of the conventions, to flick two fingers at success, and to experience as much as possible, but always on my own terms and never with acceptance in view.

Sadly, the experiences I witnessed of the few openly gay people on campus profoundly affected my perception of what it was to be gay. They were tolerated, joked about behind their backs, and often harassed: shit through the letterbox was a frequent occurrence, particularly after a rugby club piss-up. One gay man I knew well shared a campus flat with four rugby players. He slept with three of them, yet stood by while their friends threw stones through his bedroom window. I had a stronger sense of self-preservation than he. I remained locked behind my closet door. But in my third year I had a summer fling with my first woman lover and then went to the USA where nobody knew me and explored living as a lesbian further.

In my last year at university, I lived a gay life outside my old straight circle of friends. I took up with a pack of newly emerging wannabee dykes who are still my closest friends, and fell in love with a chestnut-haired Irishwoman. I had, at last, found acceptance and love, in this new world within a world.

Freedom to express my sexuality openly has always been very important to me, yet I was still convinced that there was also a need to conform to the middle-class norm; to succeed, and to be perceived to succeed. I wanted to have a career and so chose magazine publishing, because I was 26 and passionately believed that the world really needed a lesbian-orientated glossy monthly. I know better, now.

In the small, chummy, but high-pressure environment of London, I began to thrive on the thin air of optimism, ambition and greed that fed many of the graduates of 1987. I had come out to the directors, two women, during my interview. They practically begged me to take the job – all they needed then was a disabled person and someone of colour to complete their set. Within a year I was queer-bashed twice; on each occasion my caring, sharing bosses urged me to return to work as soon as possible, preferably within two days. I discussed handing in my notice once, because I was bored with the job and wary of bumping into my attackers, and in a meeting it was gently put to me that other publishing companies, indeed other companies in general, would be less than sympathetic to my maverick ways and open and unashamed lesbianism. So much for my so-called liberal bosses.

The strain of remaining in a job I grew to loathe in a city I detested led to a complete and spectacular nervous collapse. I returned home, helped by several very good friends, and began a laborious rebuilding process. Without, I wish to add, the help of therapy. Love and friends at that time were enough.

The happy ending? That has yet to happen. But I did find a woman who taught me a great deal about unconditional love, by loving me unconditionally for several years, and I 'found myself' in cooking.

My parents had reservations: they saw working as a chef as a 'step down' after my high-flying job in London. But they have seen me change, and blossom and flourish in the four years since my return from London, and they have come to accept my sexuality and all it entails.

Heterosexuals, like the middle classes, have an unshakeable belief in their right to success and in their superiority as a species. Their expectations are high at birth, and remain high, because no one tells them, 'No. You can't.' Gay men and lesbians don't have this, whatever their background. We are raised with a sense of fear and revulsion at ourselves and our sexuality.

Some may disagree, claiming that they consider themselves every bit as good as straight people. But I believe that inside every gay person there hides a tiny grain of inadequacy; a feeling that whatever we do we will never be quite good enough to be classed as 'the same'. We will never have the same status as heterosexuals, and we will, consequently, never enjoy exactly the same rights. We are condemned to be considered somehow 'not quite quite', and this is bound to affect our self-esteem, and our expectations.

We have to alter our perception of success. We have to redefine many of heterosexual society's preconceptions. Gays must re-evaluate and relearn life. Self-esteem is the only foundation upon which we can legitimately build. We must add on wisdom, kindness, honesty, trust and love as and when we can. Then we can determine our own victories and successes. The heterosexual world remains foreign and hostile, yet the safe haven we can create for ourselves on the periphery of it is one in which we can thrive and fulfil our potential, in both our professional and personal lives.

Square pegs only fit into round holes if we change their entire shape or force them in. This alteration or forcing changes the nature, the very essence of the peg. Yet that peg will never be perceived as, or accepted as, a round peg like all the other round pegs. It will be merely a square peg that has been bent out of shape or broken.

I have learnt to love being a square peg in a square hole, and that, as far as I can be aware, is the only kind of success that is worth striving for. That accepted, the rest follows.

The Politics of Pride

CHRIS SMITH – MEMBER OF PARLIAMENT

CHRIS SMITH is Britain's first out gay MP. He has been Labour member for Islington South and Finsbury since 1983. He is a former Shadow Treasury Minister and is Vice-Chair of the All-Party Parliamentary Group on AIDS and the All-Party Parliamentary Group on Drug Misuse. He is on the board of Shelter and a governor of Sadler's Wells Theatre Foundation; he is co-chair of the Stonewall All-Party Parliamentary Group.

It was in the early 1980s that lesbian and gay politics began to hit the national headlines in a big way. There had been massive publicity around the passing of the 1967 Sexual Offences Act, and vigorous national debate on the subject; but once that was safely on the statute book, the fire seemed to have gone out of the argument. Not, however, for long. Within fifteen years the whole issue had again sprung to life, and much of the response was motivated by the worst possible kinds of prejudice.

The Greater London Council dared to say that it wanted to ensure equal treatment for lesbians and gay men, and was vilified for doing so. It sought to provide modest financial assistance for the establishment of a lesbian and gay centre (on the same lines as many European capitals, only better) and was castigated by irate ratepayers who somehow forgot to notice that lesbians and gays were ratepayers too. Other local authorities tried to offer some practical assistance: Islington, for example, purchased a set of gym mats for a women's self-defence course that included lesbian participants. It was quoted endlessly as conclusive proof of loony-leftism gone mad. From that period onwards, the tabloid press began to treat lesbians and gay men as 'fair game', to be hunted, pilloried and railed against in the most wretched and senseless fashion.

And then of course, came the sorry saga of the Bermondsey by-election. Bob Mellish, the long-established sitting Labour member, former Chief Whip and scourge of the left in the party, resigned from Parliament, and the local Labour Party selected Peter Tatchell to fight the seat in his place. Peter was clearly from the left, was gay (which was known fairly widely), and had been criticised publicly by the party leadership. A viciously homophobic campaign ensued. Bob Mellish campaigned against him, using the sneering slogan, 'Which Queen will you vote for?' I can vividly remember canvassing for Peter in that by-election. In a seat that had been rock-solid Labour for decades, it was uphill work. On doorstep after doorstep I encountered voters who said yes they'd vote Labour, but I knew in my heart that in the end they wouldn't. Anti-gay posters appeared on walls. People talked about it. Other political parties did nothing to stem the tide of prejudice. And Peter lost, massively.

All of us dedicated to a politics of inclusion, a politics that seeks to draw lesbians and gays into the mainstream rights of society, were dealt a savage blow by Bermondsey. The result of that by-election fortified the bigots and disheartened the rest of us. How could a straightforward politics of equal rights be advocated in such a hostile atmosphere?

I well remember the time, less than two years after Bermondsey, when we debated the 'pretty police' problem in Parliament. Police officers dressed provocatively in tight jeans had been lounging around outside gay pubs and 'enticing' men into sexual contact. The practice of entrapment, officially discouraged, was still going on, and the gay community was rightly enraged. The issue came to a head when a Conservative MP in a Soho club was arrested by the police for soliciting. The case hit national headlines; the MP defended himself successfully; and we ended up having a tense debate in Parliament on an amendment to the Police and Criminal Evidence Bill which tried to prohibit any practice of entrapment by the police.

It was late at night, but the press gallery was packed. I was absolutely terrified when I spoke. The whole atmosphere of the Commons on that occasion was fraught. One or two brave souls from the Conservative benches spoke up in favour of an amendment to the law, but the entire presumption of the occasion was that speaking up for lesbians and gay men was somehow rather strange, and certainly politically dangerous.

Shortly afterwards, customs and excise officers raided Gay's the Word bookshop in London, impounded a range of books that had been imported, declared them indecent and obscene, and launched a prosecution of the bookshop under an antiquated piece of customs law which appeared to say that something that wasn't obscene in domestic law could nevertheless be obscene if it were imported. The raid on Gay's the Word galvanised the lesbian and gay community. Meetings were held, petitions drawn up, a fighting fund was established. And the legal action was contested every inch of the way. In the end the Customs and Excise backed down, but in the meantime they had taught us two things. First, that lesbians and gay men will continue to be 'picked on', in a whole variety of different ways. And second, that it is possible for us all to come together, protest and succeed.

It was against this background that I decided to 'come out'. A rally was being held in the town of Rugby, against the local council who had declared that they were removing sexual orientation from the list of attributes they would not discriminate against in employment. The decision had been accompanied by stark statements from the leader of the council, about not wanting men coming to work in dresses and earrings, and other similarly nonsensical stuff. I had agreed to speak at the protest rally, and when I arrived to find a hall packed with about a thousand people or more I decided, very much on the spur of the moment, to make a statement about myself.

'My name is Chris Smith, I'm the Labour MP for Islington South and Finsbury, and I'm gay,' was all I said. The rest was drowned in the most amazing standing ovation I have ever experienced. The worthy sentiments I'd prepared for the rest of my speech, about freedom from discrimination and the right to work, got rather overwhelmed in the wash. I had thought that the tabloid press would go to town over what I had said, but they uttered not a word. It took the *Sun* about four months to get round to carrying an article about it. My mailbag was almost entirely positive. What I think had been achieved was the removal of any titillating salacious innuendo-value in the whole exercise. I am led to the over-whelming conclusion that you counter prejudice and sniping criticism best by being open, clear and confident about who and what you are. It is a lesson I believe we need to keep learning and relearning as the years go by.

In the immediate aftermath of Rugby, I decided very deliberately to take a high-profile role in debates and commit-tees on subjects completely unrelated to specifically lesbian or gay concerns: the environmental problem of acid rain; the future of the British film industry; and the desperate need for more and better housing for hard-pressed inner-city areas like Islington. It is, I believe, crucially important for openly lesbian and gay figures in public life to demonstrate that they can do well in all areas of life, all subjects of politics, every bit as well as – if not better than – anyone else.

Since that time, the atmosphere for debate and discussion in the House of Commons on any lesbian and gay subject has certainly improved. The change can perhaps be most clearly seen in the profound difference between two debates we had on the issue of AIDS. The first, held shortly before the 1987 general election, was scarred by the most blatant homophobia, and betrayed startlingly little knowledge about the facts of HIV. The second, held three years later, was better informed, more progressive and far better tempered. Perhaps, after all, some people, even some politicians, can learn what reality has to teach us.

It was against this background of tabloid hostility but slightly improving parliamentary atmosphere that the shock of what we now know as Section 28 occurred. It was brought forward by a group of Conservative right-wing backbenchers, but was shamefully endorsed by the government and passed both in committee and on the floor of the House. Not, however, before a massive public protest, a couple of intense debates in Parliament, enormous demonstrations in Manchester and London, the invasion of abseiling lesbians into the House of Lords, and a remarkable sense of solidarity amongst the lesbian and gay community. And not only did the community take up political cudgels in a way never really seen before; lesbians and gay men were working together, making common cause, and fighting alongside each other in an amazingly new way.

Section 28 has never, ever been used in court against a local authority. Its malign power rests on two things. First, it makes council officers censor themselves: they warn against making a particular grant, or giving a particular permission, because it might infringe the wretched Section. This, of course, is the traditional trick of the censor: you force your victims into acts of self-censorship. Secondly, and most importantly, Section 28 is offensive because of what it stands for. It labels lesbians and gay men as second-class citizens. It rejects the principle of diversity in democracy. It seeks to impose some sort of conditioned 'normality' on everyone. Indeed, in this respect, it represents a disturbing trend of the Thatcher years: a drive for economic liberalism coupled with a drive in a completely opposite direction, towards social conformism.

I like to think that the government learnt something of a lesson from Section 28. They were genuinely alarmed at the strength of opposition they encountered, and have certainly not tried the same sort of thing again. There have even been one or two very minor victories. The government have announced that lesbians and gay men in the armed services will no longer be prosecuted for their sexuality. They'll still be dismissed, and that's bad enough; but the change is a tiny, tiny step in the right direction. There is also the amendment to the first draft of proposals about the possibility of lesbian and gay fostering of children, as well as welcome moves in some police forces to take the needs of the lesbian and gay community seriously to heart. All of this is welcome, but it certainly doesn't add up to a consistent or coherent agenda for change.

The upshot of the last fifteen years in Britain is that lesbians and gay men have far greater visibility than before. More famous people have been perfectly happy to identify themselves as lesbian or gay. Rock stars, actors, characters in soap operas have said they are, and perhaps this has encouraged other people – in the neighbourhood, in the family, in the house next door – to follow suit. The greater the visibility, the greater the public acceptance will be. I believe it is growing.

That growth is reflected in the response to politics. When the Tory right-wingers launched the Section 28 campaign, I am sure they thought of it as a sure-fire vote-winner for the Conservative Party. It wasn't. In America, the Republicans tried the same trick in 1992, with a convention that was full of so-called moral prejudice. That didn't work either. Knee-jerk, anti-gay sentiment doesn't necessarily win votes, as politicians on both sides of the Atlantic are beginning to understand.

Fighting back against prejudice, securing a better political atmosphere for debate, and increasing our visibility, are all gains that we have made in recent years. We still have a long way to go, however. Britain remains one of the most regressive countries in Europe on lesbian and gay rights. The law discriminates in the age of consent and the position of people in the armed services; and there is still a battery of ancient laws used almost exclusively against consensual gay contact. Administrative practice discriminates in housing, in employment, in custody cases, in the immigration rules. Much of the tabloid press remains vilely homophobic. Section 28 remains on the statute book. And we have no anti-discrimination protection in law either.

In New South Wales an anti-vilification law has just been passed, to protect lesbians and gay men. The fact that we can't even dream of such progress here, that we have so far to go on a much more basic agenda first, demonstrates very clearly how very far behind we really are. In twenty-five years we have made some painfully small, agonisingly won advances. But we must aim infinitely higher.

Proud of Who I Am

CHARLOTTE TAYLOR – POLICEWOMAN

CHARLOTTE TAYLOR was born in 1966, the youngest of four children. She was brought up in the Wirral. She has lived in Scotland, Brussels and now lives in London with her partner of six years. She joined the police in 1991 and passed out from Hendon Training College in November that year. She was posted to an outer London district for 2 years and is now based in North London.

I first realised I was gay when I was 13 or 14. I just had this feeling that I was different. I was a very insecure child and adolescent and I couldn't bear the thought of being shut out from the rest of society as I believed all 'deviants' were. Coming out and accepting my sexuality was a long, slow and sometimes difficult process.

I ended up having a one-night stand with my best friend at the time. I left that thinking, 'This is it, I know where I'm going', she left it thinking, 'I'm never going to do that again', but we are still friends and we've talked a lot.

I met my first real lesbian when I was 16 and she took me to my first gay club. I also had a gay male friend of my own age and he and I really supported each other. I went out to pubs and clubs in Liverpool, but it was right at the end of the butch/femme era and I just couldn't relate to the women there. I considered myself an ordinary woman who just happened to be attracted to other women and just did not feel I belonged.

Coming to terms with my sexuality took a long time. I told my parents when I was 19 and they reacted really well, but I still didn't have much confidence or belief in myself. I moved to Scotland to work as a volunteer at a Rudolph Steiner home, and it was there that I really found myself. The life there gave me a lot of time to think and to deal with all the rubbish that was going on in my head. After about eighteen months it was time to move on: I knew I was ready to start living as a gay woman, I now had the confidence to be my true self.

I moved to London and started to attend a gay group in Harrow. There I met my partner, Maggie, who lives with me now. We had a long and slow courtship. Maggie really believed in me and as a result I really began to believe in myself. I gained a lot of strength from her and regained all my self-confidence. She gave me a sense of pride.

I first thought about joining the police when I moved to London, but certainly wasn't ready for it. I didn't know if I could cope with the bigotry which I saw within the force. I find it very hard not to tell people that I am a lesbian and didn't know if I would manage to be closeted or if I could cope with the adverse reactions if I came out. But when on various TV programmes I saw that things had started to change, I felt I could be both out, and in the police.

People told me that I shouldn't be out before I joined but I was determined. I didn't realise that there would be hurdles right from the beginning. The first question on the application form was, 'Are you married or single?' I didn't know how to answer, and so ticked single – my big resolve crashed at the first hurdle.

After I had sent in my application I received a home visit by a couple of local bobbies to suss me out. The first thing they did when they arrived was to look in every room; I hadn't bothered to shut the doors or anything. There was a big double bed in one room and no bed in the spare room, so they could see the situation at once. The first question they asked was if I shared my flat with a woman. Just as they were coming to the end of the interview they asked what my relationship was to my flatmate. I said that she was my friend, which wasn't really a lie. They then asked if I was emotionally involved, which I took to mean with my friend although of course it could have been with anyone. I said no – I decided that one lie was better than loads.

I felt terrible then. It was the first time I had denied Maggie, and our relationship, and I felt awful; it was really horrible. I was very upset and Maggie said, 'Give it up, give it up.' But I was stubborn and thought, 'No, I'll carry on, I'll wait till I get into the force and then I'll come out.'

I got past the interview and was accepted. I started at Hendon in July 1991 and went through the five months' training. Another woman in my class was also gay. When I told her that I wanted to come out, she wouldn't have any of it. For the first ten weeks she desperately tried to stop me, and really started to make me doubt myself again. Other lesbians there started to pressurise me to stay in the closet too. I was feeling a lot of stress – it is a hard enough job without having to watch every word you say. I realised that I simply couldn't do it any more.

I came out by rumour. I told a person who I thought would probably tell somebody else, who would tell somebody else. One day a lesbian friend took me to one side and said 'Charlotte, I think you ought to know . . .' We were in her room and two of the other lesbians came in. They started to criticise me for coming out and threatening their anonymity. They told me I had no right to come out, which made me very angry. I was very clear that *they* had no right to make me feel guilty. It was really painful: suddenly I felt alone. I wasn't getting support from my own kind, so I could imagine what it would be like from everyone else. Now I understand why those women felt as they did – since we left the close proximity of Hendon we've talked it all out – but it was very difficult at the time.

One day I walked into the canteen and there was a massive silence. I nearly gave up, and would have walked out right then if it hadn't been for Maggie's support at the weekends, a straight woman friend who didn't give a damn about my sexuality, and my instructors who were very supportive.

But even though the rumour was going round, no one was actually prepared to talk to me about it, to find out if it was true. So everyone was nervous: I knew that they knew, but they didn't know if I knew that they knew. I started winkling people out, talking about Maggie, bringing the subject up in the pub in the evening. This started to make people relax because suddenly they saw I was comfortable about my sexuality. It is easier to deal with people face to face about being gay, even when they have problems with it, than to cope with silence. Most prejudice is based on ignorance; whatever the reason, people have no right to judge you just because you are gay.

After I finished training, I went to an outer-London station. I got on with my work, but the rumour about my sexuality came with me – it always does with this job. I didn't make a statement, I didn't go into the parade room and say, 'I think you ought to know, I'm a lesbian.' A lot of fellow officers felt that I went on about being gay quite a lot, but I don't feel I did. All I do is talk about Maggie in the same way that they talk about their partners. I know that some of my fellow officers think I pushed it down their throats. I am pushing my sexuality down their throats no more than heterosexuals push their sexuality down gay people's throats all the time. If I said nothing about being gay, I would lose my sense of identity. I am proud of being a lesbian and I am proud of who I am.

It is hard to put yourself on the line and I have found it very tiring. I feel I have to prove myself more than other officers, not only because I am a woman, but also because I am an openly gay woman. Male officers have told me that a lot of the men find me threatening because I talk openly about something they find difficult. They should start dealing with their own prejudice before deciding that I am the problem. A lot of their fear is because they know that I am not afraid to speak my mind and to question the way they do things. If they step out of line, I am not going to keep quiet. I won't follow the male party line; I am not going to pamper their egos and go along with their jokes if I don't find them funny.

I do have a circle of friends outside the police but it is hard. I find it almost as difficult to say to new gay people I meet that I am a police officer as I do telling police officers that I am gay. In some ways the gay reaction is even worse: I can feel people thinking, 'Oh, I don't think I'll bother carrying on this conversation.' It hurts. Many gay police officers feel that terrible isolation; they don't feel they belong in either camp. One of the reasons I joined the police was because change was happening and I wanted to help that change along. You have to have some people on the inside with the right ideas, otherwise change will never get anywhere.

My sexuality will always be an issue – you never stop coming out. Whenever you meet someone new you have to gauge what their reaction will be. I've just moved to a new station where I'll have to go through it all again, and I'm exhausted with it. I am not going to be closeted about my sexuality, I'm not ashamed about it, but it is nobody's business but my own.

Policing Pride is weird. I like and I don't like Pride. I like it because I do feel proud. But this year as I sat in a van full of police, a gay man stopped, turned, pointed at us and said, 'You lot are all straight.' I just raised an eyebrow and thought, 'Oh, yeah.' I felt like saying to that guy, 'How dare you assume I'm heterosexual . . .'

Out in the Open

RALPH WILDE –
YOUNG ACTIVIST

RALPH WILDE is 20 years old. He has been a Youth Ambassador for the UN in Geneva, an English teacher in China and a researcher for Senator Edward Kennedy in the US Senate. He is currently a governor of the London School of Economics where he studies International Relations. He is very closely involved in the campaign to achieve an equal age of consent for gay men and will be taking his case to the European Court of Human Rights.

It is unfortunate that the invidious combination of Section 28 and an age of consent at 21 meant that when I was at school there was scant possibility of being honest. As with all other non-heterosexual teenagers, I missed out on conventional adolescence and was spectacularly frustrated at not being able to express my sexuality. At no time, however, did I question the sexuality itself. My only problem was my perception of other people's attitudes to it and how I believed they would affect my prospects for a happy, fulfilled life.

Needless to say, sex education made no mention of

same-sex intercourse and the whole experience (with the use of clinically sterile words like 'zygotes') was an embarrassment for all concerned, not the scenario in which to ask important questions about sexuality. One contemporary, braver than me at that age, came out in the sixth form and suffered as a result. There were lots of things I wanted to do and I imagined then that coming out would prevent this. I resolved to play the game and lead a double life, such were the moral values instilled by the school.

It took the radical shift in context that came when I left school and began work to challenge my resolve on the balance between public and private honesty. After I finished my A levels I had six months to kill before I went to China, where I had a job teaching English. I decided to go for a job at the Hacienda nightclub in Manchester, and made the conscious decision not to lie any more and actively to pursue relationships with people of my own gender. My experiences at the Hacienda will stay with me for the rest of my life.

At this time there was a pink revolution afoot in Manchester, as more places became gay friendly and gay-owned bars and clubs became the trendiest places to be, whether you were gay or straight. The 1990s queers were setting the agenda in Manchester's clubland, capitalising on gay culture and creating the most exciting and dynamic scene in town. It is worth noting that it is the dance music of black gay clubs in New York, Chicago and Detroit that all the straight white clubbers were dancing to at the Hacienda at that time, yet unlike the States there was a large degree of ignorance about the heritage of such music.

The time came for gay people to reclaim this heritage. Paul Cons and Lucy Scher founded the gay promotions company A Bit Ginger (as in ginger beer = queer) and the hip Manto bar started, which soon expanded into the club Paradise Factory.

It was at the Hacienda that I came into contact with my

first successful, articulate and respected man who was also thoroughly homosexual. To see a successful gay man was worth much more than being told in an abstract way that it was OK to be gay. It was wonderful to see the possibilities on offer if one decided to ignore the received wisdom about the dire prospects for fags. I had the time of my life and am very grateful for the supportive atmosphere there which nurtured my determination not to accept any hassle and to be proud of what I am.

At the London School of Economics I pushed further at what I thought was the risky business of being 'out'. I was utterly prepared to be honest and candid if the subject came up, yet never willing to broach the subject unilaterally. Through writing for the student newspaper, involvement in student politics and then being elected president of my hall of residence, I became known in the union, but not particularly for my sexuality. My biggest fear about coming out – that I would be robbed of my identity and seen merely as 'the gay one' – never materialised and instead I became someone who was achieving things in the union. A good example without being a self-defeating stereotype.

This attitude was reinforced when I began the 'Age of consent' campaign and announced that I would be taking the government to the European Court of Human Rights. For my peers, all of us studying international law, to bring a case to the European Court was the perfect combination of academic study and political activism. They respected me for making the stand, and in the process perhaps reassessed their own perceptions of homosexuality. Many people came to me as the 'only gay friend I have' to, quite unsolicited on my part, talk about their views on homosexuality and the age of consent. A taboo subject was out in the open and people relished the opportunity to express their thoughts.

I won all subsequent elections in the union and as a result am now on the board of governors of the LSE. This has been an opportunity to influence change. The school, where the Gay Liberation Front was founded, came up with a two-tiered 'equal' opportunities statement that contained a self-defeating distinction appearing to award less than equal opportunities on grounds of, amongst others, sexuality.

In summer 1993 I went to Washington to work for Senator Edward Kennedy on gay civil rights. America, of course, contains both extremes – 'moral majority' prejudice and tremendous lesbian and gay activism. In cities like Chicago, New York, Washington, Seattle and San Francisco I saw lesbian and gay organisations that were light years ahead of what we have, sophisticated lobbying groups and vast direct action networks. I was in DC at the time of the 'lesbians and gays in the military' débâcle, when reactionary forces in Congress and the full might of the Pentagon forced Clinton to back down on his campaign pledge to lift the military ban.

Despite a media that seemed comparatively conservative (for example *Tales of the City* was finally made by Channel 4 and *The Lost Language of the Cranes* by the BBC) the climate in America's big cities was markedly different to that of the UK. Their ethos is that individuals can prove themselves, they do not have to be held back by artificial constraints. One of Ted Kennedy's counsels, the man who sat on Hillary Clinton's healthcare task force, wrote speeches for Kennedy and drafted both the Ryan White AIDS care bill and the forthcoming gay civil rights bill, has a banner above his computer proclaiming, 'Homosexual by nature, militant by choice'.

In America, people are taught about their rights and are much more willing to stand up and fight for them when necessary. Here we are so biddable, not used to the traditions of fighting for our independence and respecting a bill of rights, that we do as we are told and convince ourselves that we cannot make a difference. Not so in America. When

76

the battle to lift the ban on gays in the military was lost this summer, a battle that had seen many late nights, many desperate dashes on to the floor of the Senate to update senators on the latest, federally funded Pentagon research on the incompatibility of homosexuality and military service, one would have expected an atmosphere of disillusionment and bitterness. However, lobbyists and congressional staff soon focused on alternative strategies, in this case opposing the codification of the bill and challenging the policy in the courts, determined not to give in and accept compromise.

When I grew up, I believed that it was not possible to be out and successful and happy. This is not true. The sooner my generation realises this (and many of them already have) the sooner we will see out lesbians and gay men at every level of public and private life, rather than closeted gay people, as at present. My father's insistence that we should not allow arbitrary classifications to define our success in life (he was talking about his class) has always held true for me and much of the battle is won if we genuinely believe in ourselves. Once people sense that conviction they are unable to challenge it.

This is not to say that the prejudices that provoked the riots twenty-five years ago have disappeared, rather that more people, from all walks of life, have made the courageous decision to stand up and be counted.

Whirling and Twirling

GLENN WRIGHT –
BALLROOM DANCER

GLENN WRIGHT was born in Oldham, Lancs in 1955. He trained at Billingtons Central Dance Academy, Oldham, and qualified with the Imperial Society of Teachers of Dance in London with Gwenethe Walshe. He has danced professionally all over the world and with his dance partner, Heather, now specialises in teaching and performing authentic Latin American Dance. Glenn is the only professional teacher to openly offer dance tuition to lesbian and gay couples.

When people think of ballroom dancing, they either think of the film *Strictly Ballroom* or the TV programme, *Come Dancing*. *Come Dancing* has given ballroom dancing a bad name. Ballroom and Latin American dance is much more than some sequins your mother Shirley sewed on.

I was born in Greater Manchester in the sort of family where my mother kept the curtains closed for a week when my sister got divorced. I first knew I was gay when I was seven years old and had my first sexual experience at the age of 11. I couldn't tell anyone about being gay, but I was told that every seven years we go through a major life change. I became convinced that when I was 14 years old I would suddenly wake up straight. I both longed for and feared this approaching change and was pretty stunned when it never happened. By then, however, I had already discovered ballroom dance.

I went to my first ballroom dance class when I was six years old and right from that very first lesson, I absolutely loved it. I was the only boy in a class of thirty girls and I can distinctly remember that I never really enjoyed dancing with the girls. I really wanted to dance with boys.

I not only hid my sexuality from the other kids at school, I hid my dancing too. I knew what awful things they would say if they ever found out. When I was 12 I won a major dancing competition and my mother forced me to do an interview and have my photo in the local newspaper. I refused at first but she threatened to stop paying for my dancing lessons, so I gave in. It was agonising because I knew that once I appeared in the papers everyone would know my terrible secret. From then on, school life was hell; I was teased and taunted all the time. I got all the abuse that schoolboy minds could muster. I wasn't just the school poof or pooftah, I was the 'bum boy'. I can still hear the viciousness of those taunts today, it was a ghastly experience.

When the headmaster decided that I should teach the school how to ballroom dance, life became even worse. Secretly I rather enjoyed the power of standing in the school hall ordering my vicious schoolmates around, but it was a rather shortlived form of revenge. Shortlived, because outside class I was as reviled and attacked as ever. What kept me sane was the support and all the friendships I formed through ballroom dance.

I left school when I was 15. I knew I wanted to dance, but dance was not considered a suitable job for a young man. My parents had sent me to classes because they considered dance to be a necessary social skill, they did not see it as a viable career. I needed 'something to fall back on', as my father put it, so I went to catering college. I kept on dancing in the evenings semi-professionally and gradually dance began to take over from my catering 'career'.

When I was about 20 I was offered a job in London and became a professional ballroom dancer. I was not sorry to leave the North; I knew what I wanted to do and who I wanted to be. I am very proud to be an out gay dancer.

The competition dancing is a real rat race, full of back-biting and bitchiness. Contrary to stereotype, it's not the gay men who bitch, it is the straights; they constantly bitch about your looks, what you are wearing and how you are dancing. The ballroom dance world has always been camp, but at the same time it is immensely homophobic. I think that in the 1970s and 1980s the ballroom dance world became so paranoid about being thought of as effeminate that they went totally overboard. There has never been an out gay world dance champion and there are even judges who will mark you down if you are not married to your dance partner. I know one young dancer who has been held back every step of the way just because he is known to be gay. It is only now, when he so obviously outshines the other dancers around him, that he has started to win the prizes he deserves.

In the 1970s and 1980s gay male dancers wouldn't even be out to their dance partners. I remember going to the dance championships in Blackpool and seeing young male dancers walking arm in arm and being all lovey-dovey with their dance partners. Later you would see the same young men creeping out of their hotels or even climbing out of their bedroom windows to rush off down to the gay clubs to be among the boys. I would meet them all on the dance floor or at the bar and they wouldn't talk to me. I was too out and they were too threatened by what my outness represented.

It seems quite extraordinary to me that dancers could choose not to be out to their own dance partners. It is very difficult to describe the relationship between a dancer and his or her partner. You have got to know each other and trust each other absolutely. You have an extraordinarily intimate working relationship and you spend a tremendous amount of time together. I find it incredible that some gay dancers try to hide something as integral to themselves as their sexuality. I know of one gay man who had three dancing partners none of whom ever knew that he was gay.

I have been dancing with my dance partner Heather for thirteen years now. I was out to Heather from day one, I could never have been anything else. I think if I stopped dancing with Heather I would stop dancing altogether. We have an immensely close relationship; she is my biggest confidante and we know each other so well now that when we dance we can almost sense the telepathy between us. There are moments when we will simultaneously break from a dance routine and know exactly what to improvise.

I love dancing and know I am good at it. I am one of those irritatingly lucky people who really is doing what they always wanted to do. Ballroom dancing is immensely disciplined: everyone is taught the same steps but what marks out a good dancer is how much of themselves they can bring to that dance. I could not be the dancer I am if I had remained in the closet. I would certainly not have the extraordinary dance partnership and friendship I share with Heather.

I am glad to see that more out gay dancers are beginning to appear in ballroom dance. Gay dancers are bringing more flamboyance into dance, not in a clichéd way but because they are less inhibited and are unafraid of expressing themselves. And by setting the example, they are freeing straight male dancers to express themselves too. This flamboyance is much more in keeping with the traditions of the dances themselves. The tango was originally a man's dance, very macho, very virile and very sexual. It was only in the 1920s that ballroom and Latin American dance became so sanitised.

It is strange how, over the years, ballroom dance has become so camp and yet at the same time so horrendously homophobic. Although there are more gay men coming out in professional dance, there are no out lesbian dancers. They are deeply, deeply closet. I took a lesbian friend who is a champion dyke spotter to a recent exhibition and she couldn't spot one. This is not really surprising as they can disguise themselves in all the clothes, the make-up and those smiles.

Heather and I both lecture and do exhibition dancing. We specialise in some of the more traditional Latin American dances like the Argentine tango. We also have deliberately gone out of our way to teach lesbians and gay men how to dance. I love teaching lesbians and gay men; they get all of me, both the dancer and the queen, and I think they get a better dance education as a result.

Currently I have a mission to change one of the basic tenets of ballroom dance: men must never, ever follow. Women are able to lead and follow, but officially men can only lead. I would love to be on the board of the Imperial Society of Teachers of Dance and implement this change. Gay dancing couples will be kept on the fringes of the ballroom dance world until they can pass their dance exams alongside straight couples. I think ballroom dance is for everyone, gay or straight, and I will always do my bit to ensure that gay people can dance together.

I love watching lesbians and gay men dance together. We can subvert all the traditional roles, lesbians leading, gay men following, and we whirl and twirl without inhibitions. I have always been out, from those first terrible experiences at school to the disapproval I have faced as a gay professional ballroom dancer. I have used my sexuality as a positive force and would never give in to pressure to keep my sexuality hidden. Because I am completely open, I can face the homophobes out. It is only when you are in the closet that you let them win.

Teaching lesbians and gay men to dance, and encouraging by example more dancers to come out, is like closing the hole at the top of the egg: I can integrate both my life and my sexuality fully. And because I have seen at first hand what intolerance can do, I believe I have become more patient and more tolerant and a better teacher. I have been tormented and have suffered from prejudice simply because I am gay, but I have come through. I have never for one minute regretted being gay and never will. I would come back as anything – as a flea, if necessary – just as long as I could come back gay.

The
Lesbian
and Gay
Community

Michelle Jones

Getting Active: Lesbians Leave the Well of Loneliness

EMMA HEALEY

EMMA HEALEY came out whilst at University and since then has been involved in lesbian and gay politics in Edinburgh, London and Manchester. She now lives in Yorkshire and works as a freelance writer and part-time administrator for a lesbian and gay charity.

Many women contributed their ideas and experiences to this piece, some of whom are quoted below.

There was a time when we only came out at night. We would pull on our men's clothes and creep into the bars. We would search desperately for love and catch the last bus home to the well of loneliness . . .

These days the lesbians come out by day. We are as at home on the high street as we are in the lesbian bar. We are the front covers of glossy magazines, the storylines in rural soaps, we are out in sport and out on TV. We are in print, in the news and in the sheets. In the 1990s lesbians are everywhere.

87

This is the story of twenty-five years of lesbian momentum: how lesbians moved from the closet and emerged out and proud. From gay liberation and the women's movement to Section 28 and the politics of 'queer', we have set about destroying the lesbian stereotype. We have created our own communities on our own terms: we are shattering straight illusions.

In 1885, the Labouchère amendment criminalised male homosexuality. That lesbians escaped legislation was less about Queen Victoria and more about society's denial of women as autonomous sexual beings. Lesbianism could not possibly exist in a world where women were defined by their relationship to men. This denial of our existence was as effective as any legislation. The few lesbians who did emerge were freaks, their difference an individual and unnatural sickness. This notion of lesbianism as sickness, bringing with it the inevitability of failure and the impossibility of happiness, prevailed through most of this century. It is only when we challenged this assumption and established the reality of lesbianism as a collective sexual identity that we began to challenge the sick and sad stereotypes and to demand the rights that we had for so long been denied.

In the 1960s lesbians took the first steps to break down the individual isolation that many faced. Organisations like Sappho and Kenric began to establish lesbian networks and to organise meetings, Sappho's own newsletter and the magazine *Arena 3* were circulated throughout Britain. These organisations and magazines not only recognised the importance of communication, but also provided vital social support. Not only were many lesbians meeting other lesbians for the first time but they were also given a safe space to talk about lesbianism itself. By their very existence, these networks challenged the notion that lesbianism was an isolated and isolating illness.

If Kenric and Sappho brought lesbians together in social

networks, in 1970 the Gay Liberation Front brought lesbians and gay men together in political action. Inspired in part by American activism after Stonewall and in part by the Black Power and women's liberation movements, GLF radicalised homosexuality. For the first time, lesbians and gay men marched under the banner of 'gay'. The GLFers began to challenge accepted notions of homosexuality, they 'zapped' doctors who tried to 'cure' it and attacked hostile newspapers and publishers. With anger and energy, they began to subvert the old 'sad', 'bad' stereotypes. No longer proscribed by a homophobic establishment, 'gay' was embraced as a positive sexual identity by lesbians and gay men themselves. GLF also recognised that the oppression that lesbians faced was different to that faced by gay men, but believed that this could be challenged by collective gay action. A women's group was set up within GLF and in 1971 the women's issue of *Come Together*, GLF's newsletter, stated the lesbian position very clearly:

> We share the experiences of our gay brothers but as women we have endured them differently. Whereas the men in GLF partake of the privileges of the male – you have been allowed to learn to organise, talk and dominate – we have been taught not to believe in ourselves, in our judgement, but to act dumb and wait for a man to make the decisions. As lesbians, 'women without men', we have always been the lowest of the low. Only through acting collectively can we overcome our own passivity and your male chauvinism so that together we – the whole GLF – can smash the sexist society which perverts and imprisons us all.

Ironically, by the winter of 1971, lesbians had left GLF primarily because of a result of a dispute over right/left politics, but also because of a dissatisfaction with the way gay men were behaving within GLF. GLF may have been short-lived, but it signalled a new approach to being lesbian and gay in Britain. It also had a profound influence on many lesbians: 'I experienced more intensely than ever before, or since, my identity as lesbian' (Elizabeth Wilson).

Lesbians were also active in the women's liberation movement. 1970 saw the first National Women's Liberation Conference at Ruskin College, Oxford. At the second conference in Skegness, lesbians not only led the routing of the Maoists who had temporarily tried to take over the movement, but also ensured that lesbianism was discussed at the conference. However, over the next few years the authentic lesbian voice became silenced within women's liberation as lesbianism became subsumed by a number of political discourses. For those of us who were not politically active in the 1970s it is hard to capture a feeling for the politics of the time. There was no single feminist movement and no single set of feminist politics. You could be a Marxist, feminist socialist or separatist feminist. Radical feminists crossed ideological swords with liberal feminists, and the 'mode of production' became a debate about your relationships rather than the core of socialist theory.

But as that initial lesbian energy visible in Skegness was never fully sustained, the very plurality of the political scene swamped any specifically lesbian debate, and other ideologies, other political theories, intervened. In the mid- to late 1970s, lesbianism became highly politicised, not strictly on its own terms, but rather as a political solution to the problem of women's subordination by men.

Yet lesbians remained at the forefront of feminist politics in the 1970s and early 1980s. Indeed, the women's movement was also instrumental in bringing lesbians together in networks of support and communication and in providing the opportunity for women to explore their sexuality. The growth of women's groups and the opening of women's centres and women's spaces provided even more opportunities for lesbians to get together.

By the early 1980s a new style of lesbianism had hit the scene. It was Adrienne Rich who coined the phrase 'lesbian continuum', a notion of lesbianism that sanctified 'women-identified experience' but bypassed 'genital experience with another woman'. It was the 'lesbian continuum' that could bring women together as a positive, affirming counterweight to male tyranny, it was the sixth sense that all women instinctively shared. For lesbians, this 'hands-off' politicking created nothing more than a lesbian vacuum. Political lesbianism was an idealised solution to the problem of men but it denied the very specific oppression that lesbians faced as a result of their sexual choice.

In Britain it was the Leeds Revolutionary Feminists who made the ultimate statement of political lesbianism.

> We do think that all feminists can and should be political lesbians. Our definition of a political lesbian is a woman-identified woman who does not fuck men. It does not mean compulsory sexual activity with women.

Political lesbianism tore the women's movement apart. The movement became factionalised, heterosexual women were silenced and lesbians who had been in the movement since GLF were criticised for their 'male' ideas and their putative role-playing pasts. The political lesbians' colonising of lesbianism left many lesbians out in the cold.

For Andrea Garrigan, a young woman coming out on the bar scene in Liverpool, political lesbianism seemed totally alien to the experiences of the lesbians she saw around her. Her lesbians 'were living lesbianism on the streets and in their lives'; the political lesbian she shared a flat with was simply playing a political game.

If the 1970s had been the era of political debate and

radical action, the early 1980s brought an extraordinary purifying of the lesbian movement. The personal became more political and lesbianism became more prescribed. Real lesbians didn't have penetrative sex, real lesbians didn't believe in monogamy, real lesbians didn't . . . For many new lesbians, coming out in the early eighties seemed more about rules and regulations than about discovering the joy of lesbian sex and the joy of lesbian relationships. Cherry Smyth felt that her lesbianism was constantly held up to scrutiny and any transgressions roundly criticised. Another woman complained of the restrictiveness of debate at that time: 'If I ever spoke at a meeting, I was full of fear that I would say the wrong thing, use the wrong language. I had to police everything I said.'

The 1980s also saw the rise of 'identity' politics within the lesbian community. Identity politics not only recognised the different oppressions lesbians faced because of their colour, race, class, disabilities or religion but also was a challenge to the political exclusivity of a lesbian movement that seemed mainly white and middle class. But 'identity' politics remained problematic; black women may have been welcomed into debate, but their voices were not always listened to, while the rigid hierarchy of oppression was used by some to give an increased validity to their views over others. For Yoni Ejo, going to a lesbian meeting still meant that there were 'a number of confident white, middle-class women telling us how we should think'.

Just as many women gained their awareness of lesbianism through their involvement in women's liberation, so many more were brought together again at Greenham Common to protest against cruise missiles in Britain. Greenham Common was to become a powerful symbol of women's protest and women's peacemaking. It also gave many women a safe, non-judgmental space to be lesbian in. Jane Held did not come out at Greenham but she considers it a major stage of her 'lesbian development': in a community of women, lesbianism lost its heterosexist stigma. Inevitably the straight, male media used lesbianism to devalue and trivialise the extent of women's protest at Greenham Common but this merely illustrated the threat that Greenham posed to the pillars of patriarchy.

Lesbians and gay men were in the forefront of support for the 1984 miners' strike. From GLF and the women's movement to the creation of a lesbian and gay group within the trade union Nalgo, lesbians and gay men had gained a significant voice in the trades union movement. The inclusion of lesbian and gay issues in mainstream socialist politics both legitimised the lesbian and gay movement and highlighted the oppression that many lesbians and gay men faced.

If at the beginning of the 1980s there was a conscious belief in and striving for a lesbian community, various arguments and disputes made this single community hard to attain. Many lesbians felt constrained by the 'right-on' politics of their sisters, while many others felt threatened by the increasing discussion and indeed acceptance of sado-masochism on the scene. In London in 1985, there was an immensely damaging debate about whether S/M dykes should be allowed to use the London Lesbian and Gay Centre; later there were rows about the supposedly S/M film *She Must Be Seeing Things*. Similar rows and debates were replicated in lesbian groups throughout Britain. That lesbian sex should become such an issue was indicative of many lesbians' frustration at what they saw as a sacrifice of true lesbianism for political ends.

The mid-1980s were marked for lesbians and gay men by the arrival of HIV and AIDS. The initial backlash against homosexuality that tabloid responses to HIV and AIDS actively encouraged had been felt by lesbians too and they were in the forefront of the gay response to the disease. This working together was a further aspect of the breaking down of the lesbian separation from gay politics and, indeed, gay men.

However, lesbians and gay men were brought together more publicly by Section 28 of the Local Government Act 1988 which forbade the 'promotion of homosexuality'. Section 28 diverted the movement away from internal politicking to the very real dangers of external oppression. For lesbians, Section 28 was particularly significant as the first time that we were directly implicated in anti-gay legislation. 'Never Going Underground', the slogan of the North-West Campaign for Lesbian and Gay Equality was as revealing of the nature of lesbian and gay politics of the time as it was of a future strategy for lesbian and gay action. Lesbians had spent too much time in their women-only spaces. While they had been cleansing their community of its patriarchal attitudes, they forgot that patriarchy might turn round one day and actively oppress them.

The protests against Section 28 once again brought homosexuality into the public domain. But it was lesbians who grabbed the spotlight with two extraordinary actions. The abseiling incident in the House of Lords and the lesbian invasion of the BBC News showed that lesbians could take the political initiative. That both actions were witty and ingenious was in triumphant contrast to the media stereotype of the miserable, humourless lesbian. Section 28 did a better job of promoting homosexuality to the lesbian community than years of political meetings ever had.

Section 28 showed many lesbians and gay men that they could not rely on other political organisations or indeed the Labour Party to give us the same unconditional support which we had given them. The equal opportunities policies that gave many local authorities the chance to fund lesbian and gay organisations were not only brought into question by Section 28, but, as financial restraints increased, became less of a political priority. In London the end of the GLC in 1985, which had led the field in supporting lesbian and gay rights, not only left lesbian and gay organisations unfunded but also seemed to symbolise the end of the local government support that perhaps we had begun to take for granted.

The end of the 1980s could well have been a time of pessimism for the lesbian and gay community. Although lesbians and gay men lost the battle against Section 28, they learnt many important lessons. The Stonewall Group (fronted by a number of prominent lesbians and gay men) set itself up as a professional lobbying organisation, while Outrage took the energy and enthusiasm of Section 28 and developed it into a confrontational, 'in your face' activism.

Stonewall's desire to bring lesbians and gay men equality and justice before the law reinforces homosexuality's place on the civil rights agenda. As Angela Mason, director of Stonewall, put it: 'Our agenda is based on the premise of the oppression of the homosexual that similarly affects lesbians and gay men and that there is, therefore, a unity of interest in opposing that.' For many lesbians however, there always remains the fear that the issues important to homosexual oppression remain gay male ones. Creating a specific lesbian agenda can be equally difficult. Not all lesbians are concerned by custody or parenting issues, yet there has been a tendency to shove these issues the lesbians' way.

The politics of 'queer' has given many lesbians and gay men a new confidence and vigour. More importantly 'queer' politics has given many lesbians the chance to explore their sexuality on their own terms. 'Queer' turns the old lesbian feminist proscriptions on their heads, allowing lesbians not only access to their sexual fantasies but a voice to express them. How much further 'queer' politics can take lesbians and lesbianism remains to be seen. 'Queer' could be just another internal memo to the lesbian and gay community.

Over the last twenty-five years we have seen the lesbian

come out in style. In the 1970s and early 1980s we saw her coming out in the collective. In the late 1980s and early 1990s we saw her coming out in clubs and bars. We now see her coming out everywhere. Lesbians now make their own lesbian communities and forge their own individual lesbian identities. There is no doubt that in the 1990s lesbians have an outward confidence that they have never had before. Lesbianism is no longer an isolating and isolated sickness, it is a valid sexual option. The new emphasis on sex in the naughty lesbian nineties shows that lesbianism has moved on from being an antidote to male oppression. Far from being about male subordination, sex has become about lesbian expression. This gives lesbians and lesbianism a new and challenging freedom.

But amongst all this new sexual freedom, what is lesbian politics? And where is the lesbian community? Many women hanker for that sense of political identity that we strove for in the 1970s and 1980s; they see the lesbian community now as depoliticised and fragmented. Many are uneasy with the 1990s queer-conscious lesbians: they do not see them playing the boys at their own game but simply playing at being boys. Many other lesbians remain angry at the prescriptive lesbianism of the 1970s and 1980s: they dislike what they see as the lesbian feminist colonisation of the moral high ground. They feel that they are just as lesbian and just as feminist as their lesbian feminist sisters. Many of these differences are generational: lesbians coming on to the scene now do not have the same experiences of oppression as the lesbians who came out through the women's liberation movement, but it is wrong to think that they have no understanding of lesbian oppression at all. Not all lesbian feminists are dinosaurs in dungarees; we do owe a debt to the political lesbians of the 1970s and 1980s, just as we owe a debt to the lesbian pioneers of the 1950s and 1960s. The last twenty-five years have brought lesbians together and given lesbianism a new validity and energy. Lesbians now are taking that energy and using it with confidence and style. Informed by many different ideologies and a host of different lesbian experiences, this is confidence and identity with a very loud voice.

The notion of a single, unified lesbian community has been lost to the acceptance of lesbianism as incorporating a number of different communities and voices. The lesbian community of the 1990s is not defined by how you think and what you say, it is not the inward-looking, protectionist structure it once was. The lesbian community can be all things to all lesbians: it can be a lesbian discussion group, the Paradise Club on a Friday night, a k. d. lang concert or a dinner among friends.

But there is more to lesbianism than current fashion or media personalities. We must all ensure that lesbianism does not drift back to the well of loneliness once again. We cannot expect the langs, Navratilovas and St Clements to do all the work while we enjoy the clubs. We must keep reminding the straight world that behind every lesbian personality there are hundreds and hundreds of other lesbians waiting to appear.

Robert Workman

Out of the Closets on to the Streets: Gay Men's History

MICHAEL MASON

MICHAEL MASON is a broadcaster and journalist. He was born in London in 1947 and educated at Lancing College and Oxford. He was a member of the Gay Liberation Front and was News Editor of *Gay News* from 1972 to 1981. He was director of the Hall Carpenter Archive and was co-founder and Editor of *Capital Gay*. He was a member of the Gay Rights Media Group, and is a member of GMFA and Sadie Maisie's.

To be gay in the 1950s and 1960s and to survive unscathed, you passed for straight. You might not always be successful, heterosexuals might not be fooled, but until you were actually convicted of· the crime, they tended to choose between avoiding you or keeping an embarrassed silence on the subject. Such a burden of silence and evasion was enough to drive a queen to screaming point.

In June 1969 it did just that. When police raided New York's Stonewall bar in Greenwich Village, the dam burst and a spontaneous episode of faggot fury marked the birth of a political movement. By the summer of 1970 a new organisation calling itself the Gay Liberation Front (GLF) met regularly in the city and their meetings profoundly impressed two students on holiday from London.

In October 1970, Bob Mellors and Aubrey Walters were back at the London School of Economics where they called the first meeting of GLF in Britain. Small notices advertising the weekly gatherings began to appear in the underground press (including a new, radical listings magazine called *Time Out*) and in less than a month GLF outgrew its original basement meeting room and moved upstairs to a lecture theatre large enough to accommodate the hundreds of men and women who regularly attended. Gays and lesbians were 'coming out', as the new phrase described it.

Parliament had relaxed the laws against male homosexuality only three years before. Lord Arran, who campaigned actively for law reform, promoting the Sexual Offences Bill in the House of Lords, warned us not to regard the change in the law as a 'licence' to flaunt our sexuality; even the thought of gay clubs was anathema to him. He sought to eliminate the twin terrors of blackmail and police witch-hunts, but the reformers expected gays to know their place and to feel polite shame. The concept of gay 'pride', an idea borrowed directly from the politics of black power, was incomprehensible to them.

To those who made their way each week to GLF meetings, 'coming out as gay and proud' was in varying degrees thrilling, personally dangerous, and subversive of the social and sexual order. Much as born-again Christians share their elation at 'finding Jesus', so the men and women of GLF shared their individual experiences, first of living fearfully in the shadows and then joyfully emerging into the sunlight. Many who spoke at those early meetings were prompted by an urgent desire for personal confession after years spent living with guilt. It was both a liberating and confusing feeling to stand in front of an audience of three or four hundred people who were happy to approve your sexuality and applaud your courage in 'coming out'.

Coming out in those days and for much of the 1970s created a sense of belonging, and a collective fervour, much of it channelled into the project of creating a gay politics. The reform campaign of the 1950s and 1960s was political only in the sense that we needed MPs to approve a change in the law, but in Britain in 1970 the idea of a 'politics of sexuality' was a comparatively new one, popularised by the burgeoning women's movement. If gender was political, surely sexuality could be political too, and if so what were those politics? The terms 'gay oppression' and 'gay liberation' offered a starting point and we scoured the writings of other oppressed groups for insights. Women oppressed by sexism, blacks oppressed by racism and imperialism, workers oppressed by capitalism, all fed debate at GLF's main Wednesday night meetings and set the agenda for Manifesto Group, a cell within the Front charged with the task of stating the organisation's political philosophy and objectives. The manifesto, published in 1971, identified our oppressors (including the Church, psychiatry, the education system, capitalism and the nuclear family). It sought to explain their interest in oppressing us, and pointed to the changes needed to eradicate lesbian and gay oppression. The themes of the manifesto informed GLF demonstrations, the 'zapping' of psychiatrists in Harley Street, of newspapers in Fleet Street, of medical conferences and evangelical rallies. Labour and Tory MPs alike denounced the new militants, accusing GLF variously of corrupting the young or inviting a backlash. Vicars denounced those 'flaunting it' from the pulpit. Hard left groups like the International Marxist Group and the International Socialists (who later became the Socialist Workers' Party) denounced homosexuality as 'bourgeois decadence' and a matter of no concern to the working class.

But it was not just heterosexuals who were affronted by GLF. It is ironic now to recall that an older generation, comfortably describing themselves as 'queer' were offended by the new term 'gay'. We disturbed the old queer order with our noisy antics. On one memorable occasion the Gay Pride march, then only 8–900 strong, took a route through west London past the Coleherne (still one of London's most well-known gay pubs) where patrons pelted marchers with beer cans for exposing the secret world of the queer network to the glare of publicity.

Yet adopting the word 'gay' proved to be a small piece of political genius on the part of GLF, whether by accident or design, for although it drew the disingenuous protest that we had robbed the English language of an innocent flower, headline writers could not long resist the convenience of the three-letter word. Soon it was part of everyday speech and we had asserted, finally, our right to determine how we described ourselves, how others should describe us. It also threw a lifeline to young or isolated people, still adjusting to their sexuality; how much easier to maintain self-respect in those days by coming out to yourself as gay rather than queer.

Gay liberationists explored new ways of living together in the romantic hope of finding self-sufficiency outside the capitalist system while patiently waiting for it to rot away. Awareness groups, or consciousness-raising groups, were small cells of half a dozen people who met with severe regularity to talk about their innermost senses of identity. We talked about the most traumatic moments of our lives and the lessons we thought they taught us, hoping to distinguish those beliefs and assumptions that were truly ours from those imposed on us by a homophobic society (though the term 'homophobia' would not be coined until 1972 by Dr George Weinberg in his book *Society and the Healthy Homosexual*). Other members of the group might then offer their own sometimes acerbic interpretations of our experience, and meetings could end in tears and new trauma, feelings which only the balm of group sympathy could then soothe. Many lived in communes, renouncing private property but sharing whatever was brought into the house. It was wrong to feel jealousy; it presupposed property rights in another individual. We would sleep together, a dozen at a time, not out of sexual attraction but because preferring one sexual partner to another was a 'put-down' of that other to whom we should be showing respect and solidarity.

Significant though its history remains, GLF lasted a mere eighteen months, tearing itself apart in fierce, sectarian warfare. GLF Marxists insisted that the way ahead lay in alliance with the revolutionary left and the overthrow of capitalism. Only socialism could deliver gay liberation. Gay women, as they had called themselves recently, now reasserted their identity as lesbians. Men in GLF, they asserted, could not help but be parties to patriarchal sexism; we received privileges by virtue of our sex which we could not voluntarily renounce. Only the overthrow of the patriarchy could deliver gay liberation, they concluded. Radical feminists, male ones, agreed. Only by living round the clock in drag and thus explicitly flouting male convention could we share women's oppression.

But in its brief life and death, GLF spawned vital new enterprises. It had published its own paper *Come Together* with anarchic irregularity, but now Andrew Lumsden and its first editor, Denis Lemon, conceived and launched the fortnightly *Gay News*, arguably the most influential lesbian and gay publication produced by the modern British gay movement. The paper became a vital focus for the exchange of information and its workers soon could not cope with the volume of phone calls they got from every corner of the land, so they invited activists to a meeting upstairs at the Coleherne. Gay Switchboard, still the world's busiest, was the result. Switchboard was followed by the pioneering theatre company Gay Sweatshop, as a direct consequence of the impact that women's theatre was making on the fringe. Meanwhile personal support and counselling groups such as Friend, with its nationwide network of local branches, offered a welcoming hand to lesbians and gay men coming out and seeking an end to their isolation.

At the time of GLF's collapse, other purposefully political lesbians and gay men were engaged in a quieter, more reform-minded enterprise. Where GLF was a vanguard group, a metropolitan elite, committed to direct action, the Campaign for Homosexual Equality had evolved out of the North-Western Committee for Homosexual Law Reform, the body which fought for the 1967 Act and was establishing itself as a broader, popular organisation committed to winning public favour and bringing lesbians and gay men together, both socially and as grassroots lobbyists concerned with equal rights. CHE had been seen by GLF as too respectable by half and a sell-out of the sexual revolution. But on the fragmentation of GLF it was the only popular political movement we had, and so became the natural destination for many of the liberationists. It was a fruitful marriage, though one fraught with conflict, and produced the most effective gay organisation yet, powerful because its groups existed throughout England and Wales, interacting subversively with the local press and broadcasters, churches, women's organisations and local trade union branches, councils and constituency parties. By holding regular social events too, often in towns without their own gay pub, CHE recruited new troops with comparative ease. Hydra-headed, it proved a difficult foe for the moralists who protested that homosexuals were now 'flaunting it' and threatening fundamental moral values. Politically, it won ground through the well-tried tactic of the confrontational, CHE followed up with sweet reason. 'You're right,' said CHE, 'they're wild extremists. Why not, then, deal with reasonable moderates like us.' As the suffragists and suffragettes had shown, as Martin Luther King's civil rights movement and the Black Panthers had shown, and as Outrage and the Stonewall Group may yet show, change can be more rapidly achieved by attack on more than one front.

Though satirised as a grand bureaucracy, with its committees, constitutions and conferences, CHE learnt how to make use of the media both locally and nationally, gained audiences with government ministers, and backed several important initiatives including the setting up of the International Lesbian and Gay Organisation (ILGA) which flourishes today.

Some measure of the extent to which CHE (along with its sister organisation the Scottish Minorities Group and the Northern Ireland Gay Rights Association), together with *Gay News*, college GaySocs and Switchboard between them had woven an effective political network came in late 1976 when that dedicated opponent of gay and women's liberation, Mary Whitehouse, turned her guns on *Gay News*. Her notable stunt was to bring a private prosecution against the paper for 'blasphemous libel' over the publication that June of a poem by Professor James Kirkup, illustrated by the talented cartoonist Tony Reeves, nowadays of *Gay Times*. The poem offered a first-person account by a Roman centurion (gay, in Kirkup's account) of his feelings at the crucifixion, referring to a history of sex between Christ and the disciples. Tony Reeves had drawn an unusually well-proportioned crucified figure, with a flavour of the art nouveau about it.

News of the prosecution was greeted at first with disbelief that in 1976 any court could be asked to consider a charge of blasphemy, but when it became obvious that the survival of *Gay News* was at stake, the movement acted. In a national response lesbian and gay groups shook collecting tins, held benefit discos, and sought the support of local papers and radio stations against what they saw as a naked attack, not on a poem but on the gay community. Mary

Whitehouse's admission that she was not a frequent church-goer lent conviction to the claim. Significantly the liberal establishment, though already regarding Mary Whitehouse with distaste, was quick to support *Gay News*, if not publication of the poem itself. It was not gay money alone that poured into the paper's defence fund.

And so the match opened at the Old Bailey in June 1977 with Rumpole's progenitor, John Mortimer, battling for the defence, and with Judge King-Hamilton, a stalwart of the orthodox synagogue and well known for his conservative views, as umpire. Each day at the lunch interval, the prosecutors would gather in an ostentatious circle outside the court, bow their heads and pray for victory. The suspended prison sentence passed on Denis Lemon, the fine imposed on the paper and the subsequent unsuccessful appeal to the European Court of Human Rights were undoubted defeats. But the case created a certain sympathy for the whole enterprise of the gay movement in quarters where we had formerly been regarded as merely a sexual sideshow. It was remarkable too in demonstrating the readiness of disparate organisations within the ever-broadening 'movement' to co-operate in common action.

That broadening movement now included an effective network of groups for students. Lobbying within the National Union of Students had led to the launch of a national NUS Gay Rights Campaign, with funding for posters and leaflets, support for campaigns in universities and colleges against censorship of reading material and discrimination on the part of straight students, so that by the end of the 1970s the majority of British universities had more or less active GaySocs. For those lucky enough to get university places, GaySocs offered practical and moral support at a time in their lives when many most needed it.

In parallel, the late 1970s also saw the rapid growth of the commercial gay scene. Tricky Dicky's pioneering discos in the upstairs rooms of London pubs were now joined by West End 'super discos' such as Heaven and Bang. Gay pubs began to acquire gay landlords to replace benign, though sometimes bewildered heterosexual ones. Yet there was comparatively little contact in large conurbations between the 'political' and the 'commercial' gay worlds until the very end of the decade.

By that time, however, the growth of the commercial scene had rendered CHE's social function largely superfluous. Many were content, on coming out, to make their contacts exclusively through the pubs and clubs. CHE itself, as it saw the average age of its membership increase, embarked on what proved to be the suicidal project of splitting itself in two – a social organisation intended to promote serious commercial enterprise in order to fund a sister organisation of active political campaigners. This formalised a division of conflicting interests and broke the campaign's back.

With the collapse of CHE, a recent tendency on the part of activists to identify with people on the commercial gay scene now became commonplace. Gradually the phrase 'gay movement', with its connotations of exclusively political aspirations, lost currency and the idea of a 'gay community', with no very clear sense of what was common about it, emerged to replace it and to embrace the strictly commercial side of gay life. Political initiatives were increasingly taken not by independent gay organisations but within the broader Labour movement, in trade unions and local groups. The concentrated sexual-political energies of GLF and CHE were dissipated. The attempt to establish a new, politically active organisation, the Gay Activist Alliance, foundered for want of a clear constituency, and there was no well-organised resistance at a national level when we came under new political fire in the early 1980s.

It was the initiatives of Ken Livingstone's GLC, such as the £1.5 million spent on the much-lamented Lesbian and

Gay Centre in Cowcross Street, which first renewed public attention and hostility towards lesbians and gay men at the very time when we were beginning to be threatened by an as yet mysterious new disease, AIDS. At the same time Tory MPs, backed vociferously by the *Sun*, launched a dishonest campaign accusing the gay movement, as ever, of deliberately setting out to 'corrupt' schoolchildren. Their *casus belli* was a book called *Jenny Lives with Eric and Martin*, which was originally funded by the Danish government as a teaching aid for their schools. The captioned photo-story told of an adopted young girl being raised by a pair of gay lovers and was translated into English and published in the UK by the Gay Men's Press. A single copy of this book was purchased for a teachers' resource centre by a north London borough, though no copies were bought for classroom use by children themselves. Nevertheless that single copy was used to alternately beat 'corrupt' Labour local authorities and the gay movement. And when Labour councils in other cities began to follow the GLC's lead, offering grants to gay groups, advertising in the gay press and writing anti-discrimination clauses into their employment policies, our most fervent critics hit back, sponsoring the clause that became Section 28 of the Local Government Act 1988. That small but significant legislative gesture, which forbade local councillors to 'promote homosexuality' or to approve of 'pretended family relationships' had a galvanising effect on lesbians, gays and liberal supporters and provoked an unforeseen degree of opposition.

Though unable to stop the clause, opponents forced the government to amend it significantly on its way to the statute book, and a new generation of lesbians and gay men learnt to view their sexuality as a political matter. For what the clause did was to assert that we were not the final arbiters in determining our sexual identities, as gay liberationists had asserted twenty years earlier. Once again the assertion was made that family relations were the sole key to understanding sexuality and that our relations were invalid to the extent that we did not produce children.

Section 28 has itself initiated a new form of politics, perhaps first cousin to the power-brokering system currently winning control of politics in the American lesbian and gay community. At the time of the parliamentary battle for the Section, a group of gay journalists met regularly at Heaven before the doors opened to disco-goers. Some worked in the gay press, some on nationals, some for radio and television. It was this group, advised by senior parliamentary strategists whose members agreed that their meetings 'never took place', which was responsible for the impressive full-page advertisement that appeared in the *Independent* on the day the clause was debated warning against 'the development of a climate of persecution'. The advertisement was signed by peers and MPs, academics, clergymen, scientists and celebrities from the worlds of arts, broadcasting and journalism. Neil Kinnock, Paddy Ashdown and Michael Foot were signatories, sharing the stage with Joanna Lumley, the Pet Shop Boys and Alan Bennett, Miriam Rothschild, Anthony Quinton, Melvyn (and Billy) Bragg, Sir Michael Tippett . . . the list was long. In a few short weeks the signatures were gathered, £8,000 was raised to pay for publication, and the page duly appeared.

One of those stirred to action by Section 28 was the actor Sir Ian McKellen who, together with Michael Cashman and others, founded the Stonewall Group, another of the new breed of lobbying groups. Insisting that they do not claim to 'represent' the community, and free of the vicissitudes of election that bedevilled their forerunners in CHE, the members of the Stonewall Group rely on personal influence to open doors. Confident that the ends will more than justify the means, bringing substantial benefits to lesbians and gay men at large, members ride out the public and sometimes bitter personal attacks on their closed circle. Outrage has taken the place of GLF just as Stonewall has replaced CHE in the continuing clash of political cultures. With lesbians and gay men still battling for something more than survival, one party seeks a fight to the death, the other, peace with honour, whilst those who feel themselves outside the political fray seem content to party till they drop.

And all this against the backdrop of AIDS, the epidemic that has changed the collective psyche by injecting a renewed sense of anger, frustration and above all impatience with the continuing institutionalised oppression of lesbians and gay men. As our griefs and losses mount, so moral platitudes on the lips of churchmen, lawyers and parliamentarians sound trivial when they are not obscene. In February 1994, offered a chance to accept the principle of equality at law, MPs refused and rather than end the distinction between heterosexual and homosexual ages of consent, members rekindled the patronizing discrimination. By changing the existing age of 21 (proposed by Wolfenden almost forty years earlier, and long since disregarded completely by young gay men and widely by the police) to a brand new 18, the mind of Parliament freshly expressed itself in our own times, thereby inviting police to enforce discrimination anew. Though many had anticipated the result, few of us were prepared for the intense personal degree of anger and contempt that we would feel individually when the vote came through; the gay vigil outside the House of Commons erupted tearfully and violently in an entirely spontaneous way, almost to its own surprise, and such sentiments found their echo in pubs and clubs around the gay scene. Today's law, in short, continues to give its blessing to a Home Office that idly murders prisoners, refusing them condoms; to school governors with powers of veto over the sex education that saves lives; to the absence of safe social facilities for young gays that could be provided by local authorities and welfare agencies, were they not afraid of running foul of the law. It is understandable that we should no longer be very nice in our politics, though it is a high-risk game.

In the end we can continue to think the unthinkable. For better or worse, the circumstances of our lives have changed beyond recognition. Much of what happens today was unthinkable at the time of Stonewall; much of what happened in the 1960s would be unthinkable today. When a gay man was charged for having sex in private with a consenting adult, police interrogated him for the names and addresses of former sex partners and visited those other men at their place of work, letting it be known why. Today, there is an officer at Scotland Yard responsible for liaison with the community and local forces have stated that they do not intend patrolling certain well-known cruising areas at night. In 1976, after their trainee manager, Tony Whitehead, appeared on a documentary TV programme about CHE, British Home Stores sacked him. He later became a distinguished chair of the Terrence Higgins Trust. In the early 1970s, BBC and ITV were under persistent attack for never presenting gay characters on television other than as comedy grotesques. In the 1990s Channel 4 commissioned a weekly series of lesbian and gay programming, and screened a selection of gay programmes as alternative viewing over Christmas 1993. Ian McKellen was awarded his knighthood after publicly campaigning for gay rights, Jonathan Grimshaw an OBE for his AIDS work. A church of England minister offered services of 'blessing' to gay couples in his East End church with the full knowledge of his bishop. Gay pubs in London and Kent have come under attack from CS gas. Others have been granted 4 a.m. licences. Some 200 people took part in the first Pride march; in 1993 over 100,000 took part.

Meanwhile the armed forces cashier service personnel for being gay, the incidence of queer-bashing seems to have risen since the mid-1980s, and men and women everywhere are looking for Mr and Ms Right.

Making it Happen: The Making of the Gay Community in Scotland

IAN DUNN

IAN DUNN was born in 1943 in Glasgow and has lived and worked all his life in Scotland, firstly as meteorologist, latterly as townplanner. From 1967, stung by the Church of Scotland's opposition to gay sex reform, he has been at the forefront of Scotland's effective gay and lesbian rights movement. Both a socialist and a nationalist, sexual politics lies at the heart of his outlook.

Antisyzygy (the union or close bonding of opposites) permeates the Scottish psyche. From self-righteous Bible-thumper to murderous drunkard in the same person. Great moments of courage and far-sightedness to deep bitterness and timidity, again in the same person. In men, the cult of 'macho' is a very long time dying. Yet from such unpromising soil we have built a movement which, in its multifarious ways, is breaking down the barriers and is changing the face of Scotland.

My own sexual identity dates from the mid-1950s (I was

born in Glasgow in 1943) a time dominated by the Home
Service news on the wireless: of Montagu, Wildeblood and
Wolfenden. The newspapers were hostile and any supportive
readers' letters were anonymous. A little later I remember my
parents, devotees of Dirk Bogarde, coming home from the
cinema in tears after seeing *Victim*. Stunned by its bleak view
of homosexuality and blackmail, Mummy pleaded with me,
'I hope you're not like that?' This was 1963. I was 20 and had
just come out – well, it wasn't coming out, more confession
reluctantly wrung and heard with dread.

I was aware I could carry on being a decent, rather empty-
headed sort of person, but I developed a curiosity about
why things were the way they were. The debates in Parliament
in the mid-1960s pointed up the difference between urban
England and attitudes everywhere in Scotland. I was hugely
disappointed that Scotland was excluded from the Sexual
Offences Act 1967 and deeply offended by the Church of
Scotland's attitude against people like me. More than anything
this prompted me, on 29 July 1967, to write to Antony Grey,
director of the Albany Trust in London and secretary of the
Homosexual Law Reform Society. I was feeling alone and
wanted to meet someone with greater experience.

I went down to London by train that September. When
I got there I was in quite confident mood and I remember
being impressed with the London way and with this grand
big street called Shaftesbury Avenue and going to a little
coffee-house with Mr Grey and the waiter saying, 'Mr Grey,
the usual kind of coffee? . . . coffee for two?' Clearly Mr
Grey's waiter had seen many young fresh-faced, short-back-
and-sides homosexuals coming in with the former Coal
Board solicitor!

I wanted to set up a Scottish branch of the London
operation, but Antony Grey wouldn't have any of it. I later
learnt why: the uppity North-Western Homosexual Law
Reform Committee (or the HLRC) had been formed in 1964.

Its chairman, Allan Horsfall, had been casting working-class plain truths at over-anxious London and Tony Grey did not want a repetition of this in Scotland. Throughout 1968 and 1969 I corresponded with Franklin Kameny the pioneering gay activist in Washington, DC. Kameny was an excellent letter-writer: I followed the growth of the pre-Stonewall gay rights movement as if I was sitting at the ringside. Frank had promoted the expression 'Gay is Good' and sent me a 'button', but I didn't dare wear it then. I followed up two or three contacts from Tony Grey and the first meeting of the Scottish Minorities Committee, half a dozen very courageous souls, was held in Glasgow in January 1969.

The meeting took place in the drawing room of my parents' West End house at 13 Buckingham Street. Glasgow City Council ought to erect a pink (bronze) plaque there. We called ourselves 'Scottish Minorities' because we were too afraid to say 'homosexual', and the word 'gay' was considered to be utterly frivolous, at least by one of us who is still alive and still involved. It is interesting to reflect on who was there: a gay estate agent, a gay scientific civil servant, a straight and married social worker, a bisexual Kirk minister, a gay Post Office telephone exchange operator, a transvestite teacher and a homosexual brewery employee. We were male, mostly middle class with articulate working-class support. We were absolute beginners. We drew lessons from the black civil rights movement and early women's movement but without 'seeing' them or connecting with them.

We wanted to set up a mass membership organisation with branches in the four cities and the larger towns (eventually, by 1982, the membership peaked at 1,200) and so we called an open meeting in the Protestant Chaplaincy, Oakfield Avenue, and on 9 May 1969 the Scottish Minorities Group (SMG) was founded. There were about twenty-five present, a good representation of women, and Bob Stewart (he became a Glasgow Labour bailie but slipped to calmer Lib-Dem waters in the 1980s) moved that 'group' had a less narrow sound than 'committee' and so it was. It's strange for me today to sleep with young men who weren't even born on founding day: I can hardly believe some of the things which have happened to me as a result of setting up SMG.

The name of the group was highly appropriate: we were a bundle of minorities and didn't attempt to inflate our numbers (the dubious 10 per cent claim). We quickly agreed on four aims – counselling, changing the law, making life better and, crucially, getting 'congenial meeting places for homosexual men and women and their friends' (how quaint the language sounds in the 1990s, but I still like the 'and their friends' bit). In the first two years we didn't have honorary vice-presidents but we knew we had to work with a grain of society, to pick carefully those who would support us, who would not be fazed by supporting a homosexual organisation.

We always made sure that there were good spokes-people who knew us personally, who had sat with us and listened to us. In return we had got to know them and their interests. Some of us might work for them – perhaps to get people to vote for them if they were in a party. Our early links with Janey Buchan, David Steel and Robin Cook were made in that fashion. But we also believed in the rightness of labour organisation and we never underestimated the position of the main churches in Scotland and from them, too, we found individuals who gave solid support. We rounded off our vice-presidents with three academics.

The year 1970 was a worrisome one for SMG. I had left Glasgow (Prestwick) the previous autumn to study in Edinburgh. It was an uphill job building the group. What transformed our fortunes was largely events 400 miles south, in London: the launching of the Gay Liberation Front in October 1970. In Scotland we started the monthly newsletter, *SMG News*, in January 1971. Twenty-three unbroken years and seven editors later it is still being published with just one change of title (in 1978). *Gay Scotland* is owned by the members of SMG's successor, Outright Scotland, and is one of the longest-running gay publications in Europe.

The start of 1971 saw Scotland's first gay discos and the launch of the SMG Glasgow Women's Group, and shortly afterwards the SMG Edinburgh Women's Group and their magazine *Gayzette*. We moved from the unyielding Church of Scotland's Mound Centre to the altogether more relaxed Catholic Chaplaincy basement at 23a George Square. There in the 'Cobweb' we held our regular Monday meetings and Saturday night dancing. Three shillings to get in – and people came from hundreds of miles away. Within two years we had to transfer the disco to 'Tiffanys', a marvellous dance hall in the New Town (since burnt down). We accumulated much money and purchased our first premises, the SMG Information Centre, 60 Broughton Street, at the end of 1974 and opened the following spring. But there was an almighty row. The local Tory councillor, Mrs Sally Pringle, attempted to have our planning permission withdrawn (she successfully stopped our brass plate from going up for a year – until Secretary of State Willie Ross overturned Edinburgh District Council's refusal).

It is hard to capture in a few pages the hectic pace of the five years from 1971 to 1976 in Scotland. There were annual conferences in Glasgow ('Homosexuality: Reform or Revolution?' and 'The Homosexual in an Industrial Society'), the Edinburgh University 'Teach-In on Homosexuality' (1973) and Scottish International's 'What Kind of Scotland?' I visited the United States and Canada in the summer of 1971 and five northern European countries in 1974. The object of all this activity was to find out how others had organised, in particular how gay community centres functioned and, crucially, could we operate such centres in Edinburgh and Glasgow?

The peak of international activity in that period was the

first International Gay Rights Congress held in Edinburgh 18–22 December 1974. This was only made possible by Derek Ogg's involvement: as senior president of Edinburgh University Students' Association he had unrivalled access to resources. He collared me and said we had to have a big world meeting. Derek is one of these very good people who can catch the big idea and take it up and make it happen. About ten years later he was to do the same for AIDS by setting up Scottish AIDS Monitor. Anyway the International Congress took off, 400 turned up for the five-day event (£16 full board!) and it led to the setting up of the International Gay (later Lesbian & Gay) Association in 1978 in which Scottish delegates played a very strong part for eight years.

The congress made a big impact in Scotland and was a great fillip for the opening of the centres in Edinburgh and, in 1977, in Glasgow. The story of the Edinburgh Centre would fill volumes, but it has always been democratically owned and run by the members. The secret of its success, I believe, stems from the fact that we have never relied on public subsidy, nor did we overstretch ourselves. Sure there were lean years, but the organisation pays its way and the lessons from Europe have endured.

The Glasgow Gay Centre was also an SMG enterprise. The Glasgow branch was ambitious. It purchased an old building at 534 Sauchiehall Street and got youth training scheme labour to convert and equip the premises. The building opened in 1977, and when Tom Robinson visited shortly afterwards he pinned up a note which said: 'This is fucking marvellous!' (Sir Peter Maxwell Davies, another man of music, left similar but more genteel praise in the Edinburgh Centre.) Our centres were a huge success and attracted a much younger crowd than we had anticipated. We had a general rule that you had to be 16 before you got in. I wonder what the people who objected to the presence of our younger members would make of the Blue Moon Café in the Edinburgh Centre today where youngsters are welcome if accompanied by a parent? There has indeed been a social transformation in our community: homosexuals are also mums and dads.

The centres allowed the switchboards to expand. The first switchboard in Scotland was the Edinburgh Gay Switchboard which was put on a formal basis in 1972. Glasgow's was originally called GGAS (Glasgow Gay Advisory Service) and they published a newsletter *Ggaslight* for a year or so. While part of SMG from the start, they soon wished to be independent of what was seen as the intrusive political motives of the parent organisation. They also needed to attract council grants, and became charities.

The early years were dominated by the 'directional' vs. 'non-directional' debate. Those involved in the services by and large wished to be 'non-directional' but positive about gayness. The Scottish switchboards story is one of quiet growth: there are now four 'Friend' services in Scotland, and switchboards in Ayr and Aberdeen. A fully independent Lesbian Line started in Glasgow in 1981 to be followed a few years later by a Lesbian Line attached to Edinburgh Gay Switchboard. Today there are lesbian lines in Perth and Kirkcaldy and a Bisexual Phoneline in Edinburgh (in the centre). The telephone counselling services are for those who are being blackmailed and there are phonelines for youth, and for those with questions to ask about AIDS or HIV. All these services are free, which reflects great credit on the hundreds of volunteers.

An essay like this can never do enough justice to the less formal networks which flourished from the mid-seventies. Many were women's groups like the strongly principled St Andrew's Lesbian-Separatists. Immediately after the 1974 congress, following a silly comment I made about the 'red herring' of separatist feminism, a magazine flourished with the title *Red Herring* in Edinburgh. Although I retracted my remark the impression was made that I didn't like women. Gay men can be thoughtless or uncaring towards women, especially towards lesbians. That's sexism. I believe such division weakens our movement.

In the late 1970s, with much of the pioneering work behind us, I developed my political interests, always as an openly gay man. I joined the Labour Party in 1977 and that same year got involved with the Edinburgh Books Collective. We opened a bookshop in the Old Town of Edinburgh, and called it First of May. It specialised in alternative left-wing political thought and lifestyles and ran for ten years, until the mainstream bookshops caught up, began to sell our books and – radical stuff – open in the evenings. We left lesbian and gay material to Bob Orr and others who were working hard to build what is arguably the finest lesbian and gay bookshop in Britain, West and Wilde. Even then our personnel overlapped: Scotland really is a village.

In October 1978 SMG voted to become the Scottish Homosexual Rights Group (SHRG). We had become embarrassed with the closeted 'Minorities'. There was, of course, a lot of debate about whether we should be 'Gay' or 'Lesbian and Gay' (it has to be said that some lesbians refuse to let men have the exclusive use of the neat word 'gay' – I agreed with that view). We chose 'homosexual' because, clinical as it was (and is!), it was at least an 'in your face' word.

With our name change we unequivocally adopted 16 as the universal age of consent on the principle of equality. All our vice-presidents approved the change of name. Robin Cook, who then supported an age of consent of 18, wrote to us to say he'd have difficulty being vice-president of an organisation which had 'gay' in its title. And we lost one of our gay vice-presidents, Professor Ian Willock (of the Faculty of Law, Dundee), who thought 18 the right age. Well, he was wrong to resign on that point. To his credit Robin

Cook came round to 16 after lengthy debates in the Labour Party, which there is no space to discuss here. We also made fruitful contact with the Scottish Trades Union Congress, a labour body which has more influence in Scotland than its sister TUC in England and Wales. In 1981 the Scottish TUC adopted a pro-gay-rights position but unfortunately left it to gather dust on paper. There was a recent flurry in 1993 when the General Council called all Scottish lesbian and gay organisations together at Congress House, and Campbell Christie, the general secretary and an Outright vice-president, was interviewed in *Gay Scotland* on the support trade unions give to gay and lesbian employees.

With the growing realisation of the infectious havoc being caused by the human immunodeficiency virus, we thought the 1980s were a horrible time. The Tory government showed a callous disregard for the welfare of its homosexual citizens by introducing Clause 28 of the Local Government Act 1988 when our morale was (temporarily) at a low ebb. It was an act of deep moral cowardice to move against us at that particular time, but it has backfired. There were angry and joyful demonstrations in Scotland against the clause and, after a few years of excessive timidity, Labour councils in Scotland have begun to ignore a literal interpretation of the odious Section 28 and are stepping up their support for our activities.

In 1982 both the Glasgow Gay Centre and the licensed Glasgow Club in Queens Crescent were closed and sold off. The sudden reversal of fortunes in Glasgow came about as a direct result of SMG-SHRG's long campaign to bring law reform to Scotland. Vice-president Robin Cook's amendment to the 1980 Criminal Justice (Scotland) Bill legalised gay sex between men over 21. It was a grudging reform (the best that could be obtained at the time). But the 1980 reform opened the way for an open commercial gay scene in the Scottish cities. It is not generally known that the licensing boards in the cities refused a licence if it was known that the premises 'were frequented by undesirable persons' (that was us). Glasgow University actively moved against its GaySoc and refused to allow it until the law was changed.

For the next ten years Glasgow tried (with some success) to change its image (the substance of poverty was never adequately tackled) and this culminated in the Garden Festival of 1988 and the Year of Culture, 1990. As Janey Buchan quoted: 'It was the best of times; it was the worst of times' (from *A Tale of Two Cities*). Then, with Glasgay!, the extraordinarily successful lesbian and gay arts festival, in 1993 some people wondered if Armistead Maupin's *Tales of the City* could transfer from San Francisco to Glasgow. But it could just as well be in Edinburgh. There is a healthy and traditional rivalry between the two cities even though they're only 45 minutes apart by car or train. A new Gay & Lesbian Centre in Glasgow is just around the corner.

How did the Edinburgh centre survive the 1980s? We took the opportunity of Switchboard and the bookshop moving out to their own premises to negotiate a handsome loan from the ever-supportive Clydesdale Bank and completely remodelled the inside of the building. The improvement with the most impact was the café – first as Stonewall run by Colin Morrison and his team and now by Allan Nicholls and his staff as the Blue Moon. We have transformed *Gay Scotland* under the editorship of Dominic d'Angelo: it's a bright, colourful monthly magazine, widely on sale. The shop Drondale gives the snobs a chance to sniff – sure, Drondale sells cards with silly big (American) penises, leather knickers, poppers – but also *Harpies & Quines* and other magazines.

Everything about the centre seems always-changing. The exterior improvements are entering their final lap (after five years). The new front doors and stone steps are shockingly swanky. The frontage will be painted in time for our silver anniversary. Even non-gay organisations are leasing some of the office space: a theatre group, trustees of an old church at the foot of the street that is waiting to be converted into a wonderful multi-purpose centre for arts and architecture.

We have a choice in Scotland. We can support the UK organisations or we can invest in Scottish activities. Thank goodness enough people have felt it important to have good local gay organisations and we are reaping the benefits of that home-grown support. Much more is needed. It galls me that the larger gay bars and clubs have been so ready to take our drinking money and return so little to the community.

I can hardly believe what I've packed in and yet I've only just turned 50! I have not dared to talk about my private life or adventures: much passion (Labour Party deselection) and a strong sense of less-than-full achievement (academically) or missing out on so much music, theatre and film. But one thing's for sure – every time I devote too much energy to 'straight' things, I eventually begin to pine for 'gay' energies. I sincerely believe that we do handle relationships differently from straights (they'll catch up with us, one day).

Nothing would give me greater pleasure than to go to a packed hall where there are people shouting and crying for liberation. 'In the uncertain balance of my mind, opposites waver; I willingly submit my neck to the yoke' (Carl Orff, *Carmina Burana*).

I'd go to it: my heart is there.

The Black Perspective

Suzanne Roden

OLIVETTE COLE WILSON AND CLARENCE ALLEN

OLIVETTE COLE WILSON was born in Britain of West African parentage. She has lived most of her life in Tower Hamlets. She came to terms with her sexuality in her mid-20s and since then has been involved with black women's and black lesbian groups in London. She was a member of the Black Women Talk publishing co-operative. She was one of the first members of the Stonewall Group.

CLARENCE ALLEN is 26 years old. He was born in Birmingham and now lives in London. He is currently volunteer co-ordinator of the Black Lesbian and Gay Centre and part-time Youth Worker for an agency targeting young homeless people. He is also involved in the black gay social/discussion group 'Let's Rap'.

This chapter is based on discussions and responses to a questionnaire that was circulated to a number of black lesbians and gay men in London in 1993. Black here is being used in its broadest sense to include a wide range of people as in the Black Lesbian and Gay Centre definition, which is: all lesbians and gay men descended through one or both parents from Africa, Asia (i.e the Middle East to China, including the Pacific nations) and Latin America, and lesbians and gay men descended from the original inhabitants of Australasia, North America and the islands of the Atlantic and Indian Oceans.

*

Living and surviving in a racist society has not stopped black gay men from forging a very strong black identity. On the contrary, everyone we asked admitted to gaining strength from other black lesbians and gay men. But the difficulty with their sexuality, and coming to terms with it, in a society that is riddled with institutionalised and overt homophobia, is a very different issue. Aligning the two sides of one's life, blackness and gayness, is not always easy: 'I don't think I became fulfilled or rested until the two sides of me met.' It is never easy coming out in a society that, at best, accepts homosexuality on a superficial level (if it is kept secret, if it is the creative arts) and, at worst, physically attacks and sometimes kills lesbians and gay men. Having to open ourselves up to extra abuse or 'allow' ourselves to become doubly oppressed is not done without great thought. One man, not out to heterosexual friends, work colleagues and family said, 'It's too hard for me to do. Why give the racists another excuse to hate me?'

Some gay men admitted to having had relationships with women in the hope that their feelings would change or go away. Others were very sure of the attraction they felt for other men but, nevertheless, chose to adopt a heterosexual lifestyle as, at that time, it was too difficult or painful to adopt a gay one. This initial denial of one's sexuality is probably true of many white gay men too. What is evident, however, is that it was necessary for these black gay men to become confident about their race and their sexuality, in order to get by honestly and with the sense of personal integrity that they wanted in their lives: 'I realised that I had to forge an identity based on being black and gay, one which would allow me to be proud of both sides of myself.' Another man needed space 'to work out his black identity'.

Forging a black gay identity is not easy, especially when one finds oneself ostracised from the black community for being gay, and from the lesbian and gay community for being black. Yet it is important for these men to feel part of some community. There were different understandings and interpretations of the word 'community' but most appeared to agree that it was a place of trust, love and growth with like-minded spirits, that supports and shares (or has shared) experiences, identities, cultural and racial backgrounds. In this respect many felt distanced from the mainstream white lesbian and gay community as it does not satisfy, never mind meet, the needs of black gay men.

Many feel that issues affecting our race and our lives are at best marginalised and at worst ignored, as 'many white gay men are racist'. Virtually all of those spoken to felt that there is no understanding of what it means to be black and gay in the wider community. 'We have never been part of it,' wrote one gay man, 'but felt obliged to tag on to its coat-tails because there were no alternatives.' Nevertheless those interviewed felt that, although the wider lesbian and gay community denied their needs, black lesbians and gay men do have a diverse community, even if initially it is relatively hard to access. This community has like-minded people and safe social events, that is to say, free of racism and homophobia. This community has different support mechanisms, from friends and acquaintances to organisations such as the Black Lesbian and Gay Centre, and the black lesbian and gay club and party scene. In this respect it is believed that we have not been pushed out, but 'have pulled out', have made a conscious decision to opt out of the lesbian and gay scene. 'You can't be pushed out if you were never there in the first place,' said Haydn Kirnon.

There is an understandable resentment towards a lesbian and gay community that consistently fails to recognise a large proportion of its members. The mainstream lesbian and gay community purloins from the lifestyles and iconography of black lesbians and gay men the things that do not threaten it and then makes them their own. Dennis Carney cites 'house music, snap, black gay cultural language codes and clothes . . . The white community does not value or recognise the contribution that [we] have made to the lesbian and gay community as a whole.'

This sense of dissatisfaction with the lesbian and gay community has hastened the move to opt out of a scene that negates our experiences and feelings. 'How can I feel part of anything that embraces and rarely challenges skinhead imagery?' asked one man. Thus we have begun to create our own community on our own terms. Arguably it is not in a very strong position, and does not truly reflect the black lesbian and gay community in all its diversity, but there is a capacity for great strength. Yes, we may be fighting our own internalised oppression but we are making moves to recognise the differences of our community, which most definitely is not homogeneous. 'The day when a black person sees himself/herself in every other black person and feels the pain of every black lesbian and gay man, we will have arrived!'

It is, however, hard to become part of a community that is establishing its central roots and most of its gatherings in the expensive and alienating social scene, whether mainstream or black lesbian and gay. It is intimidating for those who cannot afford it or who are introspective, shy or lack self-confidence. Most of the men find that the social scene is limited and has the capacity to be oppressive. The 'bitching . . . lack of self-love and brotherhood can leave you wishing you had never bothered going . . . I believe that the black gay scene can be conservative and reluctant to change,' wrote one black gay man. 'I sometimes find this frustrating and try hard to challenge this in any way I can.' One man recognised that no community is ideal. It takes time, debate, encouragement, support and strength for any community to work. Black lesbians and gay men have had a fairly visible presence only in the last ten to fifteen years. 'Our community is still very new and is always developing,' said Chris Adam.

The negative experiences that we occasionally face on the black gay scene have not sent us scurrying for friendships, relationships and socialising with white lesbians and gay men. Although it is not always ideal, most of the men felt that there was something very calming and affirming about socialising with black lesbians and other black gay men. 'There's a special energy and beauty about it that is absent with white lesbians and gays.' Following on from this, few said that they would want a sexual relationship with a white gay man. There were others in cross-racial relationships who have never been happier: they feel their partners work hard to appreciate their black culture and backgrounds. Only one man in an inter-racial relationship admitted that although he loves his partner very much, if his partner could have a black skin then he would be happier.

The image of black men as 'exotic' that is rife on the scene and the myth of the priapic black stud have left some black gay men feeling angry, misused and hurt, having lived in and survived often very painful relationships. As a result they are loath to go out with white gay men. 'Never!' said one. 'Particularly when there are so many gorgeous black men around!'

It is true that on the social scene more and more black men are in black-on-black relationships. That is not to say that these same race relationships were not happening before, but it would be difficult to argue against the comment that more black–black couples are appearing on the scene. This is one of the many changes that have taken place over the last twenty-five years. Once you would have been hard pushed to see another black gay man on the scene, let alone a black gay couple.

The media seem better able to approach the topic of lesbians and gay men, but this often excludes black people. It is left to the black press, unfortunately mainly because black lesbian and gay men push the issue, to talk specifically about black lesbians and gay men. The *Journal, Asian Times, Eastern Eye*, and the *Voice* have all written fair, and in some instances very positive, articles on the black lesbian and gay experience. This was virtually unheard-of ten years ago, let alone twenty-five, when we were mostly portrayed in a negative light. Today we have out black lesbians and gay men on television. Significant programmes have included *Blackout*, featuring an African Caribbean and an Asian gay man, the series *Out* that featured pieces for and by black lesbians and gay men, a Thames Help programme featuring Black Lesbians and Gay Men Against Media Homophobia, and in late 1993 *Doing It With You Is . . . Taboo*. However, this defined its three programmes as 'men, women, lesbians and gays'. Aren't lesbians and gays women and men? We still have a long way to go: we remain the (in)significant other.

Changes at a more grassroots level have been huge. A black lesbian and gay centre could only have been imagined in 1971. The International Lesbian and Gay People of Colour Conference was held in London in 1991, again unimaginable in 1971. Pomo Afro Homos, a performance-based black trio, has appeared many times in England. Let's Rap, a social/discussion group for black gay men, would never have happened twenty years ago. Nor would black lesbian and gay picnics in central London parks, black gay men's weekend retreats, Black Gay Men United Against AIDS, Black Lesbians and Gay Men Against Media Homophobia, black lesbian and gay groups springing up around the country, from Newcastle to Bristol. It is said that change is slow but black lesbian and gay men have crushed that saying with a fierce vengeance.

In literature black gay men have *Brother to Brother* (1991), *In the Life* (1986), *Fragments That Remain* (1993), *100 Black Gay Poets* (1991), *A Warm December* (1992) and *The Visitations of the Spirits* (1989), amongst others, and have spoken to, and told of the lives of mainly African Caribbean black gay men. The year 1993 also saw Black, Queer and Fierce billed as 'the first gay arts festival from a black perspective'. Held at the Sadlers Wells Theatre, London, the Festival celebrated the creativity of black gay men with poetry, plays, performance, photography, other events and discussions for and by black gay men. The theatre has introduced positive black gay characters in plays such as Oscar Watson's *Battieman Blues* (1992), while other pieces of theatre have taken on a quasi-cult status, for example Paul Boakye's *Boy with Boy* (1991) and Pomo Afro Homos's *Fierce Love* (1991) and *Dark Fruit* (1993). Films such as *Tongues Untied* (1989), *Young Soul Rebels* (1991), *Looking for Langston* (1987), and *The Price of a Ticket* (1988) have shown black gay characters taking control and defining their own lives and sexualities.

Justin Fashanu's decision to come out also brought a dramatic change. It highlighted the fact that black gay men exist, something the wider community was loath to recognise; and just as, if not more, important, it showed that gay men exist within the black community. Equally it forced people to realise that not all gay men are effeminate and petite. We are everywhere. 'The racists and homophobes better get used to it!' wrote Eddie Mason.

In London, the social scene saw a rise in black gay events. The Pressure Zone, a popular club at the Vox goes from strength to strength, and 1993 saw the rise and fall of the Black Experience, a group of black gay men who organised parties for black lesbians and gay men. The party scene, once a labyrinth of passwords, cliques and clandestine codes, now has flyers proudly stating those two words that are so empowering for us: 'black' and 'gay'. The party scene is still with us as a valuable alternative (for some its anonymity provides the only option) to the commercial scene.

The differences are really rather startling. Most of the men realise that we have come a long way along the proverbial path to recognition and acceptance, yet there still remains much more of the way to walk. In the future we must move towards creating our own identities on our terms and not have them defined by others who know nothing about our experiences.

Despite all the evils of racism and homophobia, none of the black gay men would change anything about their lives. It was summed up best by Dennis Carney who said, 'If I was to live my life again I would definitely, without question or second thoughts, live that life as a black gay man.'

*

Discussions around coming out say a lot about how things have changed for black lesbians over the past twenty-five years. In one instance, coming out was described as 'a tortuous and very long process . . . from budding sexuality it was there . . . but there was an absolute denial . . . I thought this was a terrible thing to be, I was fucked up, genetically wrong, but the added thing is I'd bought the lie that homosexuality is a white disease or only exists among white people . . . I therefore thought I was messed up as a black woman.' Another woman's experience of coming out was 'like my worst nightmare, painful, slow, isolating, particularly as in all of it I was constantly questioning my blackness, I had never seen another black lesbian, I felt

I didn't belong anywhere and when asked on one occasion in my late teens if I was a lesbian I vehemently denied it.'

A younger black lesbian's experience was quite different: 'At college there were other black lesbians around, it made me acknowledge, yes, it is possible to live as a black lesbian', whilst another had 'mixed feelings of excitement, a new identity, fears and fantasies'.

One woman talked very positively of coming out. 'I came out in the women's movement that I was involved with at the time, I hadn't dealt with issues of "race" . . . I was 28, sixteen years ago I was immersed in a community where most of my friends were lesbians and I was in jobs that were OK, it wasn't much of a challenge, really.'

Coming out in the women's movement was supportive for some, particularly when issues of racism, culture and ethnic identity were not raised. As many of us asserted our right to be, expressed ourselves and our cultural identity, things became more complicated and to a degree our allies often became our enemies both inside and outside the movement. It was felt that race and culture were being forced on to the agenda and overtaking more important issues: the supportive community became unsupportive.

In our discussions we looked at the term 'community', what it means for us and whether we feel included in the wider lesbian and gay community. The responses were varied. One woman said, 'I think it refers to an act of imagination . . . we imagine and experience, at the level of emotion, some ties to a range of people who we've decided are like us. It might be because they are of Caribbean, African, Asian descent, it might be because of sexual politics, the point is it's actually formed in the head because we feel ourselves as part of a community – a network of people we never meet . . . community is about imagining ties . . . those passing moments . . . when we've been brought together and actually feel and demonstrate a profound unity: . . . like the Black Lesbian Group, forty women and the buzz that went round in the movement or coming together on Section 28 demos or Gay Pride or the Positive Images march in Haringey.'

One woman said: 'Thirteen years ago I feel people were more together . . . now I feel black lesbians are on the edge of the lesbian and gay community, on the periphery.' Another says, 'I spent a lot of time involved in the women's liberation movement where I wouldn't see a black face at all. There was no community in those days late in the seventies, early eighties. Things have changed, there are now communities . . . My positive image of community is my friends, people who are like-minded, share the same views about things, mainly lesbians, potentially a few gay men'. There are two issues here: wanting to be a part of a community for support, sharing, a particular need to identify and on the other hand wanting to express our cultural identities and therefore wanting to spend time with black people in our own spaces where we can have some autonomy. There is a sense of belonging and not belonging to the wider lesbian and gay communities.

According to one woman: 'When I say I feel part of the lesbian and gay community I am also making a statement to say that this thing called a community isn't white, predominantly male and outside of me, so I'm trying to disrupt racialised notions of what constitutes this community.'

Though some of us may not feel comfortable with the way the lesbian and gay community is presented or viewed, if we don't see ourselves as part of it we are denying our right to be included.

Whilst it appears that black lesbians are ambivalent about being part of the wider lesbian and gay community or communities there is, on the whole, a sense of belonging to the black lesbian and gay community at some level. 'When I haven't been with other black lesbians for a while I often wonder, am I still part of that group . . . when I meet with people, yes, I do feel connected, all I have to do is have lunch with someone and I feel a sense of history, a sense of belonging.'

As to the existence of a black lesbian and gay community another says, 'I think there is now, I can contrast it with [how] instead of celebrating another black lesbian in the late seventies, early eighties, I would avoid her gaze, thinking that the white people were waiting for us to get together. There was no community in those days. Now if I see black lesbians or gay men I have a special smile, a nod and I see that reciprocated, that recognition, I see people caring for one another in a way that I never saw before.'

In the late 1960s and early 1970s there was no black lesbian and gay community and we weren't visible to each other because of the racism we faced. It was difficult to take ourselves out of our familial surroundings and support networks and move into what was largely the unknown. 'Today we have a higher profile, people aren't scared as much, there is more support because there are more of us ... Black lesbians are educating their families more because they are prepared to go through with it ... they have left men, broken away from the norm.'

But although we have grown in strength and numbers we are still marginalised by the wider lesbian and gay communities. This is partly to do with fear and a lack of understanding. Whilst some groups and individuals recognise different cultures, they don't necessarily value them or the contributions we as black lesbians and gay men have to make. This has changed over the years but there is much more that can be done to ensure that our voices are truly heard and we are not included as an afterthought.

Yet if there are feelings that things have changed in relation to marginalisation or exclusion it is not an issue on which there is agreement: 'To be pushed out assumes you were part of something in the first place.' 'Denied a voice?

. . . only by the fact that people have been careless . . . I think the lesbian and gay community, particularly the gay community, grew out of selfishness, a need to cater for themselves; we as black lesbians and gay men had a much lower profile, it was a hell of a choice to make between our communities and our sexuality and since we knew our communities of old . . . and our sexuality probably came that bit later, many of us made the choice for our communities and never even asked for a voice within the wider community.'

Another view comes from a woman who says, 'You get two contradictory attitudes or tendencies over racialisation amongst white lesbians; one is, "Let the black lesbians speak" and anything one said could go because we were black, which meant that all possibility of communication between us was suspended: liberal guilt didn't allow it, notions of cultural specificity didn't allow it . . . that kind of practice (done out of goodwill) absolutely prevented the formation of the community. There were white lesbians and black lesbians. That was it, and it came from black lesbians too. How to speak, when to speak, who to speak with, these are constantly being negotiated, but if you use that in a paralysing way you can never have a way out of the racial boundaries . . . It's like giving a voice but denying community. The other way is "under-racialisation", where there is complete denial of difference: "We're just all lesbians and gay men together." My impression of it is that it is more the tendency with white gay men. We are divided in the world socially but the issue is homophobia – there is little debate about difference, they deny the existence of racism so they couldn't begin to talk about the effects of racism on them. They may say they are providing a space for black people within the lesbian and gay community but because they deny difference they absolutely exclude us.'

I feel that racism is still rife in the lesbian and gay communities. Over the years, there has been more honest dialogue, when people are prepared and willing to enter into it, but race does remain a stumbling block. 'I think there are some individuals who do appreciate their racism and Britain's racist history but even when people have an intellectual understanding of it they don't like the day-to-day reality of seeing themselves as racist and they don't like the emotional disturbance it sets up. The processes of denial and exclusion can take many forms. Take, for example, the dominant lesbian and gay social scene, it doesn't tend to cater for black lesbians and gay men.' 'In terms of the commercial environment they don't cater so well because they only choose one aspect of our music, the bits that the white people have chosen . . . but we have our own scene at other people's houses'.

This seems to be quite a common response, but it was also felt that 'There are more black lesbians and gay men who realise that we should not feel chased out of these spaces that claim to be for "lesbians and gay men" and should raise the number of visible black lesbians and gay men.' Generally women spoke about not wanting to feel isolated in a social environment. If there was going to be a comfortable mix they would go to a particular venue. The existence of alternative venues, if only a few, is a major change that has occurred relatively recently.

On the issue of mixed relationships there was an acknowledgement that they were possible, but hard work if the relationship was to be equal and honest. Many individuals are prepared to look at wider issues affecting black lesbians and gay men and will work towards challenging racism; these relationships are sustained with openness and support.

It is clear that there has been a lot of movement and a lot of change. Twenty-five years ago the few black faces on television were clearly racist stereotypes and I doubt whether a black lesbian was anywhere to be seen. Black lesbians have made their mark on television and radio, and to a lesser degree in the press. But 'mostly the media constructs the lesbian and gay community as white but then occasionally you get some wonderful programmes made by black people themselves that debunk all the myths and construct us as vibrant and ordinary, resisting and claiming our right to be, our blackness, our sexuality.'

Books are emerging by and for black lesbians or including us. Whereas previously many of these were from the USA (like Audre Lorde's *Zami* (1982)), we now have *Charting the Journey* (1988), *Don't Ask Me Why* (1991) and *Making Black Waves* (1993). There could be many more, and it is important to have black people involved from the outset helping to shape and plan new initiatives. Those eminent lesbian and gay authors who often exclude black people, as well as those involved in other aspects of the media, must realise there is a wide and varied talent in the black lesbian and gay community: our voices should be heard.

Many of us are still hopeful and optimistic that things can and will continue to change. But as one woman said, 'we must never be complacent; there is masses more to do both to take ourselves forward and to keep where we are'.

We have made great strides in twenty-five years but much more can be done to raise our profile and improve our quality of life. We must begin to recognise our diversity and difference and to start talking to each other and supporting other black lesbians and gay men. We must give positive publicity to black lesbians and gay men who are doing excellent work in their/our lives, as well as giving credit to the white lesbian and gay men who support our aims and objectives. There must be consistent efforts to include us and to create more spaces for constructive dialogue between black and white lesbians and gay men. Ultimately, we must all work together to challenge racism, racist practices and oppression and to strive for true equality.

Our future as black lesbians and gay men is positive and we are laying the foundations of a black lesbian and gay community of our own definition. The explosion of black lesbian and gay activity suggests that this community will be formed sooner than we think.

The Scientific Baby and the Social Family: The Possibilities of Lesbian and Gay Parenting

Nigel Sutton

ANGELA MASON

ANGELA MASON is the Executive Director of Stonewall. She was one of the original members of the Gay Liberation Front and has also been active in the Women's Movement. She is a solicitor. She lives in north London with her partner and nine-year-old daughter.

For some time after I told my own mother that I was pregnant she referred to the putative infant, conceived by artificial insemination, soon to be born into a lesbian relationship, as the 'scientific baby'. Of course, the scientific baby soon took her place in the natural order of adored grandchildren, but I thought my mother had a good point.

When I grew up there were lots of things that I thought were natural. Heterosexuality was natural, marriage was natural, women having babies was natural. In referring to the scientific baby my mother was marking the important distinction between what we see as natural and what, in the most generalised sense, we see as our own doing, our mastery over nature. So by alluding to the 'wonders of modern science' my mother was able to put a positive connotation on what, undoubtedly at some level for her, was a most unnatural event.

In fact there is very little science in AID, artificial insemination by donor, or as it is more generously called, alternative insemination. The highest level of technology required is that of the spoon and the dish. But if self-insemination is so easy why wasn't it more common before? Why did I grow up thinking that lesbians couldn't have children? What has changed to make it possible to think about procreation without heterosexual sex, rather than the more traditional concern of sex without procreation?

My mother might more accurately have called the baby the 'political baby', because it wasn't so much science as politics that was responsible for her conception and life. In a real sense she owes her existence to the lesbian and gay and feminist movements of the last twenty years which have profoundly altered our understanding of sexuality, of family and marriage. The changes that have been achieved are the gifts that brought her life.

*

Today more and more lesbians and gay men are having and caring for children. These new gay families are being constructed in a number of ways. Some children are being fostered and adopted; others are born by donor insemination. In some cases, like mine, the donor is anonymous; in others lesbians and gay men have negotiated agreements about parenting. In some families the father is known but not involved, in others parenting is shared. Divorce no longer means the automatic loss of custody rights. Not surprisingly lesbians first broke the taboo on 'homosexual' parenting, but as more gay men and lesbians are choosing to have children we may be witnessing a change which will have a dramatic effect on our future lifestyles.

I firmly believe that all men and women have profound feelings about children, towards caring for them, their future and development. This is partly a tenderness towards the child in all our adult selves, partly no doubt some genetic investment in continuing the species, partly the pleasure, emotional and physical, of one of the most altruistic of human activities. But historically lesbians and gay men have had to suppress such desires or, alternatively suppress their sexuality. A recent article in the American magazine *The Advocate*, put the point very powerfully:

> All of a sudden, in sight of my 40th year, the issue of children was a big deal. I realised that I had been sold a bill of goods that assumed I was not meant to raise children. In the space of a few months a lifetime of denial and internalised homophobia was swept away. I realised that the claim that we as gays and lesbians are not fit to raise and care for children – whether as parents, teachers, social workers, pediatricians, or whatever – was one of the most vicious and destructive elements of homophobia. Excluding us from this endeavor is an outrage, a denial of our human right to participate in the continuation of the human race. The time is right to move this issue to the top of our community and personal agendas.

I think this is a fine statement, and I want to look here at the ways in which we have been able to reclaim our relationship with children, but also to think about the wider issues this raises. Are we talking about buying into marriage and the family? Or will our families be different? What does it mean to put children on our political agenda? Will all the fun go out of sex as we become tired parents like our heterosexual peers?

These questions have a special relevance for women. Historically for us biology has been destiny. Unpacking motherhood from its ideological baggage has required an intense struggle to separate sexuality from conception.

Ironically it was precisely because 'homosexual' sex did not produce babies that it was condemned by the Christian Church. Hence the prohibition on sodomy, including sodomy between a man and a woman and, in some countries, tribady. The Catholic Church has continued to object to contraception for the same reasons. However, conception without sex has never won any plaudits despite the special honour accorded to the Virgin's immaculate conception. (It can also mean grandchildren without sons-in-law, which can be a bonus.)

For me there was a very direct link between women's struggles to control their fertility and having a baby. The clinic that I went to was closely associated with the Abortion Law Reform Association, which was the main body that campaigned for the legalisation of abortion in 1967. Originally set up to provide women with advice and assistance on abortion, it subsequently set up a fertility clinic, but their commitment to a woman's right to choose was retained and the donor insemination service was always open to lesbians.

My daughter then owes a debt to those women and men who fought for contraception as well as those who rebelled at Stonewall in 1969. It seems strange to think that having a baby could be anything to do with something so public, angry and political as a riot, but without that concept of gay pride, without the strength to be 'out' it would have been unthinkable to have children. I remember that one of the things I most admired about my partner, whom I met in GLF, was that she had lived openly with another woman. That was considered brave enough – to have a child in such a situation was unimaginable.

Indeed I did not think of it for many years. And when all my feminist friends had late feminist babies, squeezed in before biological clocks started to stop, I still thought it was physically impossible without having a one-night stand or an affair with a man.

My partner first learnt about alternative insemination from a secretary at work and I remember clearly the tiny feelings of hope and joy which began to bubble up as I was 'allowed' to want and then indeed plan to have a child. I have retained this sense of suddenly being allowed into an area of life, which I never suspected I would inhabit. It gives a new meaning to passing. One can get some measure of what it is like always to be on the outside when one part of you, your motherhood, suddenly allows you to be within society.

But although it can be tempting to pass, we have found for ourselves and our child that what is most important is to retain our integrity as lesbian parents, not mummy and daddy, nor husband and wife. All the lesbian and gay families I know are, in fact, slightly different. In one family the co-parent has undertaken the larger mothering role and the child has insisted on calling both parents 'Mum'. In our situation my partner did not want to be a surrogate mother, still less a father. What she has become and what my daughter, as much as anybody, has chosen to make her is a 'parent'.

What parenting roles lesbian or gay couples take on depends on their relationships and history. They need not be all the same and they can change. Maybe there are also some lessons here for heterosexual couples. It is clearly possible to bring up a child without fixed gender stereotypes. Non-biological parents, or co-parents as they are increasingly known, can have as deep and intensive a role as any biological parent. Children will bond and negotiate their relationship with their carers in a variety of ways that suit the individual circumstances of the family. In a situation where more heterosexuals are likely to be co-parents, to be involved in caring for children when they are not biological parents, some of our experience and the skills we are learning may have a wider relevance.

Confidence in one's sexuality is important in another sense. We are often asked whether our daughter is teased at school. In fact this has not happened and research which looks at the 'teasing' of children of lesbian mothers, confirms our experience. It is clear that our ability to create a safe social space for her depends in part on our ability to negotiate a status in which our sexuality is accepted. So her schoolteachers have known about and been supportive of her family circumstances. This in part stems from their natural good sense and understanding and in part from our confidence in 'sharing' our situation and indeed seeking their support.

We have also had to think out 'in real life' some of the questions which often arise as political or theoretical issues. Would we make our children lesbian or gay like us? Would socialisation or perhaps even the 'gay gene' produce clone dykes? What does happen if a child does not have or does not know her father? For those who are fathers, how can you convince people that gay men are not paedophiles?

In fact the experiences of lesbian and gay parents have in one way been mundanely pedestrian. Our children seem likely to grow up very like everyone else. Hearing a child first learn to play the recorder is as excruciating for us as for a heterosexual parent. The dyke with the girl in a frilly frock is an increasingly common sight. My own impression is that lesbians choosing to have children are often more on the 'butch' than the 'femme' side; that the appeal of motherhood has little to do with gender roles, even among lesbians. The first lesbian mother I met was a wonderful Amazonian figure called 'Moon' with a tiny baby dangling in her strong arms who lived on women's land outside Seattle. I often wonder if Moon, like us, fought a fruitless battle against a rising tide of My Little Ponies and, dare one say it, Barbie Dolls.

Studies carried out on lesbian households suggest that there is little difference between these children and those in matched heterosexual households on measurements of gender identity, sex role behaviour and sexual orientation, although play is slightly less gendered amongst the children of lesbians (see Golombok *et al. Child Psychiatry* 1983). Perhaps Moon did fare better.

And we already know that nearly all lesbian and gay men come from heterosexual families. In the largest controlled study of its kind, retrospective accounts by homosexuals of their parenting did not differ from those of heterosexuals (Bell *et al. Sexual Preference*, Indiana University Press 1987).

Nor does growing up in a lesbian or gay household mean that you only know adults of one sex. My own view is that it is important for a child to have a sense of the world; to know a variety of adults, men and women. In the traditional family a child's relationship with adults tends to be confined to blood relations, and those immediately responsible for their care, like schoolteachers. This relatively narrow set of contacts is now massively overwhelmed by the adults children see on television and to some extent the cinema. So children today know more about adults from *Neighbours* than from their own social circle.

We, like many lesbians and gay men, do not tend to rely primarily for friendship and emotional support on our families of origin, but look to a circle of long-standing friends. This means, at least in our experience, that our daughter has a far wider contact with adults than do others in her peer group. She is more used to social life, to restaurants, parties, shared holidays. People may fear that our children will have a very partial experience of life. It seems to me quite the contrary: their experience is often richer.

Of course, we still have a lot to learn. I await the day

when my daughter talks to me, as an adult, about what it meant not to know the identity of her father. I say as an adult because we have talked to her from the time she first began to talk about how she was born and why I chose to have a child in this way. Like other parents in a similar situation we have also emphasised the generosity of the men, for example her father, who donated sperm, and all those working at the clinic who enabled her to be born. I don't think she will say hers has been a destructive experience, but she will undoubtedly have things to say. At the moment she insists on her family being recognised and on the role of my partner as parent. She also says that she would like to know something about her father, which seems to me very understandable. This desire to know seems to be separate from any sense of loss or abandonment. Regulations which are now in force in the UK under the Human Fertilisation and Embryology Act provide that children born by donor insemination provided through regulated clinics may apply for anonymous factual information about the father; this seems a sensible way of dealing with the issue and will be helpful to children. If the donor father is known the boundaries of the social role of the father still have to be sorted out.

So we are still learning and we have to be tentative about any hard and fast conclusions, but perhaps we need not be so precious or fearful about the process of gender identification even though we understand it so little. Gender and sexuality may be hardier human qualities than we have allowed. They develop with surprising ease and certainty. The restraint and control of rigid sexual stereotypes may be unnecessary in bringing up children who are happy and confident about their gender and sexual preference. At the very least, by accepting that children can grow up to be straight or gay we are better prepared to accept and affirm our children's choices than many heterosexual parents. If the experimental laboratory of the gay family suggests that gender is truly not dependent on rigid sex roles, doesn't this free us all a little?

I have talked so far about the position of lesbian mothers. More lesbians than gay men have had children, partly because biology makes it easier for us to do so, but also because 'fatherhood' is such a problematic category. Biology does not imply social responsibility. Stripped of its legal and economic significance it is not clear what fatherhood is about. Perhaps for this reason fathers are being credited with a totally spurious moral authority whilst gay men continue to be despised and denigrated as child abusers and moral degenerates. The point that gay men have to make if they wish to claim fatherhood – that it is 'manly' for men to care and nurture – is the very point that should be being made in the frenzy about fatherhood that is being whipped up in our latest moral panic about family values.

Gay fatherhood also means trying to exorcise the taint of paedophilia which still attaches to all gay men. *Less Equal than Others*, Stonewall's recent survey of discrimination in the workplace, found that teachers were least likely to be out. Exploding myths about homosexuality and paedophilia might also go some way towards improving our understanding of male child abuse and the extent to which this is a male, not a homosexual, characteristic.

Even in today's hostile climate where the father figure is being wheeled on again to police women and children these points need to be made. They demonstrate an underlying unity in the interests of gay men and lesbians. For the lesbian mother is, of course, particularly vulnerable to those arguing for the imperative of fatherhood and these issues are being contested in legislation and public policy.

During the passage of the Human Fertilisation and Embryology Act (1990) strenuous attempts were made in the House of Lords to prevent single mothers and lesbians having access to donor insemination. I have no doubt that they were motivated by homophobia, misogyny and the need to safeguard the hereditary principle, but the language was that of the welfare of the child. Fathers were defended by making them in some mysterious way synonymous with children's welfare.

After a vigorous campaign organised by lesbian mothers, feminists and Stonewall these hostile amendments fell. The legislation reflects a compromise. A regulated clinic providing donor insemination services has to show that it has taken account of the welfare of the child who may be born (including the need of that child for a father). The Act did not seek to regulate or prohibit private arrangements for donor insemination. Donors providing sperm through regulated clinics are not treated as legal fathers, although children born as a result of such inseminations have the right to discover limited anonymous details of their fathers.

Sadly, the very cost of regulation has prevented some fertility clinics operating and the Child Support Act (1991) makes private donor fathers liable to claims for maintenance, although donors in regulated clinics are not liable.

Similar battles have been fought on fostering. After considerable representations from the lesbian and gay community and a meeting between the then Junior Health Minister, Virginia Bottomley and Stonewall representatives, the Children Act guidelines on fostering state that, 'It would be wrong arbitrarily to exclude any particular groups of people from consideration.' This opens the way for lesbian and gay applicants. The particular needs of young lesbians and gay men and the potential contribution of lesbian and gay fosterers are also recognised in the guidelines.

Today the climate is more hostile and a White Paper on adoption suggests that adoption agencies should always give priority to married couples. Whilst no legislation is proposed to prevent lesbians and gay men applying, it is suggested that adoption agencies should only consider lesbian and gay couples as a last resort. This view was not supported by the official government working party on adoption, nor by professional opinion, and it remains to be seen whether this attempt by the right to play political correctness games will be successful. In fact the courts have sanctioned lesbian and gay adoptions where they have thought it in the interest of the child to do so.

We are now in complex territory where a variety of, often contradictory, moral, class and economic agendas are being fought out. In general it seems that right-wing moral values are being brought into play to attack the most economically vulnerable. At one level the present government might have less objection to a relatively well-off lesbian couple bringing up a child than a heterosexual single mother forced to claim income support. It is not yet clear whether the values of the moral right can be used selectively by this government or whether it has entered a Faustian pact which will summon an unstoppable vortex of prejudice which will wreak havoc on us all.

*

At the very moment that we are trying to gain recognition for our families the moral conservatives are making a determined effort to capture 'the family' as their territory. This sometimes forces us into rather narrow options. Do we want to be sexual outlaws or cosy mums and dads, not to say husbands and wives?

Politically too this sort of antithesis can be dangerous. An angry 'queer' agenda that despises the heterosexual family will not speak to the significant aspirations we all have to care for each other, and for children, for stability and security. It will antagonise and marginalise us. Equally, trying to recreate the heterosexual family, will risk mobilising the right against us without offering much to improve our lives and relationships. It will tend to make us silly and vulnerable and not very happy.

In a very real sense, I think, we are all, straight and gay, in the same boat. And if this is so it might be useful to try and think of some ways out which would be mutually beneficial. Parenthood is one category that is ripe for a rethink. Instead of accepting parenthood as just a biological category perhaps we could start thinking of what I call 'social parenthood'. On a personal level this means considering that at some time in our lives we may be caring for children, that this is a part of adult life, whether or not you are a biological parent. Children are going to live with different adults and we need to do more to socialise ourselves to be ready for this. In earlier times children were less exclusively the concern of the small nuclear family and there was a more extended network of social responsibility.

Social parenting means assuming a responsibility for children even if they aren't 'yours'. It means a degree of care towards children in all walks of life. In the lesbian and gay community we have a special responsibility towards those children, many of whom are lesbian and gay, whom the nuclear family has failed. The pioneering work of the Albert Kennedy Trust in providing help and fostering for gay teenagers needs stronger support from us all. In our celebrations and public events we must be aware of children, provide for their needs and let them be visible. Pride should be an occasion for our children as well.

This wider sense of caring is already strong. On a personal level, I believe, lesbians and gay men have contributed to public work and voluntary service in ways far greater than their numbers. This contribution has been essential but seldom acknowledged. That altruism and commitment has also marked the response of lesbians and gay men to the AIDS epidemic. It is a collective response which is as fiercely caring as that of a mother for her child.

Learning to take up the cause of children, opening our community to their needs, becoming advocates for our own young lesbians and gay men will not only enrich all our lives; it also suggests that we can make a special contribution to a wider human agenda in which we seek new and more satisfactory ways to cherish and care for the future generation.

Numbers and Nightmares: HIV/AIDS in Britain

Bill Short

SIMON WATNEY

SIMON WATNEY studied art history at the University of Sussex in the late 1960s. He has been actively involved in international lesbian and gay politics since the founding of the Gay Liberation movement. He was a founder member of OutRage and has worked widely in HIV/AIDS issues, with a special emphasis on gay men's health education. He has published many books, is also a well-known critic and broadcaster and is Director of the Red Hot AIDS Charitable Trust. His most recent book is *Practices of Freedom: Selected Writings on HIV/AIDS*, Rivers Oram Press, London 1994.

> Lies and lethargies police the world
> In its periods of peace. What pain taught
> Is soon forgotten.
>
> (W.H. Auden, 'The Age of Anxiety')

It is September 1988: 1,500 are already dead, with an estimated 40,000 already infected by the virus. The most common cause of death is pneumonia, brought on by damage to the immune system. Herpes-related conditions are also frequently found amongst those infected. In all of this, the mass media respond with haste, sympathy and intelligent, well-informed enquiry. How is the virus transmitted? How can the epidemic best be slowed down or stopped? What chance is there for effective treatments, or a vaccine? There is a tremendous sense of public concern about the terrible effects of the virus, and the press is full of heart-rending stories of sadness and loss. Meanwhile the government refuses to make funds available for new research, though Junior Minister Virginia Bottomley is pictured on the front page of the *Independent* – at London Zoo. For no, this is *not* a story about HIV and AIDS in Britain, but about the fate of seals in the North Sea.

British responses to HIV/AIDS and to the seal virus could hardly differ more significantly. There has been little informed debate in the UK about either HIV education and prevention strategies, or the funding and direction of medical research. Indeed, there has been little media concern on behalf of those infected by HIV, compared to our furry, aquatic animal friends. On 24 August 1988, above a headline demanding 'Save Our Seals', the *Daily Mail* insisted that: 'We have made possible a virus destroying a whole species. It is our duty to find the antidote. And there is almost no time.' According to Brendan Bourne, writing in the *News of the World*, seals 'are highly intelligent mammals and show many human characteristics. They have a sense of humour, pair for life and grieve for missing mates and friends.' Neither newspaper has ever been so understanding of or generous to gay men in Britain, who continue to experience the most devastating medical disaster to have affected any single social constituency in Britain this century. Most noticeable is the lack of any sense of the HIV epidemic as a *tragedy* in Britain. Rather, it continues to be the pretext for prejudice, scapegoating and even celebration, and this is closely related to the fact that over 75 per cent of deaths from AIDS have been amongst gay and bisexual men. Even in 1993 it was possible for newspapers including the *Sunday Times* and the *Sunday Express* to deny that there is an AIDS epidemic of any significance in the UK, with constantly repeated calls to cut HIV/AIDS funding and research altogether, and to concentrate on 'truly' deserving causes such as cot deaths and cancer. By such spurious analogies are our lives held to count for little or naught.

*

Comparison of the figures of HIV and AIDS cases in Europe demonstrates how the epidemic is shaped by varying local factors. For example, in the north of Europe the epidemic has overwhelmingly affected gay and bisexual men, whilst in the south of Europe it has principally affected injecting drug-users and their sexual partners. France has an epidemic which affects both groups more equally. Such patterns of infection and illness reflect circumstances prior to the emergence of HIV. Thus in Britain, only 5 per cent of AIDS cases have resulted from the sharing of needles by drug-users, compared to some 23 per cent of cases in France. In Britain, drug-users have long been treated in a far less punitive fashion than elsewhere in Europe, and in 1986 the government introduced an extensive national network of needle exchanges. The effectiveness of this enlightened strategy is apparent in our national HIV and AIDS statistics.

In Scotland, injecting drug-users made up no less than 81 per cent of newly reported cases of HIV up to the end of 1985, when testing first became widely available in the UK. By 1990 this had fallen to 40 per cent, and by 1992 to only 19 per cent. This was a fall in annual numbers from 209 in 1986 to only 24 by 1992. By contrast, the proportion of newly reported cases of HIV amongst gay and bisexual men *rose* in Scotland from 23 per cent in 1986, to 42 per cent by 1990, with a slight fall to 38 per cent by 1992. These figures reflect the comparative neglect of the needs of Scottish gay and bisexual men. It is instructive to compare them to the over-all UK statistics over the same period, which show a steady *decline* in the percentage of cases of HIV resulting from unprotected sex between men, from 93 per cent in 1985, to 69 per cent in 1990, and 62 per cent by 1992. All statistics in this section are taken from the *AIDS/HIV Quarterly Surveillance Tables* (No.19, March 1993) published by the Public Health Laboratory Service AIDS Centre and the Communicable Diseases (Scotland) Unit. Unfortunately this information is restricted to a very limited number of public institutions, and is not available to charities or other AIDS service organisations in the voluntary sector.

In Britain as elsewhere we are not experiencing a single epidemic which has different faces; rather, we have a series of relatively distinct epidemics of HIV running side by side, according to differing routes of HIV transmission, and differing degrees of commitment to HIV education and prevention work. In the UK 73 per cent of HIV cases have been amongst gay and bisexual men, cumulatively since the beginning of the epidemic, a total of 11,330. A further 15 per cent of AIDS cases (1,269) have resulted from unprotected hetero-sexual intercourse; 11 per cent of cases resulted from inject-ing drugs, and less than 1 per cent of cases (143) resulted from horizontal transmission from mother to baby. Unfortu-nately, in Britain there is an overwhelming emphasis on the significance of percentage increases in HIV/AIDS cases resulting from heterosexual transmission, which are few in number, and almost no attention is paid to the several thousand gay men diagnosed annually.

For some years it has been widely perceived that the epidemic had 'moved on' from gay men to other groups. Nothing could be further from the truth. Gay and bisexual men continue to make up over 60 per cent of all newly reported HIV cases annually. We need to understand such statistics because they provide the raw material on which rational policies and resourcing may be based. HIV figures provide the data necessary for developing targeted education, and for tracing possible geographical or racial changes in the course of the various epidemics. AIDS statistics also enable planning and budgeting for hospital beds, treatment drugs, community care services and so on.

Approximately three-quarters of all British HIV and AIDS cases have been in London, which reflects the special role that the city plays for British gay men, especially in a period of escalating legal moralism and publicly acceptable homophobia. The government has never responded realistically to the demonstrable HIV/AIDS situation in Britain. To date only 1.5 per cent of the Department of Health's 'ringfenced' AIDS budget has gone to the voluntary sector, which all along has provided the most basic services from legal and housing advice to buddying and phone-lines. Only a tiny fraction of this 1.5 per cent budget has ever been available for targeted HIV prevention work for gay men. Hence the extraordinary paradox that whilst the government has spent many tens of millions of pounds on so-called 'HIV education' provided by its lapdog Health Education Council and other agencies, state funding has never been available to support community-based safer sex education for gay and bisexual men, who continue to make up two-thirds of *all* new cases of AIDS annually.

Before the advent of HIV, Britain already had a fairly developed gay culture, with its own press, information services, clubs, bars and cafés. This culture was largely united across party political lines in opposition to police discrimination, homophobic violence and abuse, and discriminatory legislation such as the 'age of consent' laws. The British gay movement also benefited greatly from its close contacts with the American lesbian and gay movement, which could draw upon a far more developed notion of citizenship, and citizens' rights. Paradoxically, the prejudice embodied in Section 28, and the increasing levels of anti-gay hysteria in the press have served, if anything, to pull increasing numbers of lesbians and gay men together, and to increase our self-confidence and our organisational and communication skills. Scottish AIDS Monitor, the Terrence Higgins Trust, Body Positive, London Lighthouse, the National AIDS Manual and others all to a greater or lesser extent stand in a line of direct descent from the complex world of lesbian and gay identity politics that existed before the epidemic. The tenacity and courage of these and other such institutions doubtless explain why, together with the introduction of needle exchanges, we in Britain have suffered less than most other European countries.

*

In a reasonable world, national and local HIV/AIDS policies would be closely based on the most recent, reliable statistics. In Britain this has never been the case, and unlike other European countries, we lack a national strategy. The UK response has essentially been ad hoc, with large sums of money being squandered on largely cosmetic exercises, while areas of fundamental need such as gay men's health education, are left to a handful of hard-pressed charities. As we enter 1994, we face a large number of potential nightmares in relation to almost all aspects of the epidemic, from standards of journalism in the national daily newspapers to funding and treatment issues. For the purpose of brevity I will restrict my analysis to factors which predominantly affect gay men.

*

One of the most remarkable features of the HIV/AIDS epidemics in the UK is the scale of disagreement about their size and significance. In the early 1980s the British press exaggerated the risk of HIV infection to heterosexuals, while virtually ignoring the vastly disproportionate impact of HIV and AIDS on gay men. The government's national intervention at the end of 1986 was both belated and inappropriate. Subsequently, however, the government was unfairly criticised for responding to HIV/AIDS *at all* by those who wish to minimise the significance of the epidemic. It is a commonplace of AIDS commentary from the *Daily Telegraph* to the *Daily Express* that 'too much' is being spent on AIDS. Such commentaries usually divide total HIV/AIDS-related spending simply by the total number of AIDS cases, disregarding HIV statistics and refusing to recognise the need for adequately funded prevention work, epidemiology, medical and social science research.

The consensus view in 1993 was well represented by Dr Claire Baron, research and liaison officer for the British All-Party Parliamentary Group on AIDS, in a 1993 conference report concerning HIV/AIDS in Europe as a whole. It is worth pointing out that not one single out gay expert on gay men's HIV education was invited to speak at, or attend, this conference. According to Dr Baron 'the epidemic in Britain, in the early stages at least, affected mainly the homosexual community which already had an articulate and educated subculture to draw on'. This is of course almost entirely misleading, implying that in some later stage of the British epidemic gay and bisexual men have somehow ceased to make up the majority of cases. Yet it is clear from available HIV statistics that gay and bisexual men will continue for the foreseeable future to make up the great majority of AIDS cases, and will remain at far greater risk from HIV than heterosexuals.

It is almost as if the government and state-funded agencies prefer to talk about the epidemic as it will probably be in thirty years' time, rather than as it is in the 1990s. Furthermore, it would be unwise to assume that all gay men have access to reliable, up-to-date information about HIV/AIDS. Most gay men read the same newspapers and watch the same TV programmes as everybody else. In reality, the so-called 'gay community' is as complex and diverse as any other arbitrary cross-section of the UK population. One major task undertaken by community-based safer sex campaigns has been precisely to try to establish HIV as an issue of *collective* interest to all gay men, regardless of our known or perceived HIV status. This is crucial since most state-funded 'official' HIV/AIDS education tends to present HIV very much as a risk faced by isolated individuals, who are exhorted to renounce promiscuity, to 'choose carefully', and so on. In effect this amounts to little more than moral management, and seems almost unrelated to the major, demonstrable routes of HIV transmission in the UK. The danger of a liberal consensus which operates its own homophobic agenda is that it denies the reality of the epidemic in order to ignore gay men's entitlements, which should be given absolute priority: in some parts of London one in every four gay men taking the HIV test finds he is already infected. The most detailed analysis of British and international HIV and AIDS statistics is given by Edward King, in *Safety in Numbers: Safer Sex and Gay Men* (Cassell, London 1993).

This is what is meant by the 'de-gaying' of AIDS – the denial of the massive impact of HIV/AIDS in our everyday lives, and the deliberate 'normalisation' of the epidemic by many institutions, including leading AIDS charities. It should be remembered that the Terrence Higgins Trust was unwilling or unable to employ a single worker responsible for gay men's HIV/AIDS prevention education until 1990, and this post could not be funded by government money. As Edward King in the *Independent* on 22 May 1993 succinctly pointed out:

> By all means report that heterosexuals can and do become infected with HIV. But is it too much to ask that some sense of perspective is maintained between the hysterical extremes of those who believe that 'everyone is equally

at risk' and those who believe that 'straight sex is safe'? Gay and bisexual men are far more at risk from HIV than anyone else, now and for the foreseeable future. It is only right and proper that this indisputable fact should be taken into account by those who allocate scarce education resources, and by those who aim to record the reality of the epidemic in Britain today.

It is nightmarish to consider the implications of Health Minister Virginia Bottomley's decision in the summer of 1993 to abolish the specialist AIDS unit at the Department of Health. This unit had monitored all aspects of the UK epidemic, and directed policies which, however inadequately, at least recognised the gravity of the epidemic and the full significance of a virus which on average takes some nine years to become symptomatic as AIDS. The moral seems to be: if you don't like the statistics you are receiving, sack the statisticians and the problem will go away. Not one British newspaper even bothered to report Mrs Bottomley's decision.

*

Throughout the entire history of the epidemic, medical reporting in the British press has been woefully inadequate, largely because we have no tradition in Britain of specialist critical medical correspondents. For example, the *Guardian*'s main AIDS writer was previously a sports writer for the tabloid, *Today*. Unethical stories of 'miracle cures' continue to proliferate, together with the equally unethical reporting of clinical trials and other studies in the earliest stages of development, before there is clear evidence of either harms or benefits. The early reporting of the drug AZT is a case in point. Raising expectations of effective anti-HIV treatments is cruel, especially when these are largely illusory.

The first decade of the epidemic in Britain was predominantly an epidemic of asymptomatic HIV, rather than AIDS. Until recently, comparatively few gay men have had much direct experience of hospitalisation, acute illness and death, unlike in countries such as the USA, where epidemics are running several years ahead of ours. Set up to provide caring services, and to some extent HIV education, the leading charities have never been much concerned or directly involved with biomedical research. The *National AIDS Manual* of 1989 aimed to place an equal emphasis on education and medicine, as well as on the provision of other services. More recently *AIDS Treatment Update* appeared; published monthly by NAM Charitable Trust, it scans the scientific literature critically and accessibly.

Whilst life expectancy for people with AIDS has steadily improved, it seems that a plateau has been reached. Most AIDS symptoms can now be temporarily treated, and many prevented or delayed. But the underlying problems of precisely how HIV leads to such a bewildering pattern of illnesses is not well understood. Yet for several years the *Daily Telegraph* and other papers have actively campaigned *against* further medical research, on the grounds that 'AIDS remains tightly confined to members of high-risk groups, such as male homosexuals and drug addicts' (*Daily Telegraph*, 14 July 1991). It is vital to insist that we are not involved in any kind of 'special pleading' on behalf of gay men, but only recognising an epidemiological reality which has tragic human consequences. Most basic research is at present conducted by commercial pharmaceutical companies working closely in association with the Medical Research Council and British university research departments. We cannot conjure up effective treatments by fiat, but it is distressing that so few people are familiar with the current state of UK medical research.

It is hardly surprising that most people with HIV or

159

AIDS also turn to complementary and holistic medicine. The relationship between these and more conventional medical treatment will continue to be a site of potential conflict, not least because some prefer to see AIDS as an outcome of 'promiscuity', 'excessive' recreational drug use, and so on. See for example, Simon Watney's article in *Gay Times*, October 1993 and Keith Alcorn, writing about the *Sunday Times* in *Capital Gay* on 17 December 1993. It is vital that people living with HIV and AIDS have access to the widest range of information about therapeutic options open to them, and that professional boundary disputes respect the full range of genuine alternatives.

We urgently need to sustain a sensible centre ground between the extremes of those who seek to deny any useful role to holistic medicine, and those who deny any role to what they caricature as 'western medicine'. Certainly we do not know enough about varying standards of care and service provision available to people with HIV and AIDS in hospitals and clinics around the country. The news of the axing of one of London's training units, reported in *Capital Gay* on 17 December 1993, bodes ill for the future course of the medical management of the epidemic. But it is important not to become too fatalistic: 31 per cent of a group of 562 men in San Francisco infected by HIV at least ten years ago have not developed AIDS.

*

Central government provides funds for all types of HIV/AIDS related work in the statutory sector. This money is distributed locally by the seventeen Regional Health Authorities which in turn fund direct services in the many local District Health Authorities. HIV/AIDS funds have been 'ring-fenced' by the Department of Health, and the government claims that in 1993, £250 million pounds was spent on the epidemic.

Yet as long ago as October 1991, an official Report on HIV and AIDS Related Services by the Controller and Auditor General, revealed that millions of pounds of supposedly protected 'ring-fenced' funds intended for HIV/AIDS work were being unspent or diverted to other purposes by Regional Health Authorities around the country. The likely ending of 'ring-fencing' in 1994 will thus only serve to make a difficult situation worse. As the voluntary sector becomes increasingly caught up in the business of 'selling' its services in the new marketplace of UK health care, charities will increasingly be forced to compete as potential 'providers'. It is moreover far from clear whether or not District Health Authorities will be prepared to support necessary education work for gay men which might prove 'controversial' for example to homophobic local newspapers and politicians.

A rational policy would be based, as I have argued, on easily available HIV/AIDS statistics, on the basis of which local and national needs can be calculated in the short, mid and long term. As we move into a full-scale AIDS epidemic from an HIV epidemic, it is especially important that necessarily scarce resources should be spent prudently, and not wasted. Future suffering can only be avoided by demanding adequate and properly targeted funding now. As things stand, few if any AIDS service organisations could survive without charitable funding. Yet recent changes in government policy suggest that it is intended that instead of topping up state funding, charities should henceforth provide the basic core funding for HIV/AIDS work, to be supplemented by the state. In a nutshell, the epidemic is being privatised by stealth. Fundraisers have a special responsibility not to collude with the wider undermining of the basic principles on which the National Health Service is based. The government speaks occasionally of the need to target resources, yet it was charities such as the Terrence Higgins Trust, which until recently attempted to provide HIV education for gay men, that have had severe cuts in funding. In a world where resources are always limited, we surely have an ethical responsibility to fund adequately on the basis of demonstrable needs.

*

According to the Public Health Laboratory Service's *Monthly Aids Figures*, by November 1993 there had been 5,250 deaths from AIDS in Britain: 317 of these were women, and 51 infants. No less than 3,993 were gay or bisexual men. HIV and AIDS have had many unpredictable consequences within British lesbian and gay life, ranging from the impressive and widespread involvement of individuals as volunteers in a host of ways, to deeply personal responses to loss and stress. The great challenge has been to relate HIV/AIDS to the principal agenda that *preceded* the epidemic in British lesbian and gay politics and culture. This has been an uphill struggle, since the epidemic was evidently regarded by many as a rather inconvenient distraction from the 'higher goals' of law reform on such matters as the age of consent. Only now in the 1990s is it widely recognised that such discriminatory legislation has an immediate harmful impact by making it extremely difficult to produce or distribute supportive safer sex education materials to gay teenagers, at the beginning of their sexual careers.

In reality, safer sex is not simply 'behaviour' that is 'learnt' in one go, and from which one may 'relapse'. On the contrary, safer sex is above all a *process* requiring constant reinforcement, not least because few younger gay men have had any direct experience of acute illness and death. For many gay and bisexual men, the UK epidemic remains largely theoretical. Hence the unique importance of gay culture, from theatre and film to TV, the gay press, and of course the whole commercial 'gay scene'. Unlike other countries, most British gay bars are owned not by gay men, but by the major commercial breweries, and many pub and club managers have not provided leaflets or condoms, for fear of somehow driving their clientele away! Gay politics must relate the *realities* of the epidemic to previous political demands and campaigns. If this is not done successfully, HIV/AIDS will come to be regarded as merely an issue for 'a minority within a minority', and the implications for all gay men may not be recognised.

As we move further into the nineties, organisations claiming to represent lesbians and/or gay men must contest homophobic accounts of the epidemic, whether in newspapers or in the policies of health authorities or charities. For example, it should be plain that supposedly 'educational' materials for young people which do not acknowledge that gay teenagers are potentially at vastly greater risk of HIV than their heterosexual peers are wholly unacceptable. HIV/AIDS is never only a medical or social issue. Always there is a political dimension, since so much bad research, reporting and policy-making is rooted in homophobic attitudes which are all the more dangerous for remaining latent. As long as the leading political and cultural institutions of British public life continue either to sensationalise or to trivialise the impact of HIV on our lives, the epidemic will effectively be allowed (and tacitly encouraged) to continue and worsen. A gay politics which cannot articulate the epidemic politically, in relation to other issues of concern, tacitly colludes with those who regard AIDS amongst gay men as an inevitability. Nothing could be further from the truth. We *can* stop this epidemic, but we can only do so as a result of co-ordinated collective effort. A gay politics which fails to recognise the urgency and priority of this need has forfeited its claims to the allegiance of the constituency it reports to represent. The seals of the North Sea had much better friends and allies than we do.

Lesbian and Gay Culture and Lifestyle

Dyke Style or Lesbians Make an Appearance

ELIZABETH WILSON

ELIZABETH WILSON is Professor in the Faculty of Environmental and Social Studies at the University of North London. She has long been involved in the women's movement, the lesbian and gay movement and in left politics. She is the author of a number of books, including *Adorned in Dreams* (Virago, 1985) and *The Sphinx in the City* (Virago, 1991) and *The Lost Time Café* (Virago 1993), and contributes to the *Guardian* and *New Statesman and Society*. She lives in London with her partner and daughter.

We are all engaged in the masquerade of 'making an appearance'.

*

'Fashion must be thought of as a symptom of our taste for the ideal' (Charles Baudelaire).

*

How to be a twentieth-century dyke – a late twentieth-century dyke?

*

Baudelaire's lesbians were not dressed at all. They lay about on cushions and were prey to unquenchable desire.

*

The laws of attraction – 'What does a woman want?' (Sigmund Freud).

*

Dressing the part: lesbians have inherited a range of dress codes which form the aesthetic parameters of how we present ourselves. This aesthetic is always open to change and modification, although it is restricted by the way dress functions as a sign system in the wider society.

The twentieth-century dyke appeared on the scene at a time when fashionable dress was already undergoing a revolution. Assisted by the movements for dress reform and aesthetic dress, women gradually abandoned the extreme elaboration of the Victorian period. Even before the First World War their garments had come more closely to resemble the functional dress of the fashionable man.

Havelock Ellis described the female 'invert' as a woman with masculine characteristics and of masculine appearance, but dress itself may have contributed to the possibility of her emergence, since, although Victorian fashion had played from time to time with the idea of some men's garments for women, it was only now that a costume emerged in which a lesbian could dramatise her identity in a satisfactory way. The new fashionable coat and skirt, a suit based ultimately on riding wear, which consisted of a masculine jacket and a long, svelte skirt, could be, and was, worn with a shirt, collar, tie and monocle and was normally made in dark, masculine material.

*

The period between the two world wars was the era of the invert, when homosexuals were born, not made. How was the third sex to dress? Quentin Crisp wore make-up and hennaed his hair in the hope of attracting a 'real man'. Radclyffe Hall was the lover of a 'real woman', Una, Lady Troubridge, yet Una dressed in the lesbian dress code of wing collar, monocle and man's jacket for her portrait by Romaine Brooks.

*

How to dress as an invert (1):

> Stephen was … grooming her hair with a couple of brushes that had been dipped in water. The water had darkened her hair in patches but had deepened the wide wave about her forehead. Seeing Mary in the glass she did not turn round, but just smiled for a moment at their two reflections. Mary sat down in an armchair and watched her, noticing the strong curve of her breasts – slight and compact, of a certain beauty. She had taken off her jacket and looked very tall in her soft silk shirt and skirt of dark serge. (Radclyffe Hall)

*

How to dress as an invert (2):

> 'Poor old Hopkins,' Norah said … 'Such a pity she goes round looking and talking like the most boring kind of man. Her flat might be the bar in a golf club …'
>
> However things had been very different some years before. Then, Hopkins had thrilled Norah … with her eyeglass and her dinner-jacket and her barrack-room phrases. (Anthony Powell)

*

Who was the lesbian invert? Was she Marlene Dietrich in top hat and tails, a seductive figure with whom both men and women in the Odeon audience could fall in love – or was she the ungainly Hopkins with her hairy tweeds and gruff voice? Both were survival techniques. When the 'mannish lesbian' of the 1920s was caricatured (and Hopkins is certainly a caricature) this was because she was potentially a threat to men, claiming male privileges and an active male role not only in the workplace but also in the bedroom. Yet when the mannish lesbian dressed in a mannish way she also gained acceptance through giving up her claim to femininity. Provided there were only a few mannish women, they could be accepted as honorary, second-rate, men. For them this may have been a way of surviving.

*

Androgyny and cross-dressing were also survival techniques. Marlene Dietrich's camp is an ironic masquerade. Who is fooling whom when she, glamorous in men's evening dress, kisses a woman on the lips and throws her carnation at a man? What is desire when Garbo, dressed for hunting in seventeenth-century boots and breeches, passionately embraces her lady-in-waiting?

*

The masquerade of the visible lesbian – is the audience disarmed? Does Dietrich allow lesbian desire to seep into the mainstream, or/and does she reveal the lesbian dreams of the heterosexual culture? Subversion or inoculation?

*

As Havelock Ellis was aware, the identity of the lesbian invert, a masculine being inside a woman's body, raised unanswerable questions about the identity of the more feminine partner of the ambiguous being. He reached the unsatisfactory conclusion that this more feminine lesbian was not an invert, but was simply a woman who was not quite attractive enough to appeal to a man: an unattractive but womanly woman.

*

Womanliness could be assumed and worn as a mask ... The reader may now ask how I define womanliness or where I draw the line between genuine womanliness and the 'masquerade'. My suggestion is not, however, that there is any such difference; whether radical or superficial, they are the same thing. (Joan Rivere)

*

The lesbian trod a tightrope between glamorous ambiguity and grotesque freakishness, negotiating a new identity with the costumes that were at hand.

*

I see her even now striding along in black pants and a man's white shirt spotted with paint, her hair slicked back behind her ears ... She's wearing white sneakers, also spattered with paint, a sailor's pea coat and no makeup, although her eyebrows have been slightly plucked. She looks very scrubbed and German but also faintly glamorous; the glamour clings to her like the smell of gitanes in wool. Is it the hard defiance in her eyes or just the slicked back hair with its suggestion of the high-school bad girl that lends this dangerous aura? (Edmund White)

*

By the 1950s there had been a move away from the belief in inborn inversion. In the lesbian popular romances of that period there are butches and femmes, but their roles are no longer fixed from birth.

*

Jack grinned at her. 'You're a boy. With Marcie anyway.' Laura put her glass down. 'I'm a girl,' she said …

'Why don't you move down here where you don't have to be either?'

'Everybody has to be one or the other.'

'You're too literal, Laura. Cut off your hair. Wear those pants you look so nice in. Get some desert boots, a car coat and some men's shirts, and you're in business.' (Ann Bannon)

*

In the 1960s fashion models looked like little girls, then like dolls, then like Christopher Robin. Hippie androgyny meant that men could look more like chicks. Dykes in suits were no longer à la mode. Now everyone saw Mick Jagger looking back at themselves from the mirror. By 1970, when everyone wore curls, flares and tie-dye what did it matter whether you were a girl or a boy? When everyone was in fancy dress there was no more masquerade, only effeminacy. Meanwhile, in the fashion spreads of *Nova*, models lounged together in lesbian poses, looking like Baudelaire's *femmes damnées* only with the damnation written out of the scenario.

*

Then came gay liberation.

Autumn 1993. I visit the Biba exhibition in Leicester. Oddly enough, I was living in Leicester when Biba happened. I couldn't wait to get back down the M1 to Kensington High Street.

It's all there: the ostrich feathers, the fringed satin lamp-shades, the droopy frocks, the sludge coloured T-shirts. There's a lump in my throat. Middle-aged women wander round. They're all reminiscing. Biba was when it really all happened for me. Being a boy and a girl all at once. Knee-high suede boots in aubergine, flowing curls, a dandy's frock coat in chocolate brown over a brickdust grandad vest.

Later on I gave my Biba Jean Harlow cream satin bias-cut evening gown to a radical drag queen.

*

Beautiful things started to happen. It was fabulous to see Richard walking around in Lorna's cardigan; Jenny in Richard's underpants; and Julia in my shoes. (*Come Together*, Gay Liberation newspaper)

*

Soon this polymorph perverse acceptance wasn't enough. In the 1970s the radical lesbian and gay community rejected a feminine androgyny in favour of the short-haired clone in boots and denim. All feminists were supposed to look dykey. (Every woman *can* be a les*bian*, after all.) The crew-cut lesbian feminist in dungarees terrified the life out of the media and politicians, but she was only making a statement about equality between women.

*

With flat shoes, baggy trousers, unshaven legs and faces
bare of makeup, their style combines practicality with a
strong statement about not dressing for men. (Inge
Blackman and Kathryn Perry)

*

In the late 1970s Glam rock and punk changed the terms of
gendered dressing. Women shaved their heads, both sexes
got tattoos, men could wear make-up.

*

Punk fashion was especially good at injecting a kind of
violent aura into femme chic that made it trashy and threatening instead of submissive and vulnerable to wear a skirt.
(Anon.)

Paradoxically, mainstream fashion soon took up the look. In
the 1980s city 'swells' (single women with lots of lolly) were
wearing hard haircuts, punk earrings and startling amounts
of lipstick.

*

Then one day Julie Burchill noticed the lipstick lesbians.
Beautiful women in love with each other.

*

But to subvert her heterosexual femininity she ... may have
a severely short haircut and wear aftershave. (Inge Blackman
and Kathryn Perry)

*

In 1993 the theme of the lipstick lesbian was taken up in such unlikely places as the *Evening Standard*, while dyke performers such as Lea de Laria and k.d. lang are the toast of the (straight) town.

*

The latest issue of *Vanity Fair* is running a series of spectacular photographs of the lesbian country singer k.d. lang cavorting with supermodel Cindy Crawford, thereby proving that lesbianism is currently at the very acme of the fashionable world. The pictures are camp, flirtatious and funny with the two girls looking quite beautiful – and fixing each other with frank looks of adoration. The traditional lad's view that lesbians all wear boiler suits, bovver boots and Number One haircuts – and that they only hang out with women because they're so ugly no right-thinking man would look at them – must now be laid to rest forever. (Louise Guinness, *Evening Standard*)

I already thought it rather peculiar when British television audiences were being treated to torrid scenes of lesbian sex in *Oranges Are Not the Only Fruit*, and *Portrait of a Marriage*, Nigel Nicolson's account of his mother, Vita Sackville-West's passionate relationship with Violet Trefusis. This interest in dyke love could only mask a crisis in heterosexuality, a crisis which in turn has something to do with the (slowly) growing independence of women. The rising divorce rate and the growth in numbers of single mothers has something to do with this; interesting how often the panic is voiced in terms of dress – recently a male journalist wrote plaintively in the *Guardian* of his confusion and dismay now that he could no longer be sure that a woman in a miniskirt was begging for sex.

Yet why should a heterosexual 'world turned upside

down' look to lesbians for salvation? Is it just the style? Is it just a replay of the old soft porn ploy of lesbians to titillate men? Nothing very subversive, after all, about Cindy Crawford fooling around with k.d. lang. Everyone knows she's married to Richard Gere; and lang in a gangster suit with Crawford playing the role of gangster's moll reinforces rather than questions the stereotypes.

*

Yet these days stereotypes have become just another masquerade. *Vogue* and haute couture fashion play with images of women dressed street sharp as men. Fashion has abandoned heterosexual obviousness. These days it speaks, however, superficially, for a woman of style who is independent of men, whose allure depends as often on an undercutting of femininity as on an exaggeration of it. There will always be some radicals for whom this can be interpreted only as divesting style of any subversive potential it ever had, for whom being taken up by the mainstream is always treachery, always a defeat. I am not so sure. The sign system of fashion often speaks what cannot be spoken in so many words, and if lesbian style takes fashion by storm that must be at least partly because heterosexuality has become so manifestly problematic.

*

One of the great struggles of the twentieth century has been to change the definition of what it means to be a man or a woman. As this century closes and we approach the millennium, we may look back and say that it has been the gay century, that it has been the century in which the figures of the dyke and faggot have come out to challenge the inevitability of heterosexuality. Their very insistence on their being in face of unrelenting oppression – from the Oscar Wilde trials through the Holocaust to the anti-commie/queer McCarthyism of the 1950s – proves that fundamental questions are being asked not only about sexual orientation, but about the masculine and the feminine.

Even about what is sex.

*

'I've marked the pages in *Sex* which are thrilling: ... the cross-dressed aristocrat who shelters a little blonde girl inside her suit jacket like a real dyke daddy; the teeth caught in a tit-ring and the tongue lavishing attention upon a fetish ballet slipper with a seven inch-heel ... (Pat Califia)

*

Is dress about eroticism or is eroticism about dress? Throughout the queer century we have disguised and revealed our deviant desires in dress, masquerade, disguise. Now that everyone's caught on in a postmodern world, what do we have to do to invent a new dyke style?

*

A bisexual dyke comes round to visit. She's wearing a cassock. Martin Margiela got there first, but hers comes from the Portobello Road. Wonderful ribbed silk, dull black, hundreds of tiny buttons, skirts sweeping the ground. This is beyond butch and femme. Now we can do anything.

Fashioning Change: Gay Men's Style

RICHARD DYER

RICHARD DYER teaches film studies at the University of Warwick. He is the author of *Now You See It: Studies on Lesbian and Gay Film* and other books and has published in *Screen* and *Playguy*, *New Statesman* and *Gay Left*, *Sight and Sound* and *Square Peg*, among others.

Twenty years ago there was nothing in the world more hilarious, nothing more naff, than a man wearing baggy khaki shorts that reached to his knees. Seven or so years ago, it was a real head-turner. Now it's delightfully routine, and thus probably on the way out. I don't know for certain that it was a gay man who first saw the stylish potential of long shorts, but I'd be willing to bet on it and on the assumption that it was gay men as a group who turned them into a fashion item.

Gay men have always played a leading role in the male (as well as, of course, the female) fashion industry. If the vast majority of gay men have had nothing particular to do with it and may dress or decorate as ineptly as the next straight man, still enough of us were into such things visibly and triumphantly enough to constitute a distinctive and recognisable gay culture. There are various possible explanations for this. In practice, fashion was a form of employment that was relatively relaxed about us (though also one of the first places that blackmailers, police and yellow journalism would look for queer material). It was also a job that allowed us to pay physical attention to men, most of the time unemphatically and inexplicitly but occasionally blossoming into changing-room fumbling and more (I shall never forget that time in Harrods . . .)

Behind such explanations lies a broader one, to do with the nature of being gay in a homophobic society. Fashion and the other style trades gave us a space to exercise a skill we have had to be very good at, namely, presentation. Surviving as a queer meant mastering appearances, knowing how to manipulate clothes, mannerisms and lifestyle so as to be able to pass for straight and also to signal that we weren't. To stay alive and unharmed we had to handle the codes of heterosexuality with consummate skill; to have any erotic and sentimental life we had to find ways of conveying our otherwise invisible desires. As I say, not all gay men managed both, or felt happy with either; but enough have, making the stereotype of gay men's investment in style not so utterly wide of the mark.

It's an investment by no means confined to people professionally involved with clothes, décor, design and so on (and from here on I'm going to talk pretty well exclusively about clothes style). It pervades our everyday life. I am conscious of trying to tread the thin line between passing and flaunting. I rarely have other than casual dealings with people who don't know I'm gay but I'm aware of wanting simultaneously to express the fact that I am and yet also to fit in. I recently had an interview for a good job and had a wonderful discussion with a friend about what I should wear. It had to be a suit, of course, one knows the rules; a

179

plain black one makes a statement about conscious choice over attire that the indeterminate brown and grey mixes of most men's clothes disavow. More difficult to decide upon was the obligatory tie. How ironic should it be, how over the top should I go to signal that I know that ties are just a piece of manly frippery; how far back from over the top should I withdraw in order not to appear to be sending the panel up? On such precipices of decision is gay style lived.

The importance of gay men in setting male fashions has given the whole question of masculine style in most western cultures a particular ambiguity (though what I have to say is a lot less true of Black and Latin, and especially Italian, cultures, where being stylish and macho are not seen as so contradictory). Concern with appearance is so associated with gay men in this society that not to be concerned with it has often been taken as a badge of real/heterosexual masculinity.

Clothing is an issue for straight men, yet one they cannot be seen to have any expertise in. Much clothing for heterosexual men has been chosen by women, (mothers and spouses), but the latter could not try the fashions out, could not themselves pioneer male styles. So, over the years, it is from gay men's interest that straight men and women have learnt, our soft white shirts, our suede shoes, our 501s, our baggy shorts. The trouble is that such stylishness has thus always been tainted by queerness. Straight men have often resisted the purchases of their womenfolk because they've thought they would make them look like pansies; and straight women have been heard to say that they don't like a man who takes too much interest in his appearance.

Yet the styles have caught on all the same. Time and again straight men have adapted to the gay-led fashions. What is going on here? In part there has been nowhere else to look: gay men have tended, literally, to corner the market on male style innovation. But we may also underestimate the element of fascination with homosexuality which is the inevitable accompaniment of something so strenuously abominated. I mean this in two ways. First, homosexual men, because they are not involved with heterosexual relations, embody a potentially enviable alternative to such relations, for both sexes. For straight men, we may represent the possibility of being free of the restrictions of domesticity and the responsibilities of breadwinning; for straight women, we are men who are not going to force ourselves upon them, we are not part of the coerciveness and power play of heterosexuality. Secondly, our sexuality is a matter of enthralled, if also appalled, interest. Many straight men have had some gay experience and fondly wish for some more on the side. In short, for all the opprobrium cast on us, there is also a great deal of envy and fascination and desire. The most visible sign of our social and sexual identity is style. When straight men adopt our style it's not just to please women or because the fashion industry (like any other capitalist industry) has to have new products to sell, it's also because of the *frisson* of the association with gay sexuality.

All this has, if anything, become more explicit in recent years. While Levi ads or the Chippendales are resolutely heterosexual in their address and attendant publicity, their gay style resonances are too explicit to be dismissed as unconscious. In the world of pop, gay association (whether or not strictly 'true') has not only not done any harm to the appeal of, for instance, David Bowie, Freddie Mercury, Erasure, Marky Mark or Take That, but seems to be very much part of their appeal. At the time of Jason Donovan's case (against the *Face* for reprinting a poster outing him), it was clear from interviews that many of his adolescent female fans not only didn't care if he was gay but felt that would all be part of what made him sexy. Similarly, Take That still carry very clearly the signs of their early career, entertaining in gay clubs, into their mainstream success.

Gay style has then always been, indeed is, *the* influence

on straight male style, in a fascinatingly ambivalent process. There has however been a profound shift in the nature of gay style. Up until some time in the 1970s, gay style was about feminising male attire; since then it has been about quoting mainstream masculinity.

Feminisation of male attire did not mean wearing women's clothes but a readiness to wear bright or pastel colours, to put extra flounce or decoration to an outfit, to do things, in short, that only women were supposed to do.

Oscar Wilde's descriptions of beautiful young men have recourse to flower similes, speak of ruby lips and golden curls, and indeed of 'beauty', a term rather dodgy in relation to men until perhaps recently. In the novel *Teleny*, apparently written by Wilde and some other men around 1893, the descriptions of the attractive and homosexual men's attire always stress both their difference from the other men and those added notes of colour and swish. One character, for instance, has 'faultless' but 'a trifle eccentric' dress – he wears a white heliotrope in his lapel. Another, who has 'a most lovely neck and throat', stands out because 'when every gentleman was in black, he, on the contrary, wore a white flannel suit [with] a very open Byron-like collar, and a red Lavallière cravat tied in a huge bow.'

Queens in Berlin in the 1920s pushed things further. Magnus Hirschfeld (a thorough cross-dresser himself) described one gay man who 'received his guests in an indeterminate garment made by himself, a cross between a ball gown and a dressing gown'. Another observer, Curt Moreck, wrote this description of the styles in the gay bars, which, though homophobic in intention, is, in its last sentence at least, utterly captivating:

In the more refined West [End of Berlin], resemblance to the opposite sex is achieved through powder puffs and lipstick. They are somewhat profligate with perfume and

coquettish in their pretty coloured silks. They have plucked
their eyebrows and crimped, sleek, shiny hair in soft quiffs.
They look at you yearningly, dreamily, out of Belladonna
eyes.

The 'Belladonna' effect was described by another observer
as 'the febrile sparkle of eyes darkened by kohl', a fashion
associated with movie stars like Theda Bara – and Rudolph
Valentino.

The attractive and outrageous young men of Greenwich
Village, New York City, in the 1930s were no less fascinated
by feminine grooming, if the 1933 novel, *The Young and the
Evil* by Charles Ford and Parker Tyler is to be believed.
Make-up, doing and discussing it, is a major preoccupation
of the group of young queers at the novel's centre. One
evening they are preparing for a party:

> Julian wore a black shirt and light powder-green tie. His dark
> hair had been washed to a gold brown and fell over his
> forehead [this is a period when real men kept their hair well
> slicked back].
>
> Karel, as he had promised, came by three hours before
> the others bringing his box of beauty that included eyelash
> curlers, mascara, various shades of powder, lip and eyebrow
> pencils, blue and brown eyeshadow and tweezers for the
> eyebrows.
>
> [Karel's] eyebrows … could be pencilled into almost
> any expression: Clara Bow, Joan Crawford, Norma Shearer,
> etc. He thought he would choose something obvious for
> tonight. Purity.

Such goings-on were only possible, of course, for a
screamingly courageous minority in a few metropolitan centres, but whether Victorian heliotropes, Weimar Belladonna
eyes or Greenwich Village beauty boxes, gay male style

involved incorporating markers of the feminine into male clothing. The history of straight adoption of such styles has yet to be written and will centre on such weighty matters as pomade (butched-up to Brylcreem), perfume (aka after-shave), floppy hair ('natural') and suede shoes (an absolute queer give-away in the 1950s that few new queers would be seen dead in today). It was not really until the 1960s that a gay-led male style emerged which crossed over so swiftly that at the time its queerness was evident to all, although in the mythologisation of the period it has tended to be forgotten.

Carnaby Street and the swinging sixties were a turning point in sartorial history, the moment of men's rediscovery of the pleasures of unabashed dress and display – the 'rebirth of the peacock', as journalism of the day had it. Carnaby Street was originally a group of very queer little shops or 'boutiques', a word borrowed from female fashion marketing and only one of the many steps taken to incorporate the feminine into male clothing in what turned out to be a last, florid burst of this particular dynamic of male gay style. Carnaby Street went mad on colour, not only pinks and pur-ples and powder blues and other sissy colours, and not only on ties but on shirts and, most shocking of all, jackets and trousers. Nor were garments just of one colour, as male clothes tend to be (when they are not a mix of sludge and drab); colours were thrown together in riots, most thrillingly in flower patterns. Shirts were waisted, fitting tight to the body; trousers were flared, creating a flowing line at odds with the military precision and control of straight legs (though no doubt revelling in the naval overtones). My most delirious memory of indubitably queer gear passing if not unnoticed then at any rate unmolested is strolling out of a Carnaby Street boutique and through London in a newly acquired pair of white lace trousers.

Such style lingered on in the 'radical drag' of the early

gay liberation movement – unshaven men wearing frocks or men going to work wearing skimpy women's jumpers with flower motifs on them. Yet this happened at the very same time as the other gay style began to emerge which has now become dominant: the quoting of traditionally male styles. Indeed radical drag highlighted a terrible truth: that effeminacy was right-on but didn't get you men any more.

Macho men had of course always been objects of desire. Alongside the heliotropes, the kohl and the lace trousers, there had always been lads, rough trade, hunks. Yet there had always been an ambiguity about them – were they really queer? The preening and grooming involved were not in doubt and certainly raised question marks about their heterosexual masculinity, but it was doubts rather than indubitable queer association. What happened, alongside the last puff of effeminacy as a gay style in the sixties and seventies, was gay men's decision to start looking like these other objects of desire. Hence the turn to 501 Levis, bodybuilding, leather, short hair, boots, white jockey briefs, as well as the rediscovery of the suit and tie, worn with new panache, braces and matching socks and shirts (an almost feminine note), and later such things as the adoption of gym gear, and baggy shorts.

I call this quoting male styles because there is a self-consciousness about the way gay men adopt these styles. Much of the gay repertoire of the seventies and eighties drew upon two traditional arenas for the forging of (straight) masculine identity: work and sport. Jeans, short hair, boots are practical gear for men's work (by the same token, there was even for a crazed moment the wearing of construction workers' hard hats at discos); muscles are a product of both work and sport, something (real) men just have; leather has long been associated with 'hard' masculinity (perhaps because so directly evoking the slaughter that has made such adornment possible or more generally because of the association of masculinity with beastliness), while jockey briefs are seen to be manlily functional, right down to the rather dysfunctional front opening.

All these items are (or were) entirely normalised in everyday life, just what men wear in an unreflective, seemingly unchosen, nay, natural sort of way. Gay men on the other hand select them, and wear them in the context of fun and sex – and wear them with care, ironing 501s and leaving one button ostentatiously undone, making sure muscles obviously acquired by machine show, keeping briefs spankingly white, playing endless more and more self-conscious variations on short hair (shaved, tufted, dyed and so on). While the degree of grooming involved may suggest the feminine, the signs remain resolutely butch – no pastels, laces or lipsticks here, though the quoting effect is often enhanced by wearing a brooch or earring, drawing attention by its sudden effeminacy to the butch regime of the rest.

The result is gay in a number of different ways. First, these are acts of queering: they find or put in the homoerotic at play in straight life, they bring out the gay while leaving enough reference to the straight to be at once exciting and disturbing. Secondly, they insist on clothes as performance: they give the lie to the notion that clothes really make the man, that clothes are in any sense natural or inevitable; they proclaim that the only things clothes are appropriate to is our fantasies of gender and sexuality. Thirdly, they celebrate masculinity as erotic, they flaunt the pleasures of male exhibitionism and narcissism, they get off on the supposedly asexual signs of manliness. In this last way they are, in terms of sexual politics, unruly, for they are not just a statement about masculinity, they are also utterly absorbed and fascinated by it too: they may destabilise its supposed naturalness but not to the point of undercutting it altogether, and I sometimes find something remorselessly virile in the endless black clothes, scratchy heads and faces and clomping shoes. The feminine, above all the effeminate, has lost out in this development and we are the poorer for it.

When gay men out male fashion and when it eventually gets taken up by straight men, two processes are at work. One is the transformation of naff into style. No word is harder to define than naff (itself a term from queer slang taken up by straights). I often think of it as almost interchangeable with the word 'straight'; it's above all what happens when straight men make an inept lunge at being stylish. The magic of gay style is that it is capable of taking the very essence of naffness, to return to baggy shorts, and somehow make it seem stylish. It's a product of deciding to see something as stylish, to quote it with confidence, to wear it with irony: baggy shorts become stylish by the very act of its being taken up as stylish by gay men, as part of a way of relating to clothes and style that gay men are so skilled at. (Though again it's important to remember that not all, perhaps not even most, gay men are so skilled; but the culture is.)

Secondly, the gay take-up of straight style makes it sexy. Much gay style has been sexual in the most obvious way from groomed and adorned penises (shaved groins and cock rings) through bikinis and white, white jockeys to tight jeans worn with elaborate and gravity-defying genital arrangements to one or other side of the fly, and on to Lycra, gay men have seldom held back from making a spectacle of their sexual parts. Other styles have spectacularised other parts: the tight T-shirt, with sleeves rolled right up, or else the shortlived 'muscle shirt' with next to no sleeves at all; and most trousers, skilfully selected for the way they hang over the buttocks, involving years of practice in looking down over one's shoulder into a mirror. What is more extraordinary, even heroic, is gay men's ability to make clothes sexy that do not cling or reveal. Which takes us back to baggy shorts, and indeed very loose jeans and floppy shirts. Of course, they too look better on a better body (baggy jeans look best with cinched-in waists), but they are not exclusively about that: they are sexy without making direct sexual reference.

The dynamic of gay style is unpredictable. After baggy shorts, can floppy jumpers and sports jackets be far behind? Or are there still some new variations to play on denim and short hair? Could we even hope for a return to pastels and flow? It will be delightful to see and to behold the ripple of queerness as one or another gay style spreads back out into society.

Harriet Logan

Show and Tell: The Emergence of Lesbian and Gay Theatre

DAVID BENEDICT

DAVID BENEDICT has worked as a writer, director and actor since 1980 for companies including the New End, Hampstead, Red Shift, the National Theatre, Channel Four and Gay Sweatshop for whom he was an Artistic Director. He was script consultant on BBC's lesbian and gay night (*Saturday Night Out*) and is currently writing for *Attitude* and the *Independent*.

Growing up in a heterosexual world, lesbians and gays learn to act. The 'gay gene' debate notwithstanding, childhood experiments in dressing up, stealing make-up and playing fantasy roles are both universal and the stuff of gay folklore. Vast numbers of children both young and not-so-young (myself included) fall in love with songs from the shows and dream of resplendent careers in the musical theatre in a process which could be described as Oklahomosexuality. Nonetheless, for all of us who spent our childhoods dancing around our living rooms dreaming of growing up to become Barbra Streisand (only to discover that her career is safe and that we are simply gay) there are legions of others for whom theatre in its widest sense would appear to have little bearing

189

upon their lives. Yet, by their very nature, lesbians and gay men are practised, skilled actors.

Unlike members of other minority groups, most lesbians and gay men have to come to terms with a hostile society, not only outside their immediate family but within it. Our 'difference' is usually strikingly at odds with our upbringing. A host of other factors from peer-group pressure to stereotypical negative images combine to produce a uniquely internalised self-hatred. Faced with the realisation of one's sexuality but unequipped to deal with the consequences, most of us adopt a role and teach ourselves to act straight. Casting an eye down the lonely hearts columns and seeing the number of people seeking 'straight-acting' partners bears witness to the fact that not only is acting a way of being for those unable or unwilling to come out, but that it is not recognised as an act.

It is hardly surprising then that professional theatre is fairly well stocked with lesbians and gay men, be they running box-offices or lining up at auditions. Yet a strange paradox exists whereby the press and the public consider most theatre people to be gay – indeed 'theatrical' is often used as a straight euphemism for gay – while falling over in a bizarre mix of astonishment, glee and horror when an actor is outed.

But if theatre is overflowing with gay talent, is it actually gay? Historically it has been seen as a breeding ground for unspecified vice, arising from early religious concerns over the immorality of disguise and dissembling, coupled with a not unreasonable fear of insurrection promoted by historical plays which pointed to contemporary ills. Actors were officially seen as rogues and vagabonds and were refused the right to be buried in consecrated ground. The outbreak of the Civil War in England in 1642 provided the Puritans with the excuse to close the playhouses and acting was forbidden, the theatres not reopening until 1660.

The century that passed from the coining of the term homosexuality in 1869 to the Stonewall riot of 1969 saw the proliferation of theatre in hundreds of new guises and forms, many of which were created by lesbians and gay men. Through fear, ignorance and censorship, however, much of our contribution has been silenced. Following the 1927 lesbian melodrama *The Captive*, the Wales Padlock Act was added to the New York State penal code banning plays 'depicting or dealing with the subject of sex degeneracy, or sex perversion', remained in force throughout the US until 1967. In 1737 in the UK the Lord Chamberlain was made responsible for the licensing of plays. The portrayal of homosexuality was banned until 1958 when the door was opened a crack to allow in the subject, 'when essential to the plot' (?) but not if the play was 'violently homosexual' or campaigned for changes in the law. Embraces and 'practical demonstrations of love between homosexuals' had to wait until the abolition of the Lord Chamberlain's office in 1968, a year after the decriminalisation of homosexuality for men over 21. Given this historical framework, the relative absence of 'gay theatre' begins to make a certain sense. Scouring pre-Stonewall theatre history and texts for examples of our presence would therefore appear to be a fairly fruitless exercise. Or would it?

Any assessment of gay theatre has to ask a number of crucial questions, most succinctly outlined by writer/performer/director Neil Bartlett in his book *Who Was That Man? A Present for Mr Oscar Wilde*: the question was, and is, who speaks, and when, and for whom, and why? Is the author gay, the character(s), when was it written, is there a 'meaning'? All these questions, easily asked by both a work's creators and its audience, are often oddly ignored. A straight director can ignore subtextual gay relationships. Closeted actors fearing for their careers can stereotype lesbian and gay characters in order to distance themselves from a role. In

1992 Neil Bartlett and Nicolas Bloomfield's *A Judgement in Stone* was castigated by one gay critic for failing to conform to the authors' roots in 'radical gay theatre', despite its central depiction of the classical gay formula of an outsider destroying the heterosexual nuclear family, in this case literally gunning them down.

The twentieth-century cult of biography has revealed the unofficial sexuality of many major theatre figures, past and present (often in the face of fierce opposition). All manner of theatre has been reassessed in the light of such knowledge. Texts have been reread, plays revived, and suppressed works rediscovered. Productions have highlighted passages which reflect upon the sexual concerns of the author from Shakespeare to Joe Orton. In 1992 the Almeida Theatre revived Terence Rattigan's *The Deep Blue Sea*, first performed in 1952. According to Nicholas Wright's illuminating programme notes, the play was sparked off by the suicide of Rattigan's former lover, Kenneth Morgan. The central character of the play, however, is a woman, Hester Collyer, who leaves her entirely respectable husband and comfortable home for a shame-filled life with a lover. In the late 1960s, Rattigan wrote to John Osborne deploring his 'Lord Chamberlain-induced sex-change dishonesty'. Clearly, if he wanted the play produced, 1952 was not the time to declare all. In the letter he goes on to lambast 'the chorus of voices shouting the love that once dared not speak its name', a remark which should be read in the light of his generation and class.

Prior to Stonewall and the abolition of censorship, gay writers such as Tennessee Williams (*Cat on a Hot Tin Roof*, 1955; *A Streetcar Named Desire*, 1948) and Edward Albee (*Who's Afraid of Virginia Woolf?*, 1962) wrote dramas of absence. In detective-story fashion, gay themes and characters were buried inside their texts with subtly planted clues for discerning audiences. Homosexual love was off limits and off-stage, but it was there in the eye of the beholder. Gay audiences mastered the art of translation, interpreting images and signals a straight audience needn't notice. Williams's *Streetcar* was subsequently reworked in 1991 into *Belle Reprieve*, a dazzling and hilarious piece of contemporary gay theatre in the sophisticated hands of Bette Bourne and Paul Shaw (from the radical drag company Bloolips) and Peggy Shaw and Lois Weaver (from the New-York-based women's company Split Britches). For liberal straight writers wishing to tackle the subject, generally classified by mid-century society as mad, bad and dangerous to know, homosexuality usually ended up as a study in isolation and martyrdom. Inheritors of the late nineteenth-century realist tradition, they wrote domestic dramas in which homosexuality was 'the problem'. For playwright Martin Sherman, pre-Stonewall drama was a series of plays in which 'people either flapped their wrists or slit them'.

The chorus of voices which Rattigan inveighed against included those directly involved in theatre. Freed from the necessity of concealment and the fear of revelation and following the example of women's, ethnic and other civil rights groups, lesbian and gay writers and performers set about reclaiming and creating their own culture. Previously highly encoded, dying through neglect or frankly ignored, a new voice began to be heard. Tired of (at best) tolerance, lesbians and gays began to strive for acceptance. Its very visibility, the frankly public nature of theatrical performance, made theatre an ideal form as distinct from the more private arts. After years of subterfuge, allegories, hints and innuendo, we were suddenly free to literally show and tell.

In March 1974, following an advert in *Gay News*, a group of gay men met and gradually formed a theatre company which set out to respond to the way homosexuality was represented on stage and to counteract the way in which gays in theatre were forced to collude in these portrayals.

Their opening season, provocatively entitled *Homosexual Acts*, at the Almost Free Theatre in 1975 was a huge success. The company became Gay Sweatshop and by the end of the year had toured the country with *Mister X*. An invitation from the ICA for a second season saw women coming into the company with Jill Posener's *Any Woman Can* (1975). Both plays and the company itself were pioneers. Audiences had never seen work in which gay self-image was so honestly and ruthlessly portrayed. Not only was the content gay, but the casts also. For many gays who saw those and indeed later productions, seeing out gays presenting complex positive images of gay lives enabled them to define and develop their sense of identity. As a guilt-ridden schoolboy I chanced upon a review of the company in *Plays and Players* and experienced the visceral thrill of recognising myself through the image of the company while being terrified that I would be discovered reading about them.

Sweatshop, unlike nearly every other company from the 1970s explosion of fringe theatre, has survived into the 1990s. Clearly, there is still a need for a separate space for lesbians and gay men, not to mention an audience around the country still facing negative stereotypes and starved of inspirational images of their lives and aspirations. In order to survive and to challenge prevailing ideas the company has changed and developed over the years. Early work often centred on the rediscovery and re-evaluation of lesbian and gay history (Noel Greig and Drew Griffiths's *As Time Goes By*, 1977), while other plays contextualised contemporary gay lives (Philip Osment's *This Island's Mine*, 1988), Carl Miller's *The Last Enemy*, 1991). In 1986 it put AIDS on the British theatrical map with Andy Kirby's *Compromised Immunity*. It has also proved hugely influential in affording actors, writers and directors the opportunity to work on their own terms, allowing their sexuality to inform their work, rather than forcing it to fit within a heterosexist framework.

Martin Sherman's play *Passing By* was produced by the company in 1975. (Simon Callow, who was in the cast, has written of the profound effect of working with the company in his book *Being an Actor.*) The quality of the production and his subsequent work with the director and founding member Drew Griffiths led Sherman to write one of the key works of gay theatre, *Bent.* Following its première at the Royal Court with Ian McKellen in 1979, *Bent* has been performed in over thirty-five countries. The play, a portrayal of gay defiance in Nazi Germany, managed to appal most theatre critics (including those who were gay or Jewish or both). It was revived by the National Theatre ten years later where its resonances were particularly strong following the coming out of McKellen and his co-actor Michael Cashman and its presentation under the shadow of Section 28. Milton Shulman, in an extraordinary double-think, observed in his review for the *Evening Standard* that the revival could be considered as being in bad taste at a time of German unification.

Despite his unequivocal portrayals of gay sex, Sherman has consciously pursued a career in the commercial theatre, which is famously loath to address the subject of gay sexuality, particularly when it comes to lesbians. As I write, Eileen Atkins's play *Vita and Virginia* is opening in the West End, which the publicity tells us deals with the real relationship between Vita Sackville-West and Virginia Woolf. Whatever the merits of this (as yet unseen) play, it is at least written by a woman, unlike the only two previous lesbian plays ever to surface in the West End: Andrew Davies's *Prin* (1990) in which the central character ends up lonely, and Frank Marcus's *The Killing of Sister George* (1967), in which the central character ends up lonely. Isolation may well be a significant factor for many lesbians and gay men, but we could do with something a little more visionary. Both these plays opt for the slice-of-life, realist approach (although Marcus's play was conceived as a farce). Unfortunately, this can only straitjacket gay characters. Perceived by heterosexuals as somehow 'other', there can be no place for us within the conventions of bourgeois melodrama which exists to establish order by the end of the play.

The ultimate example of this was the West End arrival of Jimmie Chinn's comedy *Straight and Narrow* (1992) which exemplified the 'don't frighten the horses' approach by having a pair of gay lovers on stage for most of the play without so much as a touch. While one could applaud the attempt to present gay life in a family context (albeit in the never-never world of Sitcomland), its liberal depiction of gay life being as 'dreary and respectable' as that of the rest of the characters was doomed to failure. Chinn's play suggested that we are essentially the same as heterosexuals and that prejudice against us therefore is unjust. This plea for toler-ance collapses however, when you pause to consider that if we are just the same, then we need not exist as gays, and if we don't then what was all the fuss about in the first place?

Chinn clearly had a mainstream audience in mind. Much recent lesbian and gay work has recognised the inherent problems of this approach and jettisoned the veiled pleas for acceptance which continue to bedevil much of the work of mainstream dramatists. Ironically, Section 28 galvanised lesbian and gay theatre workers into producing more explicit and stimulating work. Critics have complained that gay theatre preaches to the converted, but dramatists have recog-nised that theatre by straight white men does exactly the same thing. Affirmation and inspiration for lesbians and gays (and indeed everyone else) is in fairly short supply.

Bryony Lavery chooses to work with small and middle-scale companies around the country, producing a huge body of work from the tightly written uncertainties of *The Two Marias* to her comic tour de force, *Her Aching Heart*, the first lesbian bodice-ripper. Phyllis Nagy's almost musical command of formal structure, combined with a wholly individual grasp of theatrical language in plays like *Weldon Rising* and *Butterfly Kiss*, has silenced male critics used to reviewing the men's roles in plays by lesbians rather than the plays themselves. At the other end of the spectrum is the work derived from the performance tradition. Unfettered by the traditional workings of the literary texts, Gloria Theatre Company with *A Vision Of Love Revealed in Sleep* or the triumphant *Sarrasine* constantly break theatrical boundaries and an audience's expectations of gay theatre. Similarly, Lloyd Newson and his physical theatre company DV8 have produced a succession of works on gay themes from *Dreams of Monochrome Men* (based on the gay serial killer Dennis Nilsen), to *MSM*, his show developed from the cottaging experiences of gay men. Through theatre, dance, music and performance these works destroy the myth that an artist's (homo)sexuality, if not actually distasteful, is irrelevant.

Many of the most important pieces of gay theatre of the 1980s and 1990s have come about through the producing policies of venues keen to establish gay work as central to the culture, rather than see it marginalised. The Drill Hall Arts Centre in London has been crucial to the encouragement and growth of gay theatre, building relationships with most of the writers and companies discussed earlier (and numerous others) at a time when funding for new work has been disappearing fast. Together with Oval House Theatre in Kennington, which produced a wealth of lesbian theatre in the 1980s, and the Green Room in Manchester and the development of the It's Queer Up North Festival.

American Tony Kushner's multi-award-winning play *Angels in America* is subtitled 'A Gay Fantasia on National Themes', which serves as a rallying cry for contemporary gay theatre. Kushner rejects the problematised, pathological portrayal of gays reduced to mere symbols of their sexuality, but more importantly he confounds the age-old critical sneer that gays should stop addressing their sexuality and deal with 'real' issues (i.e. pretend they're straight), by simultaneously doing both. In common with other young writers (Nagy, Bartlett etc.) he refuses to be worried about possible homophobes drawing the wrong conclusions from mature critical depictions of gay lives. The viewpoint of this generation of gay theatre practitioners is uniquely informed by having grown up post-Stonewall. Moving away from domestic realism, they deal with concepts of identity, power and responsibility from a staunchly gay perspective and by sheer confidence pull the audience and the critical establishment up to meet them.

In Defence of Heroes: Lesbian Literature

SALLY MUNT

SALLY MUNT is a senior lecturer in English and Cultural Studies at Nottingham Trent University. She is the author of *Murder by the Book? Feminism and the Crime Novel* (Routledge 1994) and the Editor of *New Lesbian Criticism* (Harvester and Columbia University Press 1992). She is presently researching a new book on the cultural and political significance of lesbian erotic configurations such as butch/femme.

> I like to be a hero, like to come back to my island full of girls carrying a net of words forbidden them. Poor girls, they are locked outside their words just as the words are locked into meaning. Such a lot of locking up goes on on the mainland but here on Lesbos our doors are always open.
> (Jeanette Winterson *The Poetics of Sex*)

Heroes ain't what they used to be. When I was a kid I took my Action Man everywhere. I spent hours building an ornate and convoluted armoury for him, out of cornflake packets and toilet paper tubes, variations on a tank theme that I'd copied from my Saturday comic, *Victor*. *Victor for Boys* consisted of two types of cartoon strips, war stories in which the 'orrible Uns figured only as cowering victims to the relent-less march of Our Lad Johnny, and other foreigners, the Away Team, who got righteously trounced by the local Centre Forward fuelled only by tripe and chips. Before I was eight, I had a whole gallery of working-class heroes to deflect the shots of hostile forces. Being the only child in a big Victorian house with six lodgers meant I was often rattling around in an adult world without any guides, and my Action Man, and my copious tank-building, gifted me with more than a few imaginative defences.

I've always read myself out of emotional difficulty. Despite the out and proud dyke I've sometimes become, there is still a piquant melancholy attached to being irresolvably distanced from wherever the latest centre purports to be. Some part of me still wants to join up (but I don't think, even now, they'll have an Action Woman). As a child reading under the sheets by the light of my red plastic EverReady torch, my habit was to seek out those heroic narratives in which suffering was eventually recognised and rewarded, and I wasn't choosy whether triumph was clothed in leather-bound editions, or cheap, dog-eared paperbacks.

The heroic epic has survived as the most enduring style of story in western culture. André Gide put it succinctly when he said, 'Without sacrifice there is no resurrection.' Heroic narratives have validated a fair few atrocities in our time but having succeeded for the winners, they can also empower and inspire the losers, and it's this utility of heroes I want to consider here.

When I was asked for a piece on lesbian novels from 1969 to 1994 for this collection, I wanted to find some thread that would pull the piece together and realised that out of all the stuff I'd consumed over the last twelve years or so, not only were heroic narratives the most common, they were also my favourite. I had my angle. There are hundreds and hundreds of contemporary lesbian novels. The hero-protagonist on a quest for legitimation stamps the majority. Famous examples include Radclyffe Hall's *The Well of Loneliness* (of course) (1928), Ann Bannon's *Beebo Brinker* series (1957–62), Rita Mae Brown's *Rubyfruit Jungle* (1973), Audre Lorde's *Zami* (1982), Jeanette Winterson's *Oranges Are Not the Only Fruit* (1985), and almost the entire pantheon of lesbian detective novels from the mid-1980s onwards. Even if there are other complex narrative structures in place, the lesbian hero remains ubiquitous.

As is usually the case with a good idea, researching it you find that someone else has already had it, in this case Bonnie Zimmerman. In *The Safe Sea of Women* she writes:

> The lesbian hero, in all her various shapes, journeys through patriarchy to its point of exit, the border of an unknown territory, a 'wild zone' of the imagination.

This is a journey of emancipation which assumes that the imagination has a relation to the real, and that reading performs a dual function of escape and reconstruction, throwing the reader back into an imperceptibly changed world on her return. Crucially this metamorphosis takes place through a process of identification and desire – we want the hero, and we want to be the hero. Prevailing categories of the lesbian hero, according to Zimmerman, are outlaws, witches, magicians, androgynes and artists – forms adapted for contemporary circumstances and, in the novels Zimmerman describes, lesbian feminism.

Zimmerman describes how hero models have modified over the years: in pre-Stonewall literature the lesbian yearned for a return from exile, to be accepted by the dominant culture, to become normalised and assimilated (for example in *The Well*). Alternatively, in the figure of the lesbian vampire – an erotic spectacle which translated so successfully on to film – she persisted in romantic otherness (see Djuna

Barnes's *Nightwood*, 1936). After Stonewall, and the opposi-
tional movements of the 1960s, the lesbian outlaw became
more militant, a warrior whose vision is for the revolutionary
struggle (Monique Wittig's *Les Guérillères*, 1969; M.F. Beal's
Angel Dance, 1977). Science fiction was the genre of choice
for the 1970s to early 1980s, when these heroes led their
reader into utopian possibilities of new realities, new worlds
(Marge Piercy's *Woman on the Edge of Time*, 1978; the ama-
zons of Suzy McKee Charnas's *Motherlines*, 1978). Science
fiction tended to be informed by cultural feminism which
espoused a lesbianism in revolt as natural, close to Mother
Earth (Sally Miller Gearhart's *The Wanderground*, 1979). By
the 1980s social transformation became individualised, and
novels depicted moments of internal personal development.
By the late 1980s and into the present, previous experiments
with androgyny enmeshed in the 'unisex' culture of the 1970s
reappeared, reclaimed in that classic lesbian hero, the butch.

So rather than producing a general piece on lesbian
fiction since Stonewall, which would have to describe a
literary starburst, such has been its delicious, sparkling
diversity, I have chosen to focus in a more personal way on
my peculiar reading trajectory. Moments of reading are
private, often intimate, and occasionally epiphanous. The
most crying I did this year (that I am prepared to admit to)
was after finishing Dorothy Allison's *Bastard out of Carolina*
(1993); 'Bastard' is a white trash girl called Bone, from whose
savage childhood springs a particular sort of outsider status
which makes for a brittle life. But Bone, however pared
down or broken, owns that indestructible persistence of a
survivor. Allison's talent is that she neither glamorises nor
patronises, giving the appearance of realism. I'm so touched
by this kind of hero narrative because it tries to say something about life now. Novels like *Bastard out of Carolina* are
about finding the heroic in oneself.

There's a category for ideologically driven fiction called

the *roman-à-thèse*. This is realist fiction carrying a didactic message. Its intention is to convince the reader of the validity of a certain belief or truth. This is the second syndrome to be seen in post-Stonewall fiction. *Romans-à-thèse* tend to flourish in times of cultural crisis, they are overtly political and try to persuade the reader of the right course of action to take. The lesbian feminist novels of the seventies spring to mind without effort, in their attempts to produce 'real women' struggling for change. The same agenda persists and strains through novels of the 1980s and 1990s.

The *roman-à-thèse* offers us vicarious experiences which we recognise as lessons in morality. These stories provide us with a system of values in the form of a narrative quest which the hero has to uncover in order to find selfhood. The hero passes from ignorance to knowledge, from passivity into action, guided through the maze by an ethical map. The progression is upbeat, ending in victory, and also endowing upon the hero membership of a privileged (because enlightened) group. The effect is also utopian, offering a vision of how the world could be if only we got our act together. Now, doesn't this sound like an awful lot of lesbian novels you have read? I think our literature is identified so strongly with the *roman-à-thèse* because we've intelligently appropriated a model highly suitable to our ends.

Every society needs its folktales, the popular wisdom shared by its members and related in parables which tell us how to live. This is the third model I see prevalent in lesbian literature, and to my mind currently the ascendant one. Folktales are non-realist and depict sets of symbolic types. Unlike realist novels, folktales are communal texts which enjoy multiple telling. One can make parallels here with the way certain novels are accorded an iconic status, performing a bonding function within lesbian communities (Jane Rule's *Desert of the Heart*, 1964; Alice Walker's *The Color Purple*, 1982). Books are signs of legitimate membership (haven't you

203

ever checked out a stranger by scrutinising her shelves, or asking her what she's read recently?). Furthermore, the narrative impetus of a 'coming out story' is basically individualist, described in terms invariably realist; however, the closure is achieved when the newly converted lesbian finds her community, when she becomes a sign entered into a system: this is a utopian moment (see for example Katherine V. Forrest, *Murder at the Nightwood Bar*, 1988).

The scourge of lesbian representation is stereotype. Subcultures have long recognised the damage a negative stereotype can do, but stereotypes can also hold a function of self-definition for groups. They can short-circuit more complicated messages, and have the ability to communicate a lot of information quickly and concisely. A lot of lesbian pulp fiction is concerned with the processing and redefining of stereotypes. Take the sad, sick, sinful lesbian of pre-Stonewall thinking: in contemporary pulp she becomes reversed – a convert to happiness. This is not just essential for dominant culture to see, but we also need constant reassurance as we grapple with our own homophobia. Also, let's not be coy about this, lesbianism needs to be seen as desirable – positive images do seduce (Isabel Miller's *Patience and Sarah*, 1979; Mary Wing's *She Came too Late*, 1986). The plasticity of images can work for us, as rhetorical devices, as well as against. Popular cultural critics have also recognised the pleasure of predictability in formulaic fiction. It has a reassuring, encouraging function.

Amongst the lesbian and gay intelligentsia there's a certain distanced snobbery about heroes, positive images and the like. I was asked to consider the following questions for this essay:

Why are lesbian bookshelves so heavily dominated by pulp romance, detective fiction etc.? Are lesbians just incurable romantics or desperate escapists? Over the last few years many publishers have cashed in on their lesbian audiences, is this simply cynical marketing or is it a genuine response to a genuine demand?

No doubt the editor was being deliberately provocative, but the effective weight here remains strapped to the opinion that popular culture is a palliative sap, preventing critical engagement with the 'lived experience of our oppression', as they might have said in the 1960s. In fights about literary value, quality and morality the hard rigours of a masculine high culture have always come out on top. A 'heavy' read, because your brain has to 'work', is seen as intrinsically better for you. So we nestle up to a Naiad romance to mend our broken hearts and wade through a Wittig to stretch our lesbian intellects. Jeanette Winterson's quote printed on the covers of the Silver Moon pulp series 'for girls who love to be girls' serves the same purpose: it infantilises and feminises mass culture.

It's not simply a question of taste. Taste is never simple. Different texts for different subjects is a more adequate aphorism, and whilst lesbian literary theory has eulogised Gertrude Stein, H.D., Emily Dickinson, Djuna Barnes, Nicole Brossard, Monique Wittig *et al.*, it has tokenised pulp, or tackled it at a distance, by preferring treatments of books published in the 1950s. Almost any kind of attention paid to lesbian writers is welcome; the visibility issue is still paramount, but need we replicate the hidebound prejudice that popular, formulaic fiction is necessarily an immature, indulgent prototype for Literature? Some of the most recent experimental novels are fascinating (Sarah Schulman's *Empathy*, 1993; Mary Fallon's *Working Hot*, 1989; Christine Crow's *Miss X or the Wolf Woman*, 1990, and happily many others) but they are not intrinsically more political or worthwhile than pulp fiction.

For me, books have been the building bricks of my

butch orientation. Back in my 'confused bisexual' days, after a completely closet affair with a woman who is now a priest, I combed Weymouth bookshops looking for a different kind of bible which might bring insight and comfort to my 'condition'. Settled on the stones of the beach I read Marge Piercy's *The High Cost of Living* (1979) at one sitting, holding a brown paper bag around the cover so that no one would see it. The illicit, embarrassed fascination – obsession, really – I had with this book was because in it I'd met my first lesbian hero, a figure for my imagination to go flip over. Leslie drinks herb tea, thinks sugar is a drug, has a black belt in karate, has muscles, a penchant for 17-year-olds, and is hostile to gay male culture. Those people who know me will wonder what on earth we had in common; well, Leslie is also a soft-butch bottom and a working-class academic. Mainly though, Leslie was a lesbian, the first incarnation of all my nightly inarticulate pinings.

Over the years I've sought out butch buddies with whom to test out my imaginative mettle: Lee Lynch's *The Swashbuckler* (1988) and Jane De Lynn's *Don Juan in the Village* (1990) gave me permission to be a bar dyke; Joanna Russ's *On Strike Against God* (1980) and Fiona Cooper's *Rotary Spokes* (1988) taught me how to wear leathers, stomp around, and have a sense of humour; Antoinette Azolakov's *Cass and the Stone Butch* (1987) helped me to orientate lesbianism and feminism, and threw in one of the best heroes in fiction; Radclyffe Hall's *The Well of Loneliness* (1928) converted me from Christianity and inspired me with a new mission; Sarah Schulman's *After Delores* (1988) turned me around with an anti-hero whose drifting anomie sent me searching for a solution.

Every lesbian has her own list. Top of mine at the moment is Leslie Feinberg's novel *Stone Butch Blues* (1993). In its narrative structure it incorporates some of the points I've tried to introduce here, and I want to explain how consequently it arouses almost religious feelings of identification in me. I was born in the time and place of the New British Cinema of the late 1950s and early 1960s, into the culture of *A Kind of Loving*, *Room at the Top*, *A Taste of Honey*, tough stories about working-class heroes on a quest for legitimation, staking out the turbulence in the British class system, and prefiguring the turmoil of the later decade. I was brought up in a socialist family not coy about our place in the world, and whilst there is in these fictions (and, I'm glad to say, sometimes in 'real life' too) an ethic of solidarity, there is also an ethos of estrangement. *Stone Butch Blues* is a story about a similar girl, growing up in the blue-collar city of Buffalo, New York State. One question persecutes her childhood: 'Is that a boy or a girl?'. At school she is too poor to join the middle-class Jews, and too white to join the working-class blacks: she is an outsider in every respect – the classic alienated hero.

As she grows up as a butch, then as a he-she (a passing woman), *Stone Butch Blues* employs the rhetoric of an epic, pulling the reader into a story of heroic tragedy, of battles lost and won, of courage, vision and suffering. It is an instructional novel for the reader, not just in its delivery of lesbian history but in its insistence on the politics of coalition. Jess's constantly invoked outsider status is in effect a plea for inclusion, concluding with a *roman-à-thèse*-like moment of political revelation: 'Imagine a world worth living in, a world worth fighting for.' *Stone Butch Blues* is an apprenticeship novel – Jess learns from the older butches how to comprehend and fight the enemies of homophobia and heterosexism. It explores the complexity and contemporaneity of lesbian identity, it is lesbian history of the 1960s, 1970s and 1980s written with the benefit of the queer 1990s. *Stone Butch Blues* is a sophisticated text in that it draws on a variety of narrative resources, disguising the complicated procedures of ideological persuasion and conversion with an appearance of simplicity.

I think lesbians are superheroes. Cast out from the bosom of 'normal' family life we have a moment of transformation, and then spend the rest of our days fighting for justice. Sometimes when I'm queuing for pool in the corner of the bar I gaze around me in that sentimental glow at least two beers brings, and I ponder the amalgam of courage which has brought each woman here, to the lesbian homeland. A ghetto, if you believe in a mainstream, but still a community of (all)sorts. We get stuck in competitive point-scoring, in moral proscriptiveness, we have ideological/romantic tiffs, we disapprove/dislike/disappoint/discredit each other, but being in that bar continues to be a statement of bravery, perseverance and solidarity, and our entry ticket was expensive.

I don't want to trivialise or dismiss the success story of queer activism in raising awareness about AIDS, attacking narrow definitions of sexuality, and highlighting the cultural politics of representation. But I think we've been underestimating the intransigence of the opposition. Queer doesn't deliver a vision for structural change. Heterosexist society fails to get the message because the relationship between straights and lesbians and gays is never challenged. I think we need to re-evaluate lesbian and gay liberation as an expedient, complex and appropriate counter-ideology for the present. My oppression as a lesbian is very specific, and my resistance has a particular subcultural history to inform it. *Stone Butch Blues* is so effective as a political novel because it has integrated the complexities of queer without sacrificing the specificities of lesbian history, and without losing the utopian vision of liberation. What we are being liberated from, where liberation takes us, these things are always changing, and we require the fiction of liberatory struggle, of emancipation and progress, to steer that change.

Jewelle Gomez has written a novel, *The Gilda Stories* (1991) which proffers the black lesbian hero as a vampire. Elsewhere she describes her difficulty in finding black women characters of heroic dimensions, reasoning, 'we have been trapped in the metaphor of slavery . . . [therefore] we are at a loss as to how to extrapolate an independent future'. Gomez tracks the development of two literary archetypes in black fiction, explaining: 'just as the bitch makes her own existence the center of her life, the hero makes survival of the whole an extension of herself, the center of her being'.

Gomez's hero is no individualist, but a woman grounded in her community. Changes in her existence occur because of a dialectical interaction between her community and its collective imagination. In parallel to this, I wonder to what extent the restraints of our own homophobia inhibit our potential to dream, and to crystallise a common purpose. 'Difference' also facilitates isolationism.

The lesbian hero strides out from the page. She is a radical myth, a lesbian success story, an icon of struggle, and both we and 'mainstream' culture need her versatility. Lesbians like heroes, they buy them by the truckload. This must mean something other than the tainted suspicion that we are passive victims of publishers' profits. We are not naive readers. We don't always need to look to the avant-garde for an inspirational ethic. Our literature has admirable plurality, and we make it suit our political needs. Heroism has clarity, it can carry a complex statement of identity and struggle. Tina Turner got it wrong: we do need another hero and another, and another one; in fact, the more the merrier. Does it really matter whether it was a diesel dyke who threw the first punch at a police officer outside the Stonewall Bar, way back in 1969? The image is symbolic, and has an important function as a legend. My bottom line is that to live as a lesbian today, even after twenty-five years of attempted liberation, is still an heroic act.

Hot off the Press: Gay Men's Publishing

GARY PULSIFER

GARY PULSIFER spent many years as publicity director at Writers and Readers. He also worked at Random House in New York, and as literature officer at Riverside Studios in West London. He now handles publicity, rights and commissioning at Peter Owen Publishers.

Gay writing and publishing has gone mainstream, much as happened with feminist publishing and bookselling, but to a lesser degree. Gay writers – and gay publishers – have always been around, but it was the publication of Edmund White's novel *A Boy's Own Story* that marked the cross-over point from a writer who was gay to a gay writer heavily hyped and marketed by a mainstream paperback publisher. Now many publishers boast gay authors on their lists, and market them not only to gay and lesbian readers but to a wider audience.

Gay publishing in Britain grew out of the gay movement of the seventies, from the seeds sown by the Gay Liberation Front, an activist group similar in nature to today's confrontationist Act-Up organisation. Three members of Gay

Liberation Front, David Fernbach, Aubrey Walter and Richard Dipple, decided in the late seventies to follow the example of newly established publishers such as the feminist house Virago and the socialist Writers and Readers Publishing Cooperative. In 1979 the trio formed Gay Men's Press. Initially the press operated from a house the three shared in Hornsey, north London. Their aim from the start was to raise the profile of gay writing and writers, and to tackle the issues of gay rights. Some inside the gay community took exception to the idea of a 'gay men's press'. What about our lesbian sisters? went the argument. But as the press explained, they were gay men publishing for gay men. And, as it turned out, a number of lesbian presses were to spring up in Britain and the United States, including Onlywomen Press, Naiad Press and Scarlett Press. Gay Men's Press, however, did publish women, Brigid Brophy and Kay Dick among them.

The early GMP list broke down into new writing, the re-issue of 'gay classics' (following the successful example of the Virago Modern Classics), social issues and a pioneering art series. Richard Dipple took on responsibility for their fiction list, and before his death from AIDS in 1991, aged 39, garnered an impressive list of writers including Francis King, James Purdy, John Lehmann, Robert Ferro, Tom Wakefield, Christopher Bram and Edward Carpenter, not to mention Oscar Wilde. David Fernbach soon took on the mantle of managing director, and concerned himself with the social issues side of the list. Aubrey Walter developed the GMP art list, now an imprint called Editions Aubrey Walter. Here, popular, semi-explicit gay photography books, usually strong sellers, rubbed shoulders with more serious artists such as Mario Dubsky and Philip Core. More recently, the press has published a photography book, *Love Bites*, by Della Grace, that depicts female sadomasochistic acts. A number of feminist booksellers refused to stock it.

211

Gay Men's Press were pioneers in the field of gay publishing and attracted the attention of the tabloid press, notoriously homophobic. One particular title, *Jenny Lives with Eric and Martin*, about gay parenting, attracted rabid attacks yet has been a steady seller, going into several reprints. Another strong seller for the press has been David Rees's story about adolescent sexual awakening, *The Milkman's on His Way*, which prefigured *A Boy's Own Story*. Today Gay Men's Press books are found in bookshops up and down Britain. Their books are distributed worldwide.

Britain's second gay press, Brilliance Books, had a brief flowering in the early eighties. The firm was run by a writer who called himself by the exotic name Tenebris Light, and his partner. Brilliance attracted a certain amount of attention in the gay world; but the Light soon faded from sight after the demise of the Greater London Council, one of his press's main funders. One of Brilliance's more amusing titles was a reprint of *The Alice B. Toklas Cookbook*, with Brion Gysin's recipe for hashish brownies. Ms Toklas recommended serving the brownies to ladies' bridge clubs, or to chapter meetings of the Daughters of the American Revolution.

Two other gay publishers have established themselves. Millivers Books, an imprint of *Gay Times* magazine based in Brighton, is run by the author and *Gay Times* features editor, Peter Burton. At present Millivers has limited itself to publishing about a half dozen titles per year, both new fiction and reprints by writers such as E.F. Benson. Third House, established by David Rees and Peter Robins, was set up to publish the works of these two writers among others.

Gay publishing has not been confined exclusively to gay publishing houses, and more gay writers are published by mainstream publishers now, and have been so published in the past. John Lehmann, himself gay, published gay writers fifty years ago under his imprint John Lehmann Ltd, and was the first British publisher of Paul Bowles's contemporary classic, *The Sheltering Sky* (later republished by Peter Owen). Faber, Methuen and André Deutsch have all published gay writers (although Faber's Charles Monteith, served a dinner of sardines and rice followed by treacle and rice by Joe Orton and his murderous lover Kenneth Halliwell, turned down publishing Orton with the memorable comment 'several degrees too odd'). Peter Owen has published many gay writers over the years, including Paul and Jane Bowles, Jean Cocteau, Gertrude Stein and Yukio Mishima. More recently Owen has published David Herbert, Jeremy Reed, James Kirkup, Noel Virtue, James Purdy and Monique Wittig. A particular success has been the reissue of fiction by Robert Liddell, whose work has consequently been 'discovered' anew by the critics. John Calder published William S. Burroughs and introduced Yves Navarre to Britain; while at Quartet the editorial director Stephen Pickles, author of *Queens*, has published a variety of international writers, many of them gay. Cassell publishers have recently established a gay list; while at Fourth Estate Christopher Potter is publishing books as diverse as *A Queer Reader* and Maureen Duffy's life of Purcell. My own tiny imprint, Pulsifer Press, has published novels by Desmond Hogan and Peter Sheldon, and yes, prospective writers and would-be publishers, it can be done.

Today, gay writers are more visible in the mainstream publishing houses. Picador publishes Edmund White, whose work has made it on to the small screen. Chatto has had a great success with Armistead Maupin's *Tales of the City*, which celebrates a (largely) gay Californian lifestyle, and has also published Edmund White's long-promised biography of Jean Genet. Penguin, in one of 1992's publishing surprises, brought out *A Matter of Life and Death*, Oscar Moore's explicit novel about AIDS, which the author had originally published himself under a pseudonym. Publishers have awakened to the fact that, even in a recession, single gay men (and gay women), often highly educated, are willing to spend money on books – gay books. It has been argued that gay men and lesbians spend a higher proportion of their income on books than do heterosexuals. A gay myth? What can't be argued, however, is that the pink economy is thriving, and that publishers want a share of it.

One result of the AIDS crisis is that gay people have a higher profile in society now than at any other time in recent memory. Gay issues are frequently aired in the press, where – especially in Britain – an alarming amount of homophobia remains. This higher profile is also reflected in bookshops. Britain has only two gay bookshops, both popular community meeting-points. These are Gay's the Word in London and Edinburgh's West and Wilde. They provide newsletters for their customers, import books and magazines from the United States and other countries and sell 'bargain' gay books. Gay books are also found in a number of gay shops, not only in London. These shops, such as the small chain Clone Zone, sell books, magazines, cards, clothing – and sexual toys. *Gay Times* provides a mail-order service, as do the gay newspapers the *Pink Paper* and *Boyz*. Independent bookshops, such as Camden Town's Compendium Bookshop, have long had a gay section and have sold imported American titles in addition to stock from British publishers.

But it is the Waterstone's chain, a pioneer in so many ways, which has led the way in the retail selling of gay books in Britain. Before Waterstone's, it was unlikely that a chain bookshop would feature a separate gay section – even though by the eighties many gay books were being published. Waterstone's hired gay staff and promoted them, the management allowing and encouraging its employees to feature gay writing. The results today are there to be seen: knowledgeable gay staff, separate well-stocked gay sections (and window displays), high-profile bookshop readings by gay and lesbian writers. The Waterstone's example has been followed by its competitors, although Waterstone's remain the market leader in gay bookselling.

Gay publishing and bookselling, and the gay press, have flourished outside of Britain, and can be found on the continent and elsewhere, particularly in Amsterdam and Berlin. Gay publishing is especially active in the United States, where gay people have a higher public profile as a minority than do their counterparts in Britain. Americans are tackling their homophobia by public debate and legislation, which varies from state to state, and which is now being addressed on a national level by the Clinton administration. AIDS has brought a shift in public consciousness, similar perhaps to that experienced by black people during the sixties. As in Britain, gay publishing and bookselling is both specialised and mainstream. The primary gay publishers, Alyson Books, based in Boston, have published fiction, 'coming out' books, controversial books about paedophilia, and have served as a focal point in both gay publishing and the gay community at large. Sasha Alyson, their publisher, has indicated that he now intends to concentrate his energies on the AIDS crisis and it remains to be seen in what direction the press will now head. A high-profile publisher of gay (and other) books is Michael Denneny of St Martin's Press. He has consistently and successfully published many gay writers over the years and is also associated with the gay monthly, *Christopher Street*.

Another star on the US gay publishing circuit is Ira Silverberg who runs Ira Silverberg Communications, handling publicity for William S. Burroughs and others. Ira, together with Amy Scholder, now commissions books for a Serpent's Tail imprint, High Risk Books. These books aim to shock. Dennis Cooper in particular writes novels that can only be described as the literary equivalent of a snuff film. This writing goes directly for the jugular, and is in sharp contrast to more politically correct or escapist gay writing. The Putnam Group publishes gay books, including the popular *Men on*

Men and *Christopher Street* anthologies. Grove Press too has consistently published gay writing over the years.

American gay publishers present a higher public profile than do publishers in Britain. They meet as a caucus at the American Booksellers' Association conventions each year; they give annual Lambda awards for excellence in gay writing; and they are to be seen at AIDS fundraising events. Gay editors also write with some regularity for the gay press. One striking aspect of bookselling in the United States is the wide range of gay bookshops to be found not only in big cities but in smaller towns as well.

Much recent gay literature has concerned itself with the AIDS crisis, a trend that seems likely to continue. In any event, as gays as a group become more visible, and the value of the pink dollar and the pink pound becomes more obvious, undoubtedly publishers and booksellers will continue to produce and sell gay books, and in increasing quantities.

Standing Up and Standing Out: Lesbian and Gay Comedy

Len Cross

SIMON FANSHAWE

SIMON FANSHAWE is a broadcaster and writer. For a decade he was a topical comedian. He once won the Perrier Award for Comedy at the Edinburgh Festival and the nearest he has ever got to a New Year's Honour was a mention in the phone book. He is a founder member of the Stonewall Group. He dedicates as much of his time as possible to the fight for equality and justice but thinks it is important to campaign for affordable after-shave as well.

There is an erroneous, but often repeated, theory that comedians and comedy need a victim – mothers-in-law, stammerers, dribblers, Jews, blacks, gays, the list is endless. No. What comedy needs is laughter. And standing on stage trying to get it is one of the toughest exercises there is in a democracy. It's no good one or two friends laughing in an otherwise hostile crowd. Put bluntly, you need the votes. Unlike our current system for electing the government, in a comedy gig you have to get at least 50 per cent and probably

217

a good deal more, depending or not whether those whose votes you don't win are a noisy and significant opposition or merely an innocuous late-night version of Plaid Cymru or the Greens. What you have to do is to convince an entire audience that you are speaking their language, literally, emotionally and socially.

So what comedy needs is not victims but the creation of the feeling of communality. The singling out of a victim is just the tactic used, it's not the essence. In the way that Margaret Thatcher understood how to stay in power by orchestrating the popular prejudices and patriotism of an entire nation (and the Tory Party), so the comic quickly learns the skill of mobilising the common recognition of an audience. It is only because so many people are racist or homophobic that singling out the blacks or the queers is a swift and efficient route for many comics towards this goal. Thankfully now it's becoming harder. As Billy Connolly once remarked: 'You used to be able to come on stage and make a couple of anti-gay jokes to get the crowd going. Now if you do that gay people just beat the shit out of you.' Lovely man.

Every gig is a by-election and to win the votes the skill of the comic is to universalise his or her thoughts or experiences for the whole audience – 100 people if you're in the Comedy Store on a slow Thursday, or several million people at home if you happen to be Victoria Wood. Which depressingly few of us are.

That comedy is a recognition and often repetition of common experience can be seen by the simple test of ear-wigging any office party in any centre town pub, in any city. There will be gallons of hysteria spilt, judiciously mixed with Pina Coladas, G & T and Big Boys' extra-strong lager, all with umbrellas in them, simply at the mention of names and events from the office, that nonetheless remain stubbornly and entirely incomprehensible to any outside observer. The laughter locks those people together in a group that even excludes the most intimate people in their lives: their girlfriends, boyfriends or spouses. Unless of course, like the gloriously modern and professionally impaired Richard and Judy, they work together. And that is why someone who is dead funny in the pub isn't a huge hit the first time they try it in public. They forget to explain the joke to the rest of us.

So what of black humour, Jewish humour, gay humour? Well in the history of modern comedy they are all joining the mainstream. They are all transforming from private group experiences into public ones. They are all beginning to explain the joke to the rest of us.

For many years gay humour, out and explicit, was much like the office party. Incomprehensible to the outsider. There were a few exceptions. There was the occasional straight man and the less occasional straight woman who knew that 'Riah' was 'hair' backwards, that someone who was 'Serena' on the scene was 'Sir Ian' in public, and that when Kenneth Williams and Hugh Paddick, as Sandy and Julian in *Round the Horne*, did a sketch which began: 'Hi Ho, I'm the Palone Ranger and this is my horse, Sylvia', they weren't talking Italian. The gays and their friends knew they were talking Polari, the secret language of the velvet-jacketed queens of the forties and fifties cocktail circuit. And as the broadcasting studios howled at the innuendo and the camp: 'Oooh, look at the parquet floor, Sand. If I'd known, I'd have brought my tap shoes', you got the distinct impression that the writers and performers understood all of it, the audience got most of it but the top brass at the BBC understood absolutely none of it. Gay humour existed in precisely that space between public acknowledgement and private understanding. Part of what made it so funny was the fact that its gayness was never actually acknowledged. It was subversive. In humour, as in life, gay people were a *double entendre*. Ambiguity was all.

From Mrs Shufflewick, 'star of stage, screen and off-licence', to the 'ooh madams' of the lopsided Frankie Howerd,

'My trousers are sticking to me tonight. Are yours, Madam?', gay comedy is what Kenneth Tynan called all comedy: 'the exposure of what is womanlike in a man'.

All comics expose the chaos that lies beneath the order that we hope contains our lives. People without a sense of humour are those who cannot bear to believe that what they see is not what there is. Gay comics operate in one of the most fertile areas of ambiguity.

With the coming of what has been described as the 'making of the modern homosexual', sex defines us. We are who we sleep with. Society sees us not as people who just perform homosexual acts, we are seen as homosexuals. This makes bisexuals particularly confusing for them, not to mention people who are 'gay' who reproduce and have children. We are defined by our statistical deviation from the norm.

I mention this because it seems significant to me that the mere mention of homosex and homosexuality raises a laugh. In straight company, either hostile or friendly, the quality of the laughter differs, but it rings out with more than racing certainty as soon as the love that dare not speak its name pipes up. Inside the camp, where we laugh a great deal with each other, the laughter is also provoked by two main things: sex and gender. Hardly surprising, since we've been brought up to feel that we are who we screw.

So, why?

For a number of years I have been trying to write a gay lightbulb joke. This year, for a gay Christmas show on Channel 4, I finally did. 'How many gay men does it take to change a lightbulb?' 'Lightbulb? Don't let's talk about the lightbulb, darling. Let's talk about the shade.' Or take another gag, this one not one of mine. 'How can you tell if you've been burgled by a gay man?' 'Because when you get home you'll find the furniture's been rearranged and there's a quiche in the oven.' Why are they funny? Well because they suggest men who might be interested in interior decoration. There will be equivalent jokes which posit women in pit stops and heavy engineering.

What jokes do is to disrupt the natural order with a kind of chaos. They don't necessarily challenge that order, they merely provoke a common memory and understanding of what that order is. Jokes about sex are funnier when they suggest that the teller of the joke isn't getting any or is getting an excessive amount when they shouldn't be getting any at all. Broken things are funnier than mended things. Gay comedy in particular introduces a sexual and gender role uncertainty into a strictly organised structure. His and His matching pink tracksuits or Hers and Hers identical Harley Davidsons.

Gay comedy has come in two packages. There has been Camp, high in the case of Frankie Howerd, Julian and Sandy and Noel Coward and low in the case of John Inman and Larry Grayson. And there has been Drag. To be broad in a generalisation, the first is seldom overtly homosexual, merely suggestive, and the latter almost without exception is Out. It is significant that until very recently many gay men could find a public comic voice only when dressed up. On stage they could find 'the womanlike in the man' only when actually dressed as a woman. In private, off the stage, in clubs and new curtained homes all over the country, however, gay men were unremittingly camp. Depressingly low camp in the main, but with a few flashes of splendid baroque brilliance. My favourite overheard: one queen to another in a club about a third, 'Fuck her, dear? I'd rather shut my cock in a handbag.'

Camp binds gay men together in our unmasculine and unfeminine world. Never mind how butch we may dress or how tough, or even violent we may be in bed, we can all scream with the Marys down the club. For lesbians, I imagine, it is the same. Privately they are as camp as Christmas (or the winter solstice as I'm sure they called it in the early 1980s, when we still had cat-sitting rotas). Roles interchange and identities are played with. That is part of what being gay is about.

The overtness and gayness of our private humour and the covertness of our public face reflect the division that has existed in our lives. Our humour is something that binds us together in private and also shields us in public. There is a private language, things that only we on the inside understand, things that we would only dare to say in the safety of that inside.

There is both a danger and an opportunity in that state of affairs. The danger is that in using our difference as a weapon we separate ourselves off from the rest of the world. And we've been there before. We've done the separatist bit, we've been professional victims, we've constructed a lifestyle around being the permanently downtrodden. We did that after the first great outburst of frocks, nuns and rollerskates of gay liberation. The opportunity we have now is to enter the mainstream with our comedy. We have the opportunity to universalise our experience.

Compare and contrast, as they used to say in exams (on one side of the paper only, as they used to say in *1066 and All That*), our experience with the journey of Jewish humour in the States since the 1940s. Out of vaudeville came comedians looking for work. The Jewish ones to a person, including Lenny Bruce, went to the Catskill Mountains in upstate New York. There the Jews from the city took their holidays together in little Israels of entertainment. Then what happened, because we comics are genial and affable types, is that they started to mix and work together. And by the early 1950s they were all involved with Sid Caesar's *Show of Shows*. And we are talking not just a few of them, some of them, most of them, but *all* of them, Mel Brooks, Woody Allen, Mort Sahl, Lenny Bruce, Jackie Mason, Jerry Lewis, Neil Simon and so on and on.

222

What they did, unwittingly I'm sure, was to create the lingua franca of modern comedy. They moved from jokes to routines and articulated a world of modern angst which we accept as our own. It was, to start with, an entirely Jewish world. Jackie Mason, a former rabbi, was told time and again that he was 'too Jewish'. He is, but the point is that he has turned his 'Jew' into Everyman. When Mason talks about the trouble Jews have with videos, maps, machines, each other, life, he's talking in a way all of us, Jew or non-Jew, understand.

Can any of us under the age of 50 go to bed with anyone (in a hetero or homo situation) and not feel a debt to Woody Allen's narrative of anxiety about modern sex? This may be truer for men than it is for women, but the general point stands. Woody Allen and Jackie Mason with the others created a common cultural understanding, albeit western and possibly middle class, which has defined comedy for at least two generations.

In a way, gay humour is already embedded in the traditions of theatre in Britain. I don't just mean the tail feathers on the girls in the final scene of *Crazy For You*, much as we all desire them. But in the language created by a list of writers that peaks with Coward and Orton. They are of different generations. In Coward the characters create chaos and then run away from it, in Orton, they create it and then bathe in it. But they both put on stage an ambiguity of behaviour which is entirely gay. Coward's plays are, as John Lahr pointed out, 'a battle between gravity and high spirits' in which the focus of worship is frivolity and its refusal to suffer. Orton is more earthy. One might say, post the *Orton Diaries*, more lavatorial. He is, by his own admission, 'an acquired taste'. But as he said about *Entertaining Mr Sloane*, 'Eddie's stalking of the boy's arse [must be] as funny and wildly alarming as Kath's stalking of his cock.' He uses the power of gay sexuality, and its reflection in unconventional heterosex, to subvert.

223

Disguise has been the mainstay of gay comedy. But now as we come forcefully out of the closet and into the political mainstream, so does our humour. There are now comics working the ordinary club circuit. And most significantly they are both gay men and lesbians. When I first went to the States and Canada to work I was invited to a dinner party in Toronto with two other gay comics where we plotted another dinner at which we were going to gather all the other gay comics in North America. As we went through the list we could only find three others whom we knew would come happily and bring no professional fears with them. We may of course just have been very badly connected or not very good cooks. But now the situation has changed, despite our address books remaining the same. Sandra Bernhard is in *Roseanne*. And as a lesbian. Scott Thompson of *Kids in the Hall* is openly gay on a major US comedy series. And Lea de Laria has been on Network TV, out of the goldfish bowl minority spot, and been asked back more than once. There are a number of others. As Arsenio Hall said, introducing Lea on his show, 'The next comic is openly lesbian. But we didn't book her for what she does lying down, we booked her for what she does standing up.'

Lea has taken Bette Midler and made her a 'Muff Diva' (to steal the title of her first Edinburgh Festival show). The delivery is fast, furious, shocking, jokey. At speed and shouting all the way she harasses audiences in a style that is a cross between Italian mama and bull dyke. She gets her laughs more from simple shock tactics than from great writing and is simply such a naughty girl on stage that men willingly stand and shout at the tops of their voices, on her command, 'I am a lesbian.' She has no truck with political correctness, once laying into 'the fascist feminists who say you can't be a lesbian unless you eat houmus'. As she correctly points out, 'there's only one thing that you have to eat to be a lesbian and it's not houmus'. It is tempting to say that she is more

American than lesbian. I don't mean to set one against another, but merely to highlight the way she has of being herself on stage. She is a lesbian, so that takes care of her subject matter, but she speaks like Ethel Merman sang. She makes fun of lesbians as much as she makes fun of Catholics. But she also revels in her dykedom.

In the defiant bad girl behaviour there is definitely a trace of the difficulty that being lesbian in a straight world causes to everyday living. She is sometimes just a little too shocking for her own good. While gay men use ambiguity and camp to slide a little more unobtrusively between the sheets of the straight world, she is in some kind of confrontation.

In this country gay voices too are emerging, men and women who are being taken seriously in the mainstream of comedy, without dressing up. And they are playing to mixed, and mainly so-called straight audiences. They are working to universalise their experience as humans for other humans. For some long time it's felt like it's just been me, but it's great now to be joined by Donna McPhail, Maria Esposito, Rhona Cameron, Huffty and others. And like Lea de Laria, they seem to have rejected the comedy of whinge for simple professionalism. Not for them the self-victimisation of British lesbian humour from the Caves of Harmony in the early 1980s. When it occurs, which is less and less often in McPhail's case, lesbianism is a source of identity in their comedy and not a source of complaint.

What of the men, then? Julian Clary has been out there for a long while. But he is not a stand-up. In the public perception he is perhaps 30 per cent drag, 30 per cent game show host and the rest stand-up. The material has always looked as though it belonged as much to the Grayson and Inman school as to anything more modern. But unlike them, he rules the roost and retains considerable power. It is safe to say that his show has always been a bit of a one-joke act.

225

He has, by his own admission, made a pretty good living out of 'telling jokes about buggery'. But what's the fault in that, since to millions he is an image of gayness with which they feel utterly comfortable? His extraordinary good looks have bought him the licence with the public to be a kind of gay Bruce Forsyth. How will he change as out gay men become less of an exotic rarity in entertainment? Who knows? Perhaps as we sweep into the nineties he will find a wider range of things to tempt his razor wit.

But Paul Savage is most symbolic of the changes. He has found a comedy voice through the creation of Lily which owes far more to the great traditions of Scouse comedy and stand-up than it does to the lipsynching mimicking of minor transitory icons of pop culture which is the travesty that passes for entertainment in most gay clubs. Lily proves for me that there is no gay monopoly on camp and ambiguity. When I watch the Marxist Sex Kitten of Birkenhead I see Les Dawson, I see Max Miller. I see a British comedy great. I see comedy which has been dragged from the depths of working-class experience in Britain, which found a seedbed in, and drew nourishment from the gay clubs, but in belonging to both sources in equal measure, belongs to the whole world. I'm sure that people told Paul that Lily was 'too gay' to make it on the 'straight circuit'. People told Jackie Mason and Woody Allen that.

The reason gay comedy is coming out of the closet is that we are playing by the rules of the big boys and girls now. Now it's no longer good enough to impersonate Sonia, you have to write a good act. That way gay humour will become part of the universal comedy language and not just a private joke.

Fairy Tales Fast Forward: Lesbian and Gay Cinema

JOSÉ ARROYO

JOSÉ ARROYO is a lecturer in Film Studies at the University of Warwick. He has previously worked as a journalist for the *Montreal Mirror*, as Associate Editor of *Cinema Canada* and has also written a column for *Angles*, Vancouver's lesbian and gay monthly. His academic publications include articles on Isaac Julien, gay male spectatorship and 'New Queer' Cinema. He is currently working on a book about Pedro Almódovar.

I was born to a peasant family in Franco's Spain seven years before Stonewall. I already thought myself different, before knowing how, when my family moved to Canada a year after the famous uprising which sparked the gay liberation movement. I grew up speaking Spanish at home, English at school and French on the street; an experience which taught me how exclusionary the use of 'we' can be while making me desperately eager for the belonging its utterance signifies. I knew I was gay at 13. I tried to figure out where people like me went and what they did. I knew there was a gay bookstore because it was in our neighbourhood but that put it effectively off-limits to me. I tried rummaging through second-hand bookstores for paperbacks with the word homosexual on the back cover but succeeded in finding only Jean Genet's *Our Lady of the Flowers* and John Rechy's *City of Night*, both of which seemed to condemn me to a future of darkness, marginality and death. Newspapers, radio and television, in the rare instances when they mentioned my 'condition', were equally scary. It was at the movies that I began to be able to imagine a way of being in the world that included pleasure and hinted at a certain kind of 'we'.

My first exposure to gay representation in the cinema, whilst I was barely past the cusp of adolescence, was through the avant-garde. One day, while I was walking up and down St-Laurent Boulevard, intent on figuring out a way of going into L'Androgyne, the gay bookstore, without being seen by anybody, my eye focused on a poster featuring a drawing by Jean Cocteau. A shirtless sailor with a very butch body and a very fey face is what made me discover the Café Méliès, then the showcase for avant-garde cinema in Montreal. The Café sold food, coffee and alcohol at the front in order to subsidise the films they screened at the back. I later learnt that part of its staff and a significant part of its audience were gay. Even though I had walked past the café hundreds of times as I staked out the bookstore, I had never paid any attention to it. Its clientele did not resemble the covers of *Mandate* or *Blueboy*. I discovered 1970s politically correct gay coding and the films of Genet, Cocteau and Kenneth Anger simultaneously, though I was admittedly much more proficient at decoding the former than the latter.

I did not then have the cultural capital necessary to understand avant-garde cinema and was too isolated to figure out how to acquire it. I knew that even then. But I loved going to that cinema and watching those films because each held the possibility of the fulfilment of a different desire. The films fed me indelible images I reimagined and resavoured in my bed: the face of a silent Jean Marais was that of the man I wanted; it was I being carried by a gorgeous sailor in as beautiful a way and in as aesthetic a setting in Kenneth Anger's *Fireworks* (USA, 1947); and I wanted to swallow every drop of smoke the convict offered me in Genet's *Chant d'amour* (France, 1947). Why worry about not understanding when one went home so rich? Besides, the avant-garde offered an excuse. I could speak this consumption, even brag about it. It made me seem sophisticated to my peers and precocious to my teachers.

The only other type of cinema that then seemed to offer the hope of both sex and community was porn and it was not quite available to me. There was not yet a gay porn cinema in Montreal. I used to go and see straight porn with my friends. Those cinemas were full of men masturbating; most alone, some with each other. I was sure that if they ever took one look at me they would reveal me as one of 'them'. So I used to sit in the middle of my group avoiding their gaze while I condemned what they were doing even as I symbolically did the same.

I came out in the early to mid-eighties and when I joined the GaySoc at McGill University my access to and indeed the range of gay films available to me increased dramatically. During this period documentary displaced the avant-garde (never porn) as my most personally important mode. Films like Bruce Glawson's *Michael, A Gay Son* (Canada, 1980), and Gordon Keith's and Jack Lemmon's *Truxx* (Canada, 1978) remain memorable. They're very simple talking-heads documentaries. The first film is a dramatic and tearful family therapy session as Michael comes out to his family and both pleads for and demands acceptance. The second is a set of interviews with men who had been arrested during a police raid on Truxx, a gay bar. The aim was to demonstrate the brutality and injustice of the police through a depiction of the victims as ordinary people just out having a drink.

Seeing these two films again recently I wondered what

about them moved me so the first time I saw them. They are visually uninteresting, bespeaking the meanness of their budgets; and the discourses they convey (accept me, I'm just like you) now come across as flabby and dated. It is easy to forget how the availability of those films at that time was due to a whole bundle of social relations. They were made at great personal and social risk to their filmmakers. Their financing was meagre, often personal, sometimes grassroots, with filmmakers screening portions of their work-in-progress to community members and then passing the hat. They were shown in schools or community centres where gay members of these institutions fought their own battles in order to have access to such spaces. These films were usually followed by a discussion, an exhilarating experience for me after so many years of silence. I think what I found moving about these early documentaries was the bravery of their subjects. Being out on celluloid was a dramatic exit from the closet from which there was no going back. The interviewees, and the discussions which surrounded the viewing of the films, inspired me to become an activist.

University allowed me to acquire a political analysis and offered a discursive community. Two examples, productively rude encounters with feminism, come to mind. The first is when Barbara Hammer came to show her work at McGill. I believe I had already seen *Dyketactics* (USA, 1974) and *Superdyke* (USA, 1975) at the Méliès, where the programme had told me to focus on the film's form. However, seeing them again in a huge auditorium full of lesbians was seeing something different. The audience boisterously approved of the sex and actively participated in the films. Films and audience interacted in a shared culture which was foreign to me but which I wanted to learn, indeed, thought it personally and politically important that I do so. I was upset when after the screening men were asked to leave so women could discuss the films amongst themselves.

The other incident occurred when I reviewed Lizzie Borden's *Born in Flames* (USA, 1982) for the student newspaper. Officially studying economics, my evaluative criterion for films was probably a subconscious pot-pourri of what I liked best of European art cinema, Hollywood and the avant-garde. I blithely dismissed the film as technically incompetent, badly structured, ugly and didactic. I received more feedback for that article than for any other I wrote during that period: all attacks, all from women.

These two incidents were a personal watershed. I'll always be grateful to my women friends for taking the time and having the patience (which must have been saintly) to explain to me how even men who wanted to learn might inhibit or dominate discussion; how a futuristic film about feminists (lesbian and straight, black and white) organising guerrilla warfare against patriarchy might need to develop new aesthetic strategies; how one could be oppressed and still oppress; how films circulate socially and how it is sometimes more politic and productive for them to be critiqued by members of that social formation which has most at stake in those representations.

In the early 1980s I resolved to see every film that referred to lesbians and gays. By the mid-eighties I had narrowed my aspirations to films made by gays and lesbians with a lesbian or gay theme and contemporary films that included some kind of reference to homosexuality. During this period I worked on two cultural magazines: first as an editor of the film section of the *Montreal Mirror*, later as associate editor of *Cinema Canada*. For the first time I had some institutional power in drawing attention to certain films, though never enough to satisfy my constituency of lesbian and gay friends, unaware of the limitations imposed by the magazines' internal politics.

During this time, I can remember four very broad categories of audio-visual representations of interest to lesbians and gays, each with its own mode of distribution, production, exhibition and audience: Hollywood cinema, art cinema, video art (increasingly important to me) and what I will call here the 'festival' film.

It is best to draw a veil over Hollywood when it comes to lesbian and gay representation. The few times it tried to put homosexuality more or less at the centre of the narrative, it failed. Arthur Hiller's *Making Love* (1982) left everyone indifferent; William Friedkin's *Cruising* (1980) was actively boycotted. I think to this day Hollywood's attempts at addressing a lesbian and gay audience have been through marketing rather than narration. This also applies to films like Robert Towne's *Personal Best* (1983), Hector Babenco's *Kiss of the Spiderwoman* (Brazil/USA, 1985), or Paul Bogart's *Torch Song Trilogy* (1989), each of which found fans among lesbians and gay men. At the time, within broadly intellectual/activist circles at any rate, it was thought important to keep up with, analyse, and when necessary protest about these films, as they were thought to be the most influential and insidious.

By 'art cinema' I here refer to practically every film that was produced without Hollywood financing, distributed by independents and exhibited in repertory cinemas or speciality theatres. Two types of art cinema were of interest to me: that made by informed and well-meaning heterosexuals (for example, John Sayles's *Lianna*, USA, 1982); and films by gay men and lesbians for gay men and lesbians. The latter category can, at least for my purpose here, be subdivided into documentaries, which tended to be shown for about a week or so at repertory cinemas or art centres, and the low-budget independent films, which around this time began to be shown for lengthy and popular runs at the cineplex's smaller theatres.

The documentaries of this period which marked me most are Greta Schiller's *Before Stonewall: The Making of a*

Gay and Lesbian Community (USA, 1983) and Robert Epstein and Richard Schmiecken's *The Life and Times of Harvey Milk* (USA, 1984). The former utilises commercials and old film clips, and intercuts them with interviews in order to chart the course of events that led to the uprising at the Stonewall bar. The people in it were funny, strong and wise. The film seemed to address me directly and allowed me to claim a past I hadn't even known existed.

Harvey Milk was about how its eponymous hero over-came many struggles in order to become one of the first openly gay politicians in San Francisco (the life) only to be killed by senseless homophobia (the times). I and half a dozen other gay men were invited to a test screening of *Harvey Milk* by a major distributor. At the end of the film, we all came out sobbing. 'Should it be released commercially?' the marketing officer asked. 'Absolutely,' we pleaded. 'It's an important film that will make you tons of money.' I was furious when it was relegated to the rep. cinemas. *Harvey Milk* made me cry again when it won the Academy Award for Best Documentary and the co-directors thanked their lovers in front of one of the largest television audiences in the world.

The two fiction films I best remember are Stephen Frear's *My Beautiful Launderette* (UK, 1984) and Donna Deitch's *Desert Hearts* (USA, 1985). The two are very different. *Launderette* is filmed from an original Hanif Kureishi screenplay, is set in Thatcherite London and aims for stylised grit. *Hearts* is an adaptation of Jane Rule's famous novel, is set in 1950s Las Vegas and is rather conventionally shot and structured. They are both about people from different worlds falling in love. Both involve one of the characters coming out, at least to themselves. They are also very romantic. However, the reason why I tend to think of them simultaneously is that sexual orientation is not the films' problematic *per se*. I also think of them together because they were screened in several multi-screen cinemas at around the same time. What a pleasure to see these films publicly embracing my lover without having to sit on wood! The films' popularity also indicated that there could be a substantial market for future lesbian and gay films. I interpreted this as a breakthrough.

At the risk of reductiveness I would say that many of us went to Hollywood films as watchdogs of representation; to gay and lesbian art films for identification, pleasure and illumination; and to video art for self-critique. Video art played an important role in Canadian lesbian and gay activism. It was cheap to shoot and easy to distribute and exhibit, important considerations in a colonised culture. Video also allowed for indigenous intervention into international debates on sexual politics as well as aesthetics. John Greyson's *Perils of Pedagogy* (Canada, 1985) seemed to articulate many of my feelings at the time and I was passionate about it. In the tape a young man lip-synchs to a slowed-down version of Lulu's 'To Sir with Love' as the voiceover critiques how an older generation, the gay commercial scene and gay males try to interpellate and control the identity, sexuality and aspirations of young gays. Richard Fung's *Orientations* (Canada, 1986) is equally brilliant. The video critiques gay culture as white and middle class, in its own context dominant and dominating. It wittily unmasks the commercial culture's expectations of Asian sexual desire while revealing desire's vulnerability to many types of colonisation.

What I'm here calling the 'festival' film basically refers to any film that was shown primarily at festivals and was not picked up for subsequent distribution. In the days before the prevalence of video, film festivals were an important means of reconstructing lesbian and gay film histories. It was at these events (along with the Cinemathèque and repertory theatres) that I caught up with the films of Luchino Visconti, Ulrike Ottinger, Pier Paolo Pasolini, Sergei Paradjanov and John Waters as well as milestones such as Basil Dearden's

Victim (UK, 1961), Leontine Sagan's *Mädchen in Uniform* (Germany, 1931), and Claude Jutra's *Á tout prendre* (Quebec, 1963). Festivals also offered an introduction to contemporary representations of homosexuality from other countries and programmes were eagerly scanned for any clue of queerness. I remember seeing George Katakouznos's *Angel* (Greece, 1982), Nouri Bouzide's *Man of Ashes* (Tunisia, 1986) and Lino Brocka's *Macho Dancer* (Philippines, 1988). I think access to a filmic past, combined with such different representations of homosexuality from various parts of the globe, helped reveal the constructedness of 'gay' identity and made me aware of the need to historicise the relations between sexual orientation, social formation and nation.

Of the films I saw at festivals during this period, the one I loved best was Pedro Almodóvar's *Law of Desire* (Spain, 1986). A deliriously romantic, relatively sexually explicit gay melodrama, the film tenderly explored the protagonists' relationships, giving full due to their emotional dimension while revealing joyful and sensual sex lives. The characters are easy to identify with, their emotions operatic, their actions mythic. And it is erotic.

When I came to England in the late 1980s, I thought I was coming to a gay paradise. I had vaguely heard of Section 28 but it definitely had not made much of an impression. From afar England seemed the cradle of gay culture. Among countless other things, it meant the work of Oscar Wilde, Noel Coward, Derek Jarman and Bronski Beat (to see the 'Smalltown Boy' video on television and to see the pink triangle on the cover of *The Age of Consent* album in every record store in town had been a thrill). What a rude awakening. In Quebec, sexual orientation was included in the Bill of Rights in 1977; here lesbians and gays seemed to have none. But my experience in England threw a curve on my understanding of the relation between visual representation and social conditions. Here was a culture that produced *Out on Tuesday*, a weekly television magazine by lesbians and gay men for lesbians and gay men. But fear of bashings meant one had to straighten one's wrist before leaving the house.

England's gift to me during my first sojourn here was exposure to Isaac Julien's films, particularly *Territories* (1984) and *Looking for Langston* (1988). Julien's struggle to decolonise black and gay visual images from racist and homophobic discourses via a combination of intellectual and formal rigour have been a great influence on other filmmakers (Marlon Riggs, to name but one). Just as important to me is that the beauty of the images in Julien's work, particularly those in *Langston*, remain a source of pleasure and wonder.

When I first came out I was starving for representation. In the mid-1980s I stopped trying to catch up with older works but still thought I could keep up with contemporary ones. Now, though I try my best, I've given up even that small aspiration. One would need an encyclopaedia to include everything produced in the last ten years alone, much less analyse discourses around those films or how our knowledge of them was changed by books like Richard Dyer's *Gays in Film* (1977), Vito Russo's *The Celluloid Closet* (1981) or Andrea Weiss's *Vampires and Violets* (1992). Lesbians, however, remain under-represented, evidence of women's exponentially greater exclusion from the means of production. I'm also conscious that lesbian cinema is also under-represented in this piece due to its form and my relative lack of knowledge.

In the last decade or so there has been an extraordinary proliferation of lesbian and gay movies. They are sometimes screened at a local Odeon, more often at a local art house and almost always at the lesbian and gay film festivals that seem to be sprouting up. I think this has a lot to do with AIDS. The pandemic has changed the way we see our lives. AIDS has resulted in an unprecedented degree of organisation of gay men and lesbians at all levels. Organising around health issues has developed personal skills as well as an infrastructure which can then be put to various uses. The context of the pandemic provides gay men's cinema with many types of subject matter and demands new forms of expression. This has helped create new channels for the distribution of gay and lesbian films, and helped to create a market for them.

When I saw Cocteau films at the Méliès I never dreamt I would be seeing Sally Potter's *Orlando* (1992) in London's West End. Back then I could not imagine I could live openly as a gay man. When I first began to suspect I could, I didn't think I'd need to use a condom to sleep with another gay man. When I first fell in love with the only man I ever lived with, I would never have imagined that my previous and always-loved lover would die in a few years. The movies have helped mediate and indeed sometimes reflect what amount to the metamorphoses in my life. To now be able to see Greg Araki's *The Living End* (1992) and then dance the night away is a joy, one which would not have been possible without many generations of activists, or many friends.

One Queen and his Screen: Lesbian and Gay Television

ANDY MEDHURST

ANDY MEDHURST is a lecturer in Media Studies at the University of Sussex, where he teaches courses in film, television, popular culture and lesbian and gay studies. He writes regularly for *Sight and Sound* and *The Observer*.

There are two stories that this chapter needs to tell. One is a story of industries, policies and institutions, while the other deals in a currency of dreams, hopes and feelings. This is as it should be, because television, more than any other cultural form, is where the public and the private merge and mesh. Simultaneously global and domestic, television is the medium that most envelops and informs our social lives while maintaining a direct hotline to the thoughts and fantasies that we hardly dare disclose even to ourselves. We watch collectively but we always watch alone – and it seems to me that lesbians and gay men have felt that tension with a particular intensity, developing our own devious, furious, poignant and scandalous strategies for negotiating its twists and turns.

We're fond of complaining that television either ignores

us completely or gets us all wrong, but the grain of truth inside that bitter generalisation shouldn't be allowed to obscure the fact that there have nonetheless been thousands of images purporting to depict us, in every available genre and at all points of the schedule, from well-meaning liberal drama to crassly reductive sitcom, from *Kilroy* debates on lesbian motherhood to Hinge and Bracket appearing on the women's team in *Give Us a Clue*. To try and make sense of this dauntingly diverse output, to avoid producing nothing more than a shopping list of titles, I need to find a perspective, and so I want to relate the broader cultural history of these representations to another history which interests me even more: my own.

That sounds like a recipe for hopeless self-indulgence, but even the most shamelessly autobiographical account of television cannot avoid reflecting on the wider social and public characteristics of the medium. So while the story I want to tell is in some ways nothing more than that of one queen and his screen, its narrative will be informed by and integrated into the contexts within which my own viewing history must be located. I make no pretence of speaking for everybody, but isn't objectivity a heterosexual conspiracy anyway?

When I press the rewind button on my television recollections, it's never whole programmes that are conjured up, but moments and instants, snatched glances illicitly stored away for future reference. Friends I've talked to while writing this essay confirm this belief that what we learnt to cultivate in those benighted pre-video days were two specifically attuned senses: first a lightning-fast freeze-frame memory that glued key images into our minds, and secondly a keen nose for scenting out which programmes would be likely to deliver such treasures. Perhaps this was where we learnt to cruise, scavenging through the schedules, scouring and decoding the *Radio Times* for the slight but telling clue. Our quarry? Well, it would be comforting to report that we were seeking programmes that concerned themselves with responsible explorations of the homosexual world, but the truth is gloriously grubbier.

We were looking for men, men as naked as possible, fuel for our fantasies, sights and sounds that spoke to the feelings we probably hadn't yet learnt to articulate in any language that emanated from above the waistline. Whether it was two men kissing in a BBC2 dramatisation of Angus Wilson's *Late Call* or a documentary about the Liverpool team that revealed the truth beneath the football shorts, *The High Chaparral* or *Play for Today*, modern dance or rugby league, the ostensible content was irrelevant. I remember sitting through countless episodes of a particularly tedious 1970s naval drama series called *Warship* (that may not even be its correct title – such are the fickle filters of television memory) just for those moments when the sailors shed their uniforms and marched right off the screen and into my febrile queer imaginings.

Television's potential as an erotic resource was invaluable because it could be consumed, with due and daring surreptitiousness, in the unsuspecting midst of family life. No need to sneak off to forbidden films at the cinema or furtively visit a newsagent sufficiently distant from your usual high street; TV images were beamed straight into your expectant lap, provided your choice of viewing could be justified by an excuse plausible enough to fool the parents. Programmes directly concerned with gay matters were another issue entirely, which is why it's important to insist that television's relationship with its homosexual audiences should never be reduced to only those texts demarcated as being 'about homosexuality'. For the young queer at home, such programmes were off-limits, since to nominate them as part of the evening's entertainment would be far too risky, except of course as a handy opening gambit to pave the way for coming out. Those of us still to take that plunge (and without the benefit of a bedroom TV set) could only regard gay-themed shows as exotic, impossible temptations languishing in the listings.

Yet could they ever have lived up to their mystique? In the case most dear to my heart, the answer is one big screaming yes. Call it fate, or synchronicity, or just the ministering care of a good fairy watching over me, but the fact remains that the first evening I can recall my parents attending a family function without requiring me to accompany them was the evening that Thames TV first transmitted *The Naked Civil Servant*.

Dazed by this ridiculous stroke of luck, and conscious that they might return at any minute, I sat about six inches from the screen with one finger on the 'off' button, drinking in every second as if my life depended on it – which, of course, it did. Miraculously, the parental key wasn't turned in the lock until ten minutes after the film ended, by which time I was sitting back amid my homework, the surface of fake studiousness stretched taut across the delirious cauldron of discovery beneath. No, *The Naked Civil Servant* did not 'turn me into' a homosexual (at 16 I had long been sure that I never had been or ever would be anything else), but its celebration of Quentin Crisp's unrepentant queenliness filled me with an elated, vertiginous sense of identification, belonging and defiant pride. His loneliness, lovelessness and the scorn and violence poured upon him were elements I either edited out or accepted as the price that lipsticked pioneers must pay. Although the film was set in the past, I had seen the future – and it minced.

It is, of course, the very exceptional status of that evening that made it such a swoon at the time and such a fond memory now. In the general run of events, all I could hope for was to cop the occasional eyeful of thigh and try not to wince too hard when the rest of the living room delightedly lapped up a homophobic joke spat out by some pig-ugly heterosexual comedian. This underlines the negative side of television's shared domestic context, since for every secret tingle I pilfered from the screen there were dozens more moments when thoughtless stereotypes reminded me of my isolation and vulnerability. These wounds hurt all the more because they were inflicted so routinely, part of that blithe, mundane, everyday arrogance through which hetero-sexual culture presumes its universality. Perhaps it is in such memories and in our consequent desire to spare others the pain we felt that the roots lie of the calls for 'positive images' that so regularly feature in discussions of representation.

These calls are deeply felt and well intentioned. They demand that the media show some responsibility by provid-ing supportive, balanced portrayals of minority groups, thereby catering for both the self-esteem of the group in question and the information and education of the wider public. One obvious way of facilitating this has been for politicised lesbians and gay men to become more involved in writing and producing for television. In 1979, an American gay writer called Len Richmond co-wrote a new British sitcom, *Agony*, in which the central heroine's best friends were a gay male couple whose sexuality was an uncompli-cated fact of life rather than any kind of 'issue'. This approach, Richmond hoped, would empower gay viewers and enlighten straight ones. He somewhat romantically speculated that 'some little gay boy in Scotland on a farm somewhere will see the show and realise that everyone who is gay isn't a neurotic weirdo' (*Evening Standard*, 9 March 1979).

The couple Richmond created, Rob and Michael, were certainly free of neuroses. They were admirably credible and impeccably respectable, white professional thirtysome-things with non-effeminate facial hair yet non-macho table manners, rounded and likeable and unfussily tactile with each other, cracking gags about the ridiculousness of straight men, light-years ahead of the cardboard pansies which many other sitcoms wheeled on as one-joke disposables. They were positive images without a single shred of doubt, and at the time I was profoundly grateful for them, which is why I feel rather guilty for pointing out that now they seem really rather dull, their matey house-trained politeness crying out for an injection of flamboyance and scandal. They exemplify my fear that a 'positive image' means 'an image that won't upset heterosexuals'.

Rob and Michael, you see, were part of that breed of homosexual who 'just happens to be gay', a formula much admired and advocated by the proponents of positive images – let's have gay people doing ordinary things: going shopping, washing the car, boiling an egg, reading the papers, run-of-the-mill folk who just happen to be gay. This viewpoint would restrict homosexuality to a discourse of the bedroom, reducing it to nothing more than an occasionally deployed configuration of genitalia. It's a genial, liberal framework that sees sexuality as a relatively minor signifier of difference that shouldn't be overstressed – people are all the same, really – and the textual manifestations of this argument are those most likely to be awarded the label of 'positive image'. Close your eyes and he (because on British television the positive image is almost invariably male) will gradually materialise like someone beamed down in *Star Trek* – here he comes, taking shape, kind and caring, tasteful and tidy, not-at-all-camp and not-at-all-horny, he's Colin from *EastEnders* and he bores me beyond description.

There again, he wasn't written for me, because by the time *EastEnders* began (February 1985) I didn't need him. He was written for gay men's anxious parents and for A-level media studies teachers to show their students that there are some perfectly nice men who, hey, just happen to be gay. Despite my sarcasm, I'd never deny the importance of reaching those constituencies, nor the most vital group of all: those for whom Colin was created – the mid-eighties equivalents of Len Richmond's hypothesised Scots boy. The problem with Colins, however, is that their shoulder-to-cry-on sexlessness, their don't-frighten-the-horses ordinariness, is too frequently elevated into a paradigm towards which all homosexual ·representations should aspire. They have a value as a starting-point, a focus for initial recognition and identification, but to be satisfied with them is to adopt a position of mewling gratitude which has no place in my conception of queerness. Blame my early exposure to Quentin Crisp.

The just-happen-to-be version of homosexuality is also a coded plea for a particular televisual style, a pallid, cautious naturalism in which texts with points to make function as a kind of social work. Much of popular culture, however, depends on more vulgar and downmarket genres, where gently shaded psychological credibility is rejected in favour of schematic, polarised, unapologetically two-dimensional characterisations that allow audiences a more full-blooded involvement. After all, *The Terminator* would be a bit of a bore if we were asked to accept Arnold Schwarzenegger as a fully rounded sensitive individual who just happened to be a ruthless twenty-first-century cyborg killing machine. Melodramas don't obey careful political agendas, they let us revel in excessively heightened emotional states. Any sober and rational account of Joan 'The Freak' Ferguson in *Prisoner: Cell Block H* would sorrowfully have to conclude that she was not a 'positive image' of lesbianism; but queer audiences rapturously took her to their hearts, her lying, cheating, sneering, fondling, gravel-voiced, hatchet-faced, up-yours bulldykery a bracing refusal of the condescensions of heterosexual tolerance.

The Freak's strength and impact reside precisely in her 'negativeness'; it was her loathsomeness that made her so queerly lovable. The bold, broad strokes of her villainy have

244

not been matched in British soaps, where gay characters still tend to be the Bobby Ewings rather than the J.R.s. Before Colin brought tea, sympathy and the Filofax to Albert Square, there had been Gordon in *Brookside*, the vehicle for a thoughtful if timid coming-out narrative and predictably a member of the most middle-class household in the serial.

Even earlier, and often overlooked, two daytime ITV soaps had risked the inclusion of gay men. With its setting of a Covent Garden fashion house, *Gems* was almost duty bound to supply at least one temperamentally creative queen, and generously provided three (my favourite being Paul the petulant pattern-cutter). *Together*, based around a relatively well-to-do block of flats, was under no obvious obligation, so the presence of gay couple Pete and Trevor was a laudable step, particularly for 1980. Nonetheless, their living together was the subject of great debate among their neighbours, one concluding that she didn't mind 'because there aren't any kiddies living in the block'. Thirteen years later the 'kiddies' were deemed to be ready for a gay man taking up residence in their own most popular soap, with one storyline in the 1993 series of *Grange Hill* dealing with the repercussions of a teacher's homosexuality (inevitably, perhaps, he was the art teacher) becoming public knowledge all over the school. Given the age group of its target audience, *Grange Hill*'s decision to handle the story with a didactically liberal 'tolerance' slant was excusable – the problem is that when it comes to queers, all British soaps still tend to presume they're watched by surly teenagers in need of education.

Occasional plot-lines aside, the British soap had been a lesbian-free zone until *Emmerdale* (of all unlikely candidates) took the plunge in the summer of 1993. Encouragingly, the woman in question wasn't a specially imported exotic but an established member of the existing soap community. Of course a small village in the Yorkshire Dales isn't exactly throbbing with lesbian nightlife, so Zoe the vet has had to venture into Leeds (*Emmerdale*'s preferred location for anything vaguely twentieth century) but at the time of writing she has met a lecturer from the university (note, yet again, that equation of queerness with the professional classes) and hands have been held. By the time this book is published heaven knows what might have happened down on the farm. *Brookside*, too, is reputedly limbering up for its first lesbian affair. It would be churlish to find too much fault with the gentle, gradual expansion of soap homosexualities, but perhaps they could risk a little less niceness.

For rare glimpses of lesbian explicitness, viewers have had to rely on other genres, particularly the literary adaptation. Mandy Merck's apt aphorism that if lesbianism didn't exist, art cinema would have to invent it can equally be applied to 'art television'. Later-evening scheduling, minority channel location and the all-purpose cloak of cultural respectability have meant that programme-makers can actually show lesbians between the sheets, provided it all originated between the covers of a book. In 1990, both the National Trust deviance of *Portrait of a Marriage* (where the lesbianism was not so much depicted as landscaped) and the spiky, spunky coming-of-age story of *Oranges Are Not the Only Fruit* benefited from this strategy, though in other ways they could hardly have been more different. More interesting, perhaps, than either was the achievement of Debbie Horsfield's extraordinary *Making Out*, a raucous, gutsy, moving comedy-drama about a group of female friends working in a Manchester electronics factory. In its third series one of the principal characters was seen not only at home but gleefully sharing a bath with her female lover; all this on BBC1, in a prime-time programme with a large and loyal popular following.

Television comedy is a notoriously contentious area, since humour seems particularly troubling to the guardians of

246

political correctness, understandably so when one remembers all the times when jokes provided the neatest parcels in which to wrap homophobic abuse. When I and my student contemporaries used to gather together in the late 1970s for what in retrospect look like endearingly pompous discussions of 'gays and the media' we had one taken-for-granted benchmark starting point: comic stereotypes of camp, queeny men were A Bad Thing. There were two reasons for this – first, we were not like that (except of course after we'd finished our GaySoc meetings and went out to the bars to scream our tits off); and secondly, it gave straight people the wrong impression. Yet again, we were measuring our own culture with imported and inappropriate yardsticks, policing ourselves with the anxious wish not to offend.

One figure can be taken as emblematic of those arguments: Larry Grayson. A one-time drag act from the less glamorous reaches of the variety theatre circuit, Grayson achieved sudden, dizzying fame in the early 1970s with a stand-up comedy routine that basically consisted of fey innuendo, acrobatic eyebrows and the limpest of wrists. The more successful he became, however, the greater the fury of the gay political intelligentsia of the time. When he became host of the BBC's *Generation Game*, *Gay News* moved in for the kill, labelling this

> the worst possible thing that could happen to gay rights on British television … as far as we are concerned they do not come much lower than Larry Grayson … He will earn many thousands of pounds at our expense. He will become a 'superstar' while he confuses and distresses our young teenage brothers. (*Gay News*, 143, 1978)

What was it about Grayson that prompted such a self-righteous tizzy? On one level, *Gay News* was making a useful point about the lack of range of available representations – if

Grayson's persona was the only image of homosexuality given mass circulation, the picture created would undeniably be a distorted one – but underneath there is a more complex question of class. To *Gay News*, Grayson stood for an embarrassingly persistent tradition of working-class queer culture that refused to take its lead from the well-bred radicals of the 1960s (note the giveaway use of the term 'brothers'). Beyond the campuses, camp thrived, the survival humour of the subculture. To look back at Grayson in full flow is to understand why – if straight audiences thought they were mocking his pitiful poofery, then more fool them; he was getting away with murder, hardly able to believe his luck, asserting the splendidness of not being normal by deploying the effrontery of effeminacy.

One of the most exciting aspects of the queer politics of the early 1990s has been its upsetting of historical applecarts, its insistence that the gay world did not begin in 1969, that there were older, richer, more diverse histories with which we could connect ourselves. The reclaiming of Grayson might be taken as one small symptomatic example of this. We have, I trust, now reached a stage where the importance of camp to gay male culture could be denied only by those sad folk who put 'no effems' in their personal ads, and that seventies *Gay News* paranoia about queens looks, with hindsight, like a brief defensive blip. Camp is one of the weapons we can use to make the world more amenable to our needs and perspectives; it's a language in which we're particularly and deliciously fluent, a notably witty example of its effectiveness being the way in which Channel 4's *Out* series spiced up an item comparing the laws pertaining to homosexuality in the countries that make up the European Community. A worthy topic, but potentially dry as dust, so *Out* turned it into a mock-up of the Eurovision Song Contest and (this being the little pink twist of camp that made all the difference) persuaded Katie Boyle herself to introduce it.

In many ways, the high-profile existence of *Out* was an indisputable landmark in the saga of television and homosexuality, yet it would be rash to imply that these programmes received an unqualified welcome. Indeed, some of the most entrenched, curdled and bitter arguments I have ever had about television have centred on the merits or otherwise of particular items from that series, but this in itself is a healthy sign, an index of how *Out*'s lack of a party line, its irreverence and its glitziness and its argumentativeness and its anger, fed on and into the multiple homosexualities of recent years, demonstrating an increased confidence, a welcoming of diversity and a long overdue shedding of any need to 'justify' who and what we variously are. By contrast, the shortlived, London-only, graveyard-scheduled *Gay Life*, made by London Weekend Television in 1979, was still rooted in a model of explanation rather than celebration, stylistically unadventurous and ponderously even-handed. In other words, like any television programme, it was a text of its times, exciting and crucial by the sheer fact of its being there ('At last!' cried the cover headline of *Gay News* when the series began) but inevitably cramped and compromised. In the context of British broadcasting at that historical moment, how could it have been otherwise?

There are, of course, so many more titles to name and issues to explore – I haven't even mentioned Freddie from *Eldorado*, the lesbian and gay plots in *Casualty* or Channel 4's magical, perfectly-pitched adaptation of *Tales of the City* – but the spectre of the shopping list looms large. It would be satisfying to find one final example, one sweeping rhetorical flourish, to encapsulate all the narrative strands and political tensions sketched so hurriedly above, but television isn't like that. Endlessly proliferating, it always resists definitive summary. Besides, audiences change even more rapidly than the programmes they consume: I've watched television as a secretive homosexual, a sanctimoniously right-on gay man, a screaming queen and now (just look at how they waste tax-payers' money) a queer academic, and the four of me are still fighting over the remote control – how could we ever agree on selecting a single representative image from all the thousands that we've seen? It's impossible, though the sight of Julian Clary (our wised-up, postmodern Larry Grayson) in all his take-no-prisoners, flagrant finery, descending the stairs to usher us into his *Sticky Moments* comes very, very, very close.

Talking Dirty: Putting Sex on the Lesbian Agenda

RUTH EVERARD

RUTH EVERARD was born in the Midlands and now lives in London. She has been involved with many lesbian and gay organisations and now works in local government. She is now struggling to be both a lesbian feminist and a sex dyke.

The day after I slept with my first woman lover, she turned up on my doorstep with a pile of books – The Beginner's Guide to Lesbianism. Mary Daly, Sheila Jeffries, Adrienne Rich were Susie's idea of the perfect introduction to the lesbian world. I wasn't surprised that Mary Daly reduced me to quivering hysterics but Susie was. Later she was to tell a friend that 'I was a good woman but I had no politics'. These days I have loads of politics but I have stopped being good.

Looking back on my first experiences of coming out in Leeds in the early eighties it soon became clear that lesbian sex wasn't a statement of desire, it was a political belief. I knew the personal was political, but I needed the physical to affirm my new identity. I can't have been the only dyke in town whose cunt came out before her Consciousness.

251

What should have been exciting and empowering became strangely intimidating. My years of sleeping with men had left me unsure of my sexual responses and needs. I thought that by coming out I would regain control and reclaim my sexual desires, but sex which I had always thought was a personal and private experience had become a prescribed activity, choreographed by the radical lesbian collective.

I had a new lover and I felt that at last I would gain the confidence and strength I had been looking for. She spoke the language, she wore the clothes and she had the biggest blue eyes and most beautiful breasts I had ever seen. But she also knew the rules. In that delicious post-orgasmic haze, we evaluated my orgasm: my enjoyment of penetration had been too heterosexual, my desire to make love to her heterosexist. I hadn't made the political grade.

In the 1990s lesbians have put sex back on the agenda but on our own terms. We have broken down the boundaries of sexual desire. It has been an angry, sometimes empowering debate. It has been fought in meeting rooms, cinemas, bookshops and in our pubs and clubs. In the nineties, lesbian sex is full of possibilities.

These days, it is fashionable (if not *de rigueur*) to slate the lesbian feminists as uptight and anti-sex. The lesbians of the late seventies, early eighties were breaking new ground. They had identified the enemy, patriarchy and its weapon, heterosexuality. Lesbianism was our weapon and we were making a stand. It was an exciting, dangerous and politically empowering time. But along the way we turned the battle on to ourselves. The more we identified sex as male the more fortified lesbian sex became and the purer it had to be. That purity became rigidity and exclusivity. Without acknowledgement of our sexuality, without any value given to lesbians as sexual as well as political animals, we were left desexualised, our desires unvoiceable. We may have been

252

politically out, but we were sexually closet. For decades, lesbianism had been a secret vice; now lesbianism was out in the open, but our secret vice was sex.

Lesbian feminists pointed out that you didn't even have to have lesbian sex to be a lesbian, you just had to identify with us. The notion that lesbian sex was so incidental to our lesbianism as to be quite unnecessary seems, in retrospect, extraordinary. Were we really so ashamed of our hidden desires? Or was the turning of political theory into sexual practice just too dangerous? If we unleashed lesbian sex would we simply be recreating male oppression, releasing the dread forces of masculinity on to an innocent lesbian world?

Lesbian feminists were right to talk about the mutuality of lesbian relations, but it is not just emotional or political mutuality, it is a sexual mutuality too. Lesbians have a dimension to their lovemaking that straight people just don't have: we know exactly what our lovers are feeling. This knowledge, intimate and exciting, can give our sexual relations an intensity and passion. It is the ultimate mutual thrill. The desexualising of lesbianism, however, pushed the joy of lesbian sex not only to the back of the bookshelf, but also to the back of our political consciousness: sex became a bit on the political side.

Gay men don't seem to have these problems. There are leather men, preppies, skinheads, men who have sex with men, a complete range of sub-groups, all defined by their sexual activity, all with a set of sexual behaviours and all coexisting quite happily in the same bars. Lesbians have limited their discussions to the extremes: you have S/M or you have vanilla sex, each comes with a set of assumptions and a set of value judgements. In the midst of these are the silent majority, women who have escaped or ignored the debate. They have simply got on with sex and made their own sexual boundaries, they may push those boundaries, they may experiment with their sexuality. But it is unlikely that they will ever talk about that process. The only voices you will hear raised over sex issues are the angry ones.

Gay men talk about sex, straight men talk about sex, straight women talk about sex. Lesbians don't. Whilst our straight sisters might discuss in great detail penis size, performance, did he come, did she come, lesbian tongues remain firmly tied. In the early eighties interested friends might have asked about your new lover's politics; in the late eighties, whether she had a job; in the nineties whether she liked k.d. lang; but you certainly won't have asked if she liked oral sex.

This failure to talk about lesbian sex openly only really matters when lesbians want to talk about or deal with sex openly. Lesbian feminists were not really anti-sex, they were doing it all the time, but they had made sexual debate a no-go area. They had pigeonholed sex under politics and made all the rules. In the mid-eighties and for the rest of the decade, their views, their rules were consistently challenged. Sex and sex issues have been pulled out of the closet.

The S/M debates at the London Lesbian and Gay Centre in 1985 were one of the most public battlegrounds between the lesbian feminists and the S/M dykes and gay men. The lesbian feminist interpretation of sex and more importantly the linking of objectification and violence against women was being challenged. Lesbians Against Sado-Masochism overplayed their hand. Their continued linking of S/M with fascism and oppression, and the increasingly hysterical tone of their pamphlets, alienated many women from their views. It was they who seemed oppressive.

Two years later *She Must be Seeing Things* arrived in cinemas in the UK. This American-made film featured some scenes of sex that were vociferously denounced as S/M and therefore by definition degrading to the women in the film.

254

Much more dangerous, the audience was actively oppressing women by seeing the film. Cinemas were picketed and red paint thrown at the screen. Lesbian feminists might suppress sexual desire but they sure knew a thing or two about direct action.

She Must be Seeing Things was a watershed. Lesbian feminists who had successfully organised against hetero-sexual porn were mobilising against a lesbian film made by lesbians. Whilst many lesbians had been revolted by the extremes of the straight porn industry, many of the lesbians who saw the film saw a portrayal of passion that mirrored their own experience.

The argument was becoming more complex. The feminist cry of false consciousness began to have less authority. The debate became less about the horrors of sadomasochism and more about lesbians' right to discuss sexual difference and power, openly and without fear of attack from other lesbians.

Whilst some lesbians had used the early to mid-eighties as a chance to explore separatism, other younger or newer lesbians on the scene had begun to live more closely and work more closely with gay men. The collective spirit of the 1970s had been very successfully eroded by the rampant individualism of the Thatcher 1980s. The new lesbians, rarely feeling personally oppressed by the patriarchy, felt that they could live and work with men on their own terms. They also felt they had to; as infected by the individualism urge as everyone else and equally driven by economic necessity, they knew they had to make the best of Thatcher's Britain. As style became an increasingly important factor in eighties life, many women left the women-only meetings and joined gay men in the clubs.

Thatcher's Britain soon revealed itself in its true colours. Section 28 of the Local Government Act 1988 prevented the 'promotion of homosexuality' and for the first time targeted

255

lesbianism for attack. Lesbians and gay men joined in a wave of protest. But the two best actions of the campaign against the Section were orchestrated by the dykes. Abseiling in the House of Lords and the delicious storming of the BBC Bastille (memorably described in the *Pink Paper* as 'Dykes penetrate Auntie') put lesbians firmly into the homosexual political arena.

Section 28 gave many lesbians access to gay men's lifestyles and gay men's sexuality. It also gave them a lesson in gay oppression. The straight world was no longer making a distinction between those nasty gay men with those filthy sexual habits and those sad lesbians who couldn't get a man even if they tried. Lesbians and gay men had been identified as actively and equally nasty.

If Section 28 brought lesbians and gay men together in an explosion of activism, the impact of HIV and AIDS pulled the two communities together in a rush of activity. Lesbians may not have been in the front line of contracting HIV infection but they were central to the early responses to it in this country. Working with gay men, they began the long battle against the homophobia that characterised the early mainstream response to HIV and people living with the infection.

This again had repercussions for lesbian sexuality. HIV demanded a language of sex. Coyness had no part in a world where friends and colleagues were dying in increasing numbers. Lesbians and gay men worked together to create an explicitly pro-sex language. Gay places, gay bars and gay clubs began to be crowded with sexual images. Suddenly sex was everywhere. The need to produce powerful safer sex messages to save lives overrode any qualms about pornography: this was no time for prudery.

Consciously or unconsciously, lesbians were soaking up images of sexuality and have continued to do so. In 1988, however, lesbian sex was firmly back on the lesbian agenda.

Joan Nestle came to London to launch her book *A Restricted Country*, and in her talks and readings she opened up new debates about the role of butch and femme in lesbian history. Butch and femme belonged to the twilight world of lesbian sex, it was what lesbians did before we got our consciousness raised. It was not just lesbian feminists who decried the male/female stereotyping of butch and femme, it was as if we had all swept it under the carpet as something sad and embarrassing. Nestle challenged the notion that all femmes were victimised and all butches oppressors and celebrated their courage, codes of honour and place in gay history. Some women protested, fearing that this reclamation of butch and femme might bring with it a reclamation of all the worst sorts of male-defined sexuality. Living outside intellectual London, I missed the debate about Nestle's book, but I loved reading it. I found it empowering, moving and exciting, and it had deeper resonance for me than arguments about role-playing.

In 1989 Sheba Feminist Publishers published *Serious Pleasure*. This collection very deliberately changed the semantics of lesbian sex. Gone was the 'caressed wetness', gone was the 'moist flower' or the 'wet moss' favoured by pulp writers like Katherine V. Forrest. Here was the fucked cunt. This new language was exciting and different, it was lesbian sex with the lights on.

But controversy was just around the corner. Pat Califia's *Macho Sluts* with its graphic portrayals of sadomasochistic sex, rape fantasies and violence created waves of protest. Many lesbian eyes must have been watering after 'The Calyx of Isis', but other bits were secretly stirred. Califia, a long-time, self-styled sexual outlaw, had not just spoken the unspeakable, she had shouted long and loud.

Quim Magazine, first published in 1989, had done its bit to create the British lesbian outlaw. If lesbian feminists in the early eighties had claimed the moral high ground, then women in the late eighties and early nineties claimed the sexual one. Suddenly, it seemed that the only good sex was S/M. It was a 'those who can, do, those who can't, preach' mentality. It seemed that without a penis substitute you were the ultimate party pooper. This 'I dare you to be appalled' attitude was as entrenched, as polarising as the anti S/Mers had been years before. The wheel had come full circle: now it was the lesbian feminists who were being attacked. There were pockets of anger, some meetings, some angry letters, but that collective spirit, that tangible sense of lesbian community which had fuelled so much debate was gone. Meanwhile, the antagonistic, aggressive, sexual posturing gave many lesbians a visible sense of lesbian identity, it was fashionable and fun. Sex was full of lots of exciting and tempting possibilities.

Suddenly that secret sex world became visible in our clubs, on our marches and on the streets. We were waving our dildos in the face of convention. And if some of us wondered whether a dildo really was the answer to our problems, we either kept our mouths shut and enjoyed the party or moved to Hebden Bridge.

These 'bad girls', these 'dykes with attitude' have brought us firmly into the 1990s. They have ruffled the feathers of the straight world. What could be more threatening than the well-dressed dyke with her bolshie ways and confident, obvious sexuality. And when nice straight girls start cutting their hair short and pulling on their Docs, there is definitely danger in the air.

Lesbians have more access to sex than ever before. Dildos aren't so hard to come by nowadays. From the pioneer *Thrilling Bits*, the first British mail-order sex catalogue, with its canny opportunism and infectious fun (remember 'The Jeanette', the dildo for the clitterati, or 'Flipper', the dolphin-identified dildo), we have moved to thriving sex toy manufacturers and bustling lesbian sex stalls at Pride marches.

On our lesbian bookshelves, you can find Katherine V. Forrest cheek to cheek with Susie Bright. There are new books about sex, about sexuality, you can learn how to fist your girlfriend, you can discuss the politics of queer. There are Silver Moon's modern romances and Jane de Lynn's gloomy Don Juan. You can have your Pat Califia with pride, you don't need brown paper any more.

At the Gay and Lesbian Film Festival, under the auspices of the British Film Institute, you can see Susie Bright's *All Girl Action* – if you can get a ticket. Just five years on from *She Must be Seeing Things*, there are no pickets, no cans of paint as what begins as soft-focus body rubbing ends up as full-frontal fisting.

If you want to, you can go to packed clubs with lesbian go-go dancers in miniskirts, with lesbians in lipstick, lesbians in leather, lesbians in silk and lace. You can do what you want and say so, it is getting harder to be a 'bad girl' every day.

You can even have sex with men. The politics of queer, with all of us ambi-sexual, means you can do anything with anyone as long as it's consensual. More and more lesbians are talking about their sexual and emotional relationships with men. We have moved so far from the sexual correctness of the early 1980s that we are trying to reclaim heterosexual sex as something other and uniquely our own. The territory of the sexual outlaw has been eroded: what do you do when you can buy fetish fashion at Top Shop? It is ironic that in the bid to push back the boundaries, we end up bonking the boys.

As more dykes talk about having sex with men while still proudly claiming their lesbian identities, whether they realise it or not all they are doing is echoing the lesbian feminist argument. Lesbianism is not about who you have sex with. These days it might be more trendy to talk about lifestyle choice rather than politics, but it adds up to the same thing: fucking women ain't essential to being a dyke.

But if we are all ambi-sexual what happens to the politics of oppression and power? The S/M gals know what they are talking about. Sex is about power. The lesbian feminists were dead right when they identified this power inequality in sex between men and women. If queer politics offers us a sexual free-for-all, it also offers the potential to lose the ground that women have fought for and won over the last fifteen years. Lesbians in the States are already moving away from the politics of queer as lesbian issues get lost and the boys again come out on top.

The exploration of our sexuality and our relationship to men's sexuality needs to be done on our terms. Lesbians are different to gay men. Our politics and the oppression that we experience in our lives and particularly in relation to sex is different. We can learn from the boys but we can't become them.

Exploring our relationships with men, and more importantly with their dicks, lesbians, far from being oppressed by the male definitions of sex, are seizing and subverting them. We are exploring our fantasies. Della Grace's *Lesbian Boys* challenges phallocentricity. We don't need the boys to cruise, to fuck or be fucked by. Who needs the 'real' thing when you can have the perfect shape and size that never goes soft? We are really hitting the boys where it hurts – the power of the penis as a tool of patriarchy is up for grabs.

In the 1990s we don't have to argue about sex any more, we can just get on and do it. It doesn't matter what sort of dyke you are, you can have your own sexual identity on your own terms. But it is dangerous to confuse sexual freedom within our own community as freedom in the wider world. If one of the legacies of the lesbian feminists was sexual denial, what will be the legacy of the sex-positive nineties? A dildo and some tit clamps? Sex is not all that lesbians do, it is not all that lesbians are, orgasm is not all we can achieve. Repression may be just around the corner; it would be as well to be prepared.

But for now, we can walk down our city high streets and still see a world of women mimicking our style. In amongst the straight women with their short hair, DMs and leather jackets, it is hard to spot the lesbians any more. This gives us a certain something, a certain sexual power. You may not think we've noticed but we've got you in our sights.

Bill Short

Parading It: A Revisionist History of Homosex Since Wolfenden

MARK SIMPSON

MARK SIMPSON is a freelance journalist and cultural theorist. Publications he has written for include the *Guardian*, the *Independent*, *Time Out*, *New Statesman and Society* and *Gay Times*. His collection of essays on the representation of men in popular culture *Male Impersonators: men performing masculinity* is published by Cassell (Routledge in the US).

In the dark days of 1985, George Gordon, one of that decade's legion of professionally reactionary tabloid spleneticists, gave a now famous rallying cry to intolerance. Writing about the recent death of Rock Hudson from AIDS he opined that rather than lead to an increase in understanding and sympathy as gays hoped, the film star's death 'has focused attention on AIDS and also the causes of it' (meaning gay sex). Consequently, he opined, 'The gay parades are over. So too is public tolerance of a society that paraded its sexual deviance and demanded rights. The public is now demanding to live disease-free with the prime carriers in isolation.'

To many observers at the time it really did appear as if the sexual revolution had been brought to a juddering halt by the AIDS crisis. The paralysing conjunction of this terrible new disease with New Right governments on both sides of the Atlantic committed to 'traditional values' seemed set to snuff out the gains of the 1970s. However, looking back from the vantage point of the nineties, on the twenty-fifth anniversary of the Stonewall riot, the legacy of the eighties, for all its terrible toll in lives lost to AIDS, had turned out to be quite different to what tabloid columnists eagerly predicted and lovers of liberty desperately feared.

In fact tolerance for parades of 'sexual deviance' is not only greater now than before Gordon penned his obituary to gay liberation, but also greater than it was before the onset of the AIDS frost. The AIDS crisis/panic of the eighties shattered the basis of the toleration of homosexuals which was codified in the 1967 Sexual Offences Act by placing homosexuality right in the centre of the public's gaze, but it also fatally undermined the very public/private distinction on which the repression of homosexuality depended upon. Yes, the public's attention was focused 'on AIDS and also the causes of it', and this did in turn bring about an end to sixties-style sexual 'permissiveness' – but only at the cost of a second sexual revolution, more profound than the first, which swept away the previous British attitude towards sex, an attitude which held, with typical native deference, that 'permission' was required to enjoy your sexuality.

The idea that homosexuals were diseased individuals whose private life represented a threat to public health was nothing new: 'homosexualism between consenting adults cannot be regarded as their affair alone'; Lord Longford stated in the 1960s: 'they are not just corrupting each other, but are liable to spread this infection far and wide.' Indeed the great and the good liberal reformers of Wolfenden had introduced the public/private distinction in the context of the same tabloid idea that homosexuals were 'disease carriers' who needed to be segregated. Although this designation of homosexual men as vectors of disease was meant literally, the main sense of it was metaphorical: homosexual men were carriers of a contagion of which even the worst venereal diseases were just a symptom – *homosexual activity*, that is sex between men, or what I shall call 'homosex'. Prior to Wolfenden the consensus was that homosex was the virus which homosexual men carried around in their bodies and which could spread uncontrollably if they were not quarantined. After Wolfenden homosex was still regarded as a threat to morality and health but the new consensus was that it was more modern, more humane and more efficient to concentrate on quarantining homosex itself rather than homosexuals.

By legalising only that kind of homosex which was invisible anyway (between consenting adults in private), restricting it to the absolute minimum of witnesses (two) and tightening up on so-called 'street offences' such as 'importuning', the 1967 Act sought not to lift the quarantine on homosex but rather to – in typical 'white heat' sixties style – rationalise it. As Jeffrey Weeks put it, 'by ceasing to be the guardian of private morality the law would more effectively become the protector of public decency and order'.

Also influencing the Wolfenden committee was the increasingly prevalent idea that while homosex was a universal temptation open to all, and therefore a moral concern, homosexuality, or 'inversion' as it was called, was in part a constitutional predisposition brought about by a combination of genetic and childhood influences: in other words, a medical condition.

The careful distinction between homosexuality (a condition/sickness of a few 'doomed' individuals) and homosex (a sin/crime open, in varying degrees, to all) was at the heart of the 1967 Act's obsession with the meaning of 'private': not a hotel room, not a locked toilet cubicle, not a deserted heath or wasteland, not even a private bedroom if a guest was sitting in the living room. It also provided the reasoning behind the pitching of the age of consent at 21. It was considered that the lure of homosex would prove too strong for teenage boys who had not yet developed sufficient fear of it. As a Home Office report put it at the time: 'a boy is incapable, at the age of sixteen, of forming a mature judgement about actions that may have the effect of setting him apart from the rest of society'. The major concern of the reformers, like those that castigated them in the eighties for introducing the 'permissive' society, was always the 'innocent' victims – those men/boys who were not judged to be 'inverts'.

At its heart the 1967 Act's approach to making homosex invisible depended upon not just a distinction between the homosexual and homosex but also upon the expectation that homosexuals would themselves respect this private/public demarcation and not 'abuse' the small measure of tolerance that they had been granted and thus draw attention to queer desire. As Lord Arran, pilot of the bill through the House of Lords, warned, 'any form of ostentatious behaviour . . . any form of public flaunting, would be utterly distasteful and would, I believe, make the sponsors of the Bill regret that they have done what they have done'. Of course, this reliance on the discretion of homosexuals and their willingness to remain in the shadows was to begin the unravelling of Wolfenden long before the AIDS crisis.

Only two years after the Act, the patrons of the Stonewall bar in Manhattan's Village 'flaunted it' with verve. By resisting just another police raid the patrons of that queer bar resisted the exile of them and their desire to an underworld and demanded their place in the sunshine. Soon the Stonewall spirit and its rebellion against the public/private demarcation – 'Out of the closets and into the streets' – reached Britain in the form of the Gay Liberation Front, realising Arran's worst fears. But even without the 'exhibitionist' activists and their feisty American ideas the Wolfenden strategy was deeply flawed, as Gilbert Adair, a dissenting member of the committee predicted: 'the presence in a district of . . . adult male lovers living openly and notoriously under the approval of the law is bound to have a regrettable and pernicious effect on the young people of the community'. In other words, the toleration of homosexuals could not, politically speaking, properly be separated from the toleration of homosex and queer desire.

This was proven to be the case by the massive expansion of the gay scene and the development of gay communities in the 1970s. The explosion of gay pubs, clubs and publications and the growth of gay districts increased enormously the profile of homosexuality. Consumer capitalism found itself advertising the signs of queer desire to the world (if not queer desire itself). Homosexuals might still have been ghettoised in the seventies but theirs was a ghetto bedecked with glitter and neon signs flashing 'welcome'; a ghetto with the hottest music, most with-it clothes and coolest hairstyles.

But it was a ghetto nevertheless, with homosex kept largely invisible within it. It was in the seventies that gay men began sleeping almost exclusively with other gay men instead of straight 'trade' as had previously been their habit. The clone look distinctive of that era was about eroticising/ masculinising the homosexual body and making a self-sufficient economy of gay desiré. As a result of this, anal sex – fucking – went from a minority activity to a majority activity. Meanwhile, the commercialisation of the gay scene provided gay men with a much increased opportunity for casual sex – but with a largely closed group of men travelling between the main urban gay centres of the world. Thus the very self-sufficiency of the gay male economy of desire provided the perfect conditions for the extraordinarily rapid and unseen spread of what was later to be identified as the Human Immunodeficiency Virus.

It was the AIDS epidemic that finally made the private world of homosex visible: if the 1970s was the decade of homosexuals the 1980s was the decade of homosex. The scientific interest in this astonishingly stealthy deadly disease had the effect of turning the gay world 'inside out'; science was determined to bring light to this darkness and the only way to do this in the early stages of the epidemic was to study the previously unobserved sex lives of the kind of men who were succumbing to it. Gay men found themselves faced with the first of a myriad of questionnaires ruthlessly determined to make the most intimate transactions of their lives transparent: number of partners? place where encounter occurred? insertive or receptive? anal or oral? analingus or fisting? to orgasm or not; if orgasm, inside or outside? But the quiet enquiries of science were nothing compared to the fanfared investigations of the press.

It was the press, particularly but by no means exclusively, the tabloid press, with its fascination with AIDS 'and its causes' (in their mythology anal sex/promiscuity spontaneously generated the disease), that made the most intimate details of homosexuals and homosex public in a way that the 'gay parades' and 'flaunting' of gay men never came close to. After the Hudson precedent the press moved on to exposés of gay men's sex lives, high and low, from Elton John to ratings on the Royal Yacht *Britannia*: the consenting activities of adult men in private became public property. Not for the first time the public's right to know became the public's right to gape.

The metonymic shift of AIDS into homosex, homosex into disease, was matched in the press by a slippage of scorn into voyeurism. Tabloid columnists such as Gordon and Gale fulminated for countless column inches about buggery and its 'unnaturalness', dwelling on the 'trauma' in the form of bleeding and tears that it was supposed to cause to the insertive partner's rectum. The luridness of the imagination of these middle-aged, middle-thickened men who dominated the discourse on AIDS in the popular press had a contradictory effect. The public's attention was drawn to the details of homosex in such a way that these would-be New Puritans had the effect of 'corrupting' their audience, inuring them to the very 'obscenity' of homosex which they sought to reinforce.

The government response to AIDS was equally contradictory. At first the epidemic was ignored so long as it appeared only to affect 'marginal' groups, hidden populations with private vices such as gays and drug-users. But once 'the margin' threatened to crowd in on 'the public' and the imminent danger of a 'heterosexual epidemic' was seriously mooted in 1986 by no less a figure than the US Surgeon-General, the British government was galvanised into activity. But the main thrust of this activity was to convince the public that 'AIDS is everyone's problem' – in other words, that HIV was transmitted heterosexually. So there was an attempt to make homosex invisible again. The public was offered the anodyne and heterosexually orientated advice: 'Stick to one partner or use a condom.' Such were the levels of HIV infection amongst gay men in urban areas by the mid-1980s that monogamy in itself offered no real protection; even the suggested use of a condom made homosex invisible: the special strength and lubrication requirements of condoms for anal sex were completely ignored.

This led to a curious situation where the government pursued a strategy of disavowing homosex and stressing the risks of heterosexual transmission, while the tabloids continued their campaign to expose all the details of homosex and its dangers while furiously disavowing any possibility of heterosexual transmission (unless involving bisexual men, those sexual quislings who pollute clean sexual categories).

268

In short the government was exhorting its citizens to alter their sexual behaviour to avoid a disease which their news-papers told them was a 'gay plague' spread by 'gay sex'. Unconsciously, the government's disavowal of homosex had the effect of making it omnipresent: 'everyone's problem'.

The self-defeating prudery of the government was evident in the way in which it found itself recruiting into its heterosexually orientated anti-AIDS campaigns in 1986–7 the only people who had experience of promoting safer sex and AIDS counselling: gay men. Precisely because the 'tomb-stone' leaflet pushed through every household letterbox in 1987 contained so little information on safer sex it was necessary for it to carry the numbers of the only organisa-tions equipped to give detailed advice about AIDS and safer sex: London Lesbian and Gay Switchboard (LLGS) and the Terrence Higgins Trust (at that time also effectively a gay organisation). Later campaigns were to repeat this pattern of discreet, inoffensive – and largely uninformative – copy displaying the number of the National AIDS Helpline for people to call if they wanted 'more information' (i.e. *infor-mation*). This helpline was set up initially with volunteers from LLGS and the Terrence Higgins Trust; gay men found themselves in the extraordinary position of advising mostly heterosexual callers about their sex lives.

The surprise effect of AIDS in the eighties was that what had appeared to threaten a return to Victorian values in fact produced a revolution in attitudes towards sex and sexuality that far outstretched that which occurred in the sixties. The ideology of this revolution was safer sex. Suddenly sex was a public issue for everyone, not just a few swingers in Lon-don – and this time with official sanction (for all the govern-ment's interfering prudery the Health Education Authority's campaigns did promote discussion of safer sex). If the high-tech pill was seen as the symbol of sexual fulfilment in the sixties, the low-tech condom took on that role in the eighties. Ironically, the promotion of precautions against infection by a fatal virus promoted a new view of sex as a healthy force for self-realisation. In fact the 'sex' that was now openly discussed and disseminated was 'perverse' sex; after all, the ethos of safer sex was not only the use of 'unnatural' barriers, but also implicitly the (sexual liberationist) notion of non-reproductive sex for pleasure as an individual right if not a social good.

All this benefited those who had invented safer sex – gay men. Despite the fact that their needs were ignored by the campaigns themselves, the public discussion of sex ultimately increased toleration for homosexuals. Much of the fear and loathing of homosex is due to the way that homosex tends to represent 'sex' itself. Ironically, precisely by being non-reproductive and outside the privatised institutions of marriage and the family, homosex is associated with the sexual anarchy of nature which the Christian moralist fears will burst its banks and swamp civilisation if we give in to 'unbridled lust'; the very men that decry homosex as 'unnatural' often fear it precisely for what they see as its affinity with nature. So AIDS is a metaphor for homosex just as disease is a metaphor for the 'uncontrollable force of nature'. As sex for-itself and in-itself the acceptance of homosex is by definition impossible in a society where sex is privatised.

Safer sex changed all this by firmly placing 'sex' in the public domain. But the discourse of safer sex did more than 'deprivatise' sex: it commodified it. The promotion of safer sex, often by advertising agencies, was the promotion of sex as a lifestyle and a consumer choice ('Choose Safer Sex', as one HEA slogan had it).

The most striking evidence of the 'explicit' exploitation of sex by individualist consumer capitalism occurred in 1992 with the appearance of a plethora of (semi)-pornographic videos which were passed for retail in high-street video shops by the

270

British Board of Film Classification (BBFC), the government censor. Showing how much this development owed to safer sex, these videos, with titles such as *The Lover's Guide* and *Better Loving*, were awarded '18' certificates, despite featuring scenes previously considered 'obscene' (i.e. having a 'tendency to deprave and corrupt', according to the rubric of the Obscene Publications Act 1959) because they were presented as 'educational'. The 'obscenity' of these videos can be summed up in one idea: erections. An appalled Detective Superintendent Michael Hames of the Obscene Publications Squad was in doubt. In his words the most shocking and depraved thing about these videos was that they offered the viewer, in action, 'fully aroused male sex organs'. The phallus, symbol of 'lust', of desire undifferentiated, unregulated and unprivatised, was finally unveiled (indeed one of the videos was unashamedly titled *Supervirility*).

That they were passed by the BBFC because they were educational demonstrates the victory of the new consensus that public sex is healthy sex. The BBFC statement explaining the passing of *The Gay Man's Guide to Safer Sex* reads: 'To stress the fact that safer sex can be enjoyable it is obviously necessary to show it being so.' When a government censor announces that the pleasure of 'perverse' sex must be 'shown', Wolfenden and the *ancien régime* of British prudery vanishes.

Of course, no revolution is ever complete or noncomplex in its effect. The early 1990s also brought with them a renewed trend to privatise homosex and with it desire in general. In 1991 Dr Simon LeVay claimed to have found structural differences between the brains of gay and straight men, that an area of the hypothalamus alleged to be concerned with the sex drive, INAH3, was the same size in gay men as (presumed heterosexual) women. LeVay was resurrecting the idea of the German sexologists Karl Ulrichs and Magnus Hirschfeld that homosexual men were women

271

trapped in men's bodies, or, more precisely, men with the sex drives of women. In 1993 the Human Genome Project at the US National Cancer Institute claimed to have found evidence of a gay gene, passed down the mother's side, that was strongly implicated in male homosexuality. Both LeVay and the geneticists attempt to make homosex invisible by locking it up in the homosexual's body, and by implication conceal all desire within the body. Like the Wolfenden reformers before him, LeVay, who is himself gay, believes that the best strategy to gain tolerance of homosexuality is to do away with homosex, putting in its place The Homosexual.

It is only to be expected that neither LeVay nor the geneticists saw fit to include lesbians in their studies. This is because the 'problem' that needs to be explained away is, once again, the undifferentiated male desire that homosex represents and the desiring use the homosexual makes of the masculine body (his own and others'). The coherence of heterosexual masculinity is not necessarily threatened by images (in the media or the imagination) of lesbianism; these can often be framed as existing for the voyeuristic – that is, active – enjoyment of men. Images of male homosex, on the other hand, advertise male anality and passivity in a way irreconcilable with the equation of masculine with active and desiring, and feminine with passive and desired. Biological explanations of homosex attempt to negate the threat it presents to masculinity by 'revealing' that gay men are not really 'men' at all, that same-sex desire is in fact an illusion brought about by a 'cruel trick of nature' which leaves 'red-blooded' masculinity virgo intacta.

It is one of the ironies of the contradictory effects of AIDS that the remedicalisation/privatisation of homosex which LeVay and Co. represent is intimately connected to the epidemic which has done so much to make homosex public. The 'gay gene' claims are the direct result of research into the possibility of a genetic explanation for the particular susceptibility of some gay men to AIDS opportunistic infections such as Kaposi's sarcoma. LeVay began his own researches after his lover died of the disease. What a perfect image of the remedicalisation of homosexuality! The gay scientist weighing the brains of gay men who had died of AIDS to explain their deviance. From sin to sickness indeed. The strange paradox of the scientific response to AIDS is the paradox of science's historical relationship to homosexuality: on the one hand through its researches making homosex public (and helping gay men devise the survival strategy of safer sex), and yet on the other hand a *control* of homosex which works both by intervention/observation in the bedroom and by the attempt to privatise homosex by locking it up in the homosexual's body.

What makes this more alarming is the recent strategy of leading gay activists, coinciding with LeVay's announcement, of 're-gaying' AIDS. This about-face was an attempt to make visible the gay men and the gay sex which the government safer sex campaigns of the 1980s had done their best to obscure and thus to make safer sex education serve the needs of those men the statistics showed were by far and away still the most hard hit by the epidemic. And yet this re-gaying of AIDS inexorably also represented a 're-AIDSing of gay', a claiming of AIDS by gay men as a 'gay plague'. The idea 'it's not who you are or who you do, but what you do' was inverted: sexual identities came once again to stand for sexual acts, the homosexual for homosex. As Project Sigma, the highly respected survey into male homosexual behaviour, puts it, 'the notion of the "high risk group" solidifies the search for the invisible peril by making social identities stand for physical processes'. This identification/exposure of groups and individuals who somehow, by the operation of some inner 'essence', harbour the propensity to engage in certain kinds of (unsafe) sex has usually resulted in attempts to make the practices themselves and the desire they signal 'disappear' – ironically by publicly branding the practitioners.

Talk of 'high-risk groups', however lofty the intention, will always carry with it the discourse of 'prime carriers' that those who fear sex will employ to call for the segregation of homosexuals, the erasure of homosex – the privatisation and differentiation of desire. Nevertheless the very fact that a re-gaying of AIDS strategy could be seriously and openly proposed by gay men themselves in the early nineties is itself a sign of the depth of the revolution in attitudes which occurred in the eighties, the disappearance of the dreadful, airless notion of 'permissiveness', and evidence of the resulting newfound confidence and strength of gay men at the end of a decade which was supposed to have belonged to tabloid columnists and New Puritans.

FURTHER READING

A Queer Reader, Patrick Higgins, Fourth Estate 1993

Broadcasting It, Keith Howes, Cassell 1993

Brother to Brother: New writings by black men, Essex Hemphill (ed.), Alyson Publications 1991

Celluloid Closet, The, Vito Russo, Harper and Row 1981

Coming Out: Homosexual Politics in Britain from 19th Century to the Present Day, Jeffrey Weeks, Quartet London 1977

Lesbian Talk Making Black Waves, Valerie Mason-John and Ann Khambatta, Scarlet Press 1994

Lesbians Talk Queer Notions, Cherry Smyth, Scarlet Press 1992

Less Equal than Others: A Survey of Lesbian and Gay Men in the Workplace, A. Palmer, Stonewall 1993

Making of the Modern Homosexual, The, Kenneth Plummer (ed.), Hutchinson 1981

Perverse Politics: Lesbian Issues, Feminist Review, issue no. 34. Spring 1990

Pleasure and Danger: Exploring Female Sexuality, Carole S. Vance (ed.), Routledge 1984

Policing Desire: Porn, AIDS and the Media, Simon Watney, Methuen 1987

Radical Records, Bob Cant and Sarah Hemmings (eds), Routledge 1988

Safety in Numbers, Edward King, Cassell 1993

Stolen Glances: Lesbians Take Photographs, Tessa Boffin and Jean Fraser (eds), Pandora 1991

Surpassing the Love of Men: Romantic Friendship and Love between Women from the Renaissance to the Present Day, Lillian Faderman Junction Books 1981

USEFUL ADDRESSES

ALBERT KENNEDY TRUST
Support for homeless young lesbians and gay men
23 New Mount Street
Manchester M4 4DE
061 953 4059

BLACK LESBIAN AND GAY CENTRE PROJECT
BM Box 4390, London WC1N 3XX
081 885 3543

BLACK LESBIAN AND GAY HELPLINE
071 837 5364 (Thurs, 7–10pm)

FRIEND
Social activities and support
BM National Friend
London WC1N 3XX
(also local groups)

GALOP (Gay London Policing Group)
Advice and support for gay men who have come in contact with
the police
071 233 0854 (24hr answerphone)

GLAD
Legal Advice
071 976 0840 (Mon to Fri, 7–10pm)

LESBIAN AND GAY SWITCHBOARD
For support and information, 24 hours a day
071 837 7324

LESBIAN AND GAY YOUTH MOVEMENT
BM/GYM London WC1N 3XX
081 317 9690

LONDON LIGHTHOUSE
Residential and support centre for those affected by HIV and AIDS
111–117 Lancaster Road
London
W11 1QT
071 792 1200

OUTRAGE
Lesbian and gay direct action
5 Peter Street, London W1V 3RR
071 439 2381

REGARD
For Lesbians and Gay men with disabilities
88 Maidstone Road
London N11 2JR

TERRENCE HIGGINS TRUST
AIDS information and support
071 242 1010

SHAKTI
South Asian lesbian and gay network
BM Box 3167
London
WC1N 3XX

THE STONEWALL GROUP
2 Greycoat Place
London
SW1P 1SB
071 222 9007